SCUGOG CARRYING PLACE

SCUGOG CARRYING PLACE
— A Frontier Pathway —

Grant Karcich

DUNDURN
TORONTO

Editor: Jane Gibson
Copy-editor: Britanie Wilson
Design: Jennifer Scott
Printer: Webcom

Library and Archives Canada Cataloguing in Publication

Karcich, Grant
 Scugog Carrying Place : a frontier pathway / by Grant Karcich.

Includes bibliographical references.
Issued also in electronic format.
ISBN 978-1-4597-0750-4

1. Scugog Carrying Place (Ont.). 2. Indian trails--Ontario, South Central--History. 3. Ojibwa Indians--Ontario, South Central--History. 4. Frontier and pioneer life--Ontario, South Central. 5. Ontario, South Central--History. I. Title.

FC3095.S38K37 2013   971.3'5   C2012-908605-3

1 2 3 4 5   17 16 15 14 13

Conseil des Arts du Canada Canada Council for the Arts   Canada   ONTARIO ARTS COUNCIL CONSEIL DES ARTS DE L'ONTARIO

We acknowledge the support of the **Canada Council for the Arts** and the **Ontario Arts Council** for our publishing program. We also acknowledge the financial support of the **Government of Canada** through the **Canada Book Fund** and **Livres Canada Books**, and the **Government of Ontario** through the **Ontario Book Publishing Tax Credit** and the **Ontario Media Development Corporation**.

Visit us at
Dundurn.com | Definingcanada.ca | @dundurnpress | Facebook.com/dundurnpress

Dundurn	Gazelle Book Services Limited	Dundurn
3 Church Street, Suite 500	White Cross Mills	2250 Military Road
Toronto, Ontario, Canada	High Town, Lancaster, England	Tonawanda, NY
M5E 1M2	LA1 4XS	U.S.A. 14150

In memory of Samuel Pedlar

CONTENTS

LIST OF MAPS

The trail's story also contributed to the development of the communities of Oshawa, Port Perry, Cannington, and Beaverton. In essence, the story of the trail is the story, in microcosm, of the prehistoric Native past and the early historic development of European settlement on the Great Lakes.

One reason for telling this story is to present a comprehensive history and to examine more recently acquired new information to verify, as much as possible, the various claims surrounding the trail made over the years. Additional background on the first European occupant of the Carrying Place came to light while examining the survey notes of Augustus Jones, and the origins of a French cabin at the lakeshore can now be told. During the past forty years erroneous information has placed the cabin at Lake Ontario around 1760 and linked it to the mysterious *Cabane de Plomb*, giving the misleading impression that the two were one and the same. This text assesses the precise origin of the French cabin, and attests to the true nature of *Cabane*.

Chapter 1 describes the first recorded mention of the trail and its use. Because the origin of the trail is shrouded in the prehistoric past, Chapter 2's part of the story is based on the known archaeological sites from the fourteenth and fifteenth centuries and the historical records predating the coming of European settlers. Chapter 3 attempts to clear up the misunderstanding about *Cabane de Plomb*, as described in Frost's *Forgotten Pathways of the Trent*. Early historical aspects of the trail relating to its initial discovery and settlement, primarily by American immigrants, and to the First Nations who occupied it during the late-eighteenth and early-nineteenth centuries, are addressed in Chapter 4, while Chapter 5 looks at the involvement of missionaries and itinerant circuit preachers along the trail. Chapter 6 discusses the coming of English, Irish, and Scottish settlers, and Chapter 7 introduces the beginning of more northerly settlement as the available arable land near the lake became scarce. Chapter 8 addresses the increasing marginalization of the First Nations and leads into Chapter 9, which explores the growth of commerce and industry in communities in Whitby Township. Chapter 10 introduces new villages emerging in the more northerly townships. Evolving social customs, the temperance movement, and the impact of European goods and diseases brought in by traders, missionaries, and whisky salesmen are the topics of Chapter 11, while Chapter 12 discusses the remnants of the trail that are left today.

The early surveyors were among the first Europeans to encounter the trails that make up the Scugog Carrying Place. It is through the work of such men as Augustus Jones and Samuel Wilmot that some of the first glimpses of the Carrying Place emerge. These intrepid men, frequently unacknowledged, were the ones that established the shape of the townships along Scugog Carrying Place and defined the roads that ultimately replaced it.

1

EARLY DESCRIPTION

"The settlers ... referred to this region where the trail ran as the wilderness at the time ... these Indian Trails were the only roadways of any kind through the forest."[1]

The headline in the *Oshawa Express* read "Dredging at harbour raises questions." This article in the November 11, 2009, issue of the newspaper stated that "a pile of material, resembling a berm, has been placed near Gifford Hill, the spot where FarmTech Energy Corporation is hoping to create an ethanol plant." A visit to the site revealed heavy trucks transporting loads of dredged material and gouging the terrain where the Wilson site is located.

By 1794 Benjamin Wilson had built a house and barn there, becoming the first permanent European settler in the area between Port Hope and Toronto. Previous research at Archives Ontario had verified this by yielding a map that clearly identified "Wilson's" in the area where the trucks were operating. This map, created in 1795 by surveyor Augustus Jones, was the first full survey of the Township of Whitby. However, over the years the site has been largely neglected.

There have been several public meetings both for and against the construction of an ethanol plant, which would be located at the southern terminus of Scugog Carrying Place. The current tensions between those in favour of industrialization and those who see such development as harmful to the environment or destructive of significant heritage markers are a continuation of similar conflicts that have long been part of the history of the area. During the first half of the nineteenth century there were heated exchanges between the advocates of temperance and those entrepreneurs who were building mills and distilleries along the Carrying Place.

The trail, extending from Wilson's property near the shoreline of Lake Ontario to the Ninth Concession of Whitby Township (Ontario County), is illustrated on the map developed by the surveyor Augustus Jones. Politician and historian Leslie Frost[2] referred to the trail as the "Scugog Carrying Place" in his book *Forgotten Pathways of the Trent*, but early settlers simply referred to it as the "Indian trail." Surveyor Samuel Wilmot used the description "Indian Foot Path" on his 1809–1810 map of Reach Township, north of Whitby Township. Although the date of the origin of the trail remains elusive, it appears fully-formed on Jones's 1795 map of Whitby Township.

Prior to this early documentation, the trail's history lies shrouded between the early contact with European traders and the pre-contact history of the First Nations. The trail was part of a transportation corridor connecting both Georgian Bay and the Trent River system to Lake Ontario, and it remained in use by both First Nation groups and the newly-arriving European settlers for another half-century after Jones placed it on his map. Not surprisingly, the trail helped define the location of early settlements and shaped present-day communities.

The trail wound its way north from Lake Ontario to the south shore of Lake Scugog. At that time, the southern terminus of the trail was a sandy beach on the Lake Ontario shoreline, labelled "Long Beach" on early maps, next to a peninsula called *Min-ce-nan-quash* by the Natives and near the creek just east of Benjamin Wilson's homestead. The peninsula would have been a landmark for Scugog Carrying Place and for people travelling along Lake Ontario until it disappeared under the waves of the lake in the decades following Wilson's arrival.

Lake Scugog, further north on the trail, was named *Wuh-yu Wus-ki-wuh-gog* by the Native people, meaning "shallow muddy lake." It would take less than a day for an individual to travel the trail from Lake Scugog to Lake Ontario on foot, a distance of about eighteen miles. The trail was narrow, but relatively straight, and provided the quickest connection between these two bodies of water. From Lake Scugog, travellers could canoe and portage to Lake Simcoe on either the Nonquon and Beaver Rivers, or paddle down the Scugog River, which flows into Sturgeon Lake

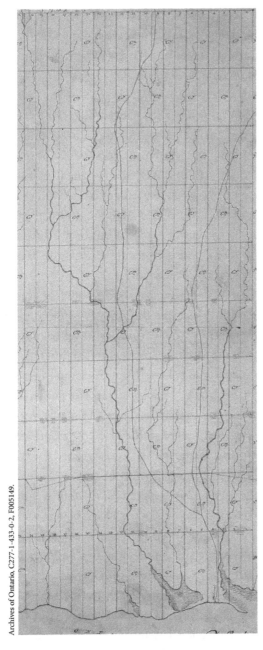

"C31" Whitby Township Plan, Augustus Jones, July 14, 1795. *The first map of Whitby Township. Augustus Jones (1757–1836) included the location of Benjamin Wilson's homestead and that of Scugog Carrying Place on his survey.*

on today's Trent Severn Waterway. From the southern end of the trail at Lake Ontario, individuals could travel west along the north shore to the Toronto Islands and on to the Head of the Lake at Burlington Bay, a route frequently taken by First Nations people.

At either end of the trail, individuals could peel off birch or elm bark and make a canoe that would suffice as a watercraft for a season or two until a new one was needed. Percy Robinson, in writing about the early history of Toronto, recounted a passage on the Toronto Carrying Place, west of the Scugog Carrying Place, that English fur trader Alexander Henry travelled on while briefly a prisoner of the Ojibwa in 1764. Henry had recalled that in a matter of two days the travellers built two canoes as they "stripped off the bark, in one entire sheet, of about eighteen feet in length ... Its ends were next closed, by sewing the bark together; and a few ribs and bars being introduced."[3]

The First Nations used the trail on seasonal migrations that took them north to south to harvest the resources found along the route. Every spring and fall they would regularly travel south to the shoreline where the Oshawa and Farewell Creeks emptied into Lake Ontario. For a number of days they would fish and hunt small mammals to supplement their food supply. Back on Lake Scugog they had access to large sections of water that produced abundant wild rice and maple trees to tap for sap.

Samuel Pedlar, who arrived in the area from Cornwall, England, in 1841, said that the first European settlers described the trail's location as "a wilderness." In his writing on the early history of Oshawa he noted that: "the settlers of the 1st and 2nd concessions of Whitby Township referred to this region where the trail ran as the wilderness at the time ... When the white settlers began to penetrate the wilderness in the Township of Whitby northward of the site where Oshawa stands, these Indian Trails were the only roadways of any kind through the forest." Pedlar had collected numerous interviews with early settlers to establish the existence of the trail, the so-called Scugog Carrying Place.

A tombstone at Myrtle Cemetery in Myrtle (now part of Whitby) reads, "In memory of John M. Fralick who settled in Whitby 1821 then an almost unbroken wilderness and endured all."[4] The first European pioneers used the term "wilderness" indiscriminately during the colonial period of North America when describing the ruggedness of the landscape surrounding them. Writing about settler life in nineteenth-century Ontario, the Strickland sisters, Susanna Moodie and Catharine Parr Traill, frequently employed the term in their respective books *Roughing It in the Bush* and *The Backwoods of Canada*.

But the region was not a true wilderness, for the land was home to various people dating back to the last Ice Age. These people had homes, villages, and extensive transportation networks both over land and by water. In fact, the early European settlers relied on the First Nations people to help them navigate their canoes between distant lakes and to show them the pathways into the interior. These indigenous inhabitants comprised various tribes speaking Algonquian or Iroquoian languages, and many of our place names come from these languages. "Oshawa" is an Ojibwa term and so are "Etobicoke" and "Ottawa," while "Toronto" is derived from the Iroquoian language.

The name "Oshawa" has been roughly translated to mean "a place where you cross the water, or leave the canoe to travel on foot." In the distant past, it is likely that the name was used to denote the entire Scugog Carrying Place, a fact that would have been well-known by the First Nations people and by the earliest European settlers.[5] In time that common knowledge was lost and the narrower use of the name for Oshawa as the "crossing of the stream" (a reference to Oshawa Creek) applied.

EARLY SURVEYS

Permanent European settlement of Oshawa, and with it the slow demise of the Carrying Place, began after Augustus Jones was hired by Samuel Holland, the provincial surveyor general, and completed his survey of the region. In 1791, Jones laid the baseline through Whitby Township, which at that time included all of present-day Oshawa and the town of Whitby. Jones is described as "a vigorous man with an iron constitution, as agile on snowshoes with a pack on his back as in a loaded birchbark canoe."[6] Jones, born *circa* 1757 (or 1758), grew up along the Hudson River in New York State where he trained as a surveyor.

Augustus Jones Jr. (circa 1818–92), the youngest son of Augustus Jones and Sarah Tekarihogen (Tekerehogen), the daughter of a Mohawk chief, inherited his father's surveying instruments.

His instructions were to cut a baseline and mark townships along the north shore of Lake Ontario from the Trent to the Humber Rivers — part of the Home District not yet surveyed. He had sufficient funds to hire nine men to work for seventy-nine days, from July 1 to September 17, 1791. Jones hired Stephen Wardell and Henry Johnson as chain bearers; David Beaty, James Everson, Henry Heartly, William Abbott, and "Billy," who is described as a "Delaware Indian," as axemen; and Burgoyne Camp as a flagman. The final person rounding out Jones's survey crew was John McEwen, employed to transport the survey party's supplies by bateaux along the lakefront.[7]

In the course of laying out the baseline from the Trent River to Toronto, Jones entered Whitby Township on August 28, 1791, working from the east and cutting his way to the Pickering Township boundary, which he reached on September 1. He crossed a marsh and then a swamp to get to a creek, which he recorded as being twenty-eight links (18.5 feet) across; this was likely the site of today's Harmony Creek. It seems he must have run across the Scugog Carrying Place on the first day of surveying in Whitby Township, but did not stop to examine the trail since the next day he proceeded to continue cutting his line to lot eighteen in the middle of the township. The third day of the survey was lost due to rain. For the next two days Jones continued the baseline from lots nineteen through to thirty-five and later continued westward into neighbouring Pickering Township and to the mouth of the Humber River — the area known today as Toronto.

His field notes indicate one person living in Whitby Township. After having crossed lot four along the lakeshore, Jones wrote: "Mr. St. John lives on the front of this lot."[8] "St. John" is the name Jones used for Jean Baptiste Rousseau, a French fur trader who regularly traversed the north shore of Lake Ontario, trading with the Mississauga. There can be only one reason for Jean Rousseau to live on the lot where the Scugog Carrying Place terminates at Lake Ontario, and that was to facilitate his trading with First Nations. Jones's reference to St. John strongly suggests that the Carrying Place was in use in 1791. Rousseau, who spoke both the Algonquian and Iroquoian languages, was employed as an interpreter by the British provincial administration. In fact, when Jones and his survey party reached Toronto at the conclusion of their baseline survey, Rousseau was there to greet the crew.

Jones did not have time to explore the Scugog Carrying Place during his initial survey. His priority was to cut a straight line through the bush and mark it by slashing the sides of trees and lay out the baseline of Whitby Township, thereby defining its breadth from east to west. Augustus Jones returned to the area in 1795 on orders from D.W. Smith, the surveyor general of Upper Canada in Newark. A letter from Smith, dated April 24, 1795, stipulated that: "the first Concession line of Township of Whitby (formerly Norwich or No. 8) on the north shore of Lake Ontario, having been already surveyed by you, I need only direct that you proceed there and complete the survey of that Township on the principals upon which it was begun."[9]

Surveys were measured with chains of fixed length. One chain is equal to sixty-six feet and was used as the width for a road allowance. The depth of a concession was equal to 6,600 feet or one-and-a-quarter miles and one acre was ten square chains. A compass for direction, plus a chain, were the only instruments needed to carry out a survey. A letter from Jones to the survey officials in Newark described how he marked the survey lines and how he would later mark the various concessions and road allowances:

> I begin at some place fixed upon, if a tree, it is blazed on four sides, with three notches, some distance from each other below the blazes, on which is wrote the number of the lot, and Concession, on the side of which they lay, this, I note down in my field Book, the small Bushes are chopped down, about the same, this is done in the Presence of the Chain bearers, as well as the Axmen who perform the work — if the Plane of beginning is a Post then the bearing and distance to the nearest great road and wholesome tree, is taken, and marked as before ....[10]

After Jones and his survey crew had laid out the nine concessions of Whitby Township, he drew a map of the lots and concessions, a map that later was labelled "Whitby C31." (See Map 1)

On lot four of the Broken Front Concession, shown on the 1795 map, Jones wrote the word "Wilson's" at the southern end of Scugog Carrying Place, at the same location where he had recorded "St. John" four years earlier. A year later, on July 17, 1796, Augustus reported that the survey was complete, at the total cost of £250. He and his crew had surveyed 114 miles of territory in the township and blazed the corner trees for each concession and road allowance.

Jones was very particular in the details of his survey in which he outlines Scugog Carrying Place. The trail is indicated on the 1795 map in red ink, while the lots and road allowances are in black ink. This distinction suggests Jones was separating the surveyed lands from the native trail. By his specific depiction of the trail, Jones seems to have recognized the importance that the Carrying Place would provide in assisting future settlers travelling north into the interior concessions.

In his field notes, Jones gives the name of the stream to the east of Wilson's as *Min-ce-nan-quash*, in the language of the Mississauga living in the region. To the west, Farewell Creek drained into this pond, which was protected by sand dunes, and emptied into Lake Ontario near Bluff Point. Both Bluff Point, to the east of Wilson's place, and today's Bonnie Brae Point to the west were considered a landmark called *Min-ce-nan-quash*. The area in between is depicted on early maps as a shallow bay called Long Beach.

The trail, used by the Mississauga in the latter part of the eighteenth century and throughout the first half of the nineteenth for travelling between Lake Scugog and Lake Ontario, runs through present-day Oshawa and helped to define the future city. At the time it was not a straight trail but rather a meandering path through the forest, roughly following the stream beds flowing into Lake Ontario. Later a section of the trail would become Oshawa's Simcoe Street, today one of the main thoroughfares in the Durham Region.

The first survey map of Reach Township (north of Whitby Township) was completed by Samuel Wilmot, who surveyed the area from November 20, 1809, to March 28, 1810. He shows the trail north of the ridge (Oak Ridges Moraine), travelling from Whitby Township down the slope to Lake Scugog. His map locates fur-trading posts at the mouth of Nonquon River, which he labelled "Mistake River," and at the mouth of Cawber's Creek he shows an "Indian Foot Path." Donald F. McOuat, archivist of Ontario in 1971, pointed out that Wilmot's field notes of the time make "four references to an existing Indian Foot Path as follows: 3rd Concession 16th Post, 4th Concession 17th Post, 5th Concession 18th Post, and 6th Concession 19th Post."[11] The trail on Jones's 1795 map clearly lines up with the survey map of Reach Township created by Samuel Wilmot a decade and a half later.

PEDLAR'S DESCRIPTION OF THE TRAIL

There is no doubt that the trail running through Oshawa was an aboriginal trail and that many pioneers travelling into the interior north of Lake

Ontario are known to have used the trail. Samuel Pedlar detailed evidence regarding the use of the trail from Lake Ontario to Lake Scugog from a number of local residents, who, in the late 1880s and early 1890s, provided first-hand knowledge of the trail and of its use by both First Nations people and early pioneers in the first half of the nineteenth century.

As Pedlar said, his intention was to put "on record the information carefully obtained in reference to these Indian Trails, to aid the work of future writers who may desire to enlarge upon this matter."[12] He goes on to discuss the southern portion of the trail as two separate trails:

> … two Trails ran from Lake Ontario northwards through East Whitby Township. The one started from the old French Block House [that] pioneer Wilson found on the bluff [and that] he took possession of at the mouth of the Farewell Creek which since Wilson settled there has been developed into a marsh, the Trail passed northward along the west bank of said creek, and along to the north part of the Township.[13]
>
> The other trail began west of Wilson's, at the mouth of the creek (Oshawa Creek), at a little landing on Thomas Henry's farm on the north side of the creek or marsh, which it now is. From there, the trail passed northwards along the east bank of the creek crossing the main road in the settlement now Oshawa, east of where the Four Mill [Warren Mill] now stands. The trail stayed along on the east bank of the creek till it reached "Settler Widdifield's" place where the Reach Road (Simcoe Street, today), crosses the stream.[14]

While Pedlar, writing in 1894, describes two southern starting points for the Scugog Carrying Place, the Jones's 1795 map shows only one southern terminus on lot four by Lake Ontario where Wilson had his homestead. The 1795 trail bifurcates in a northerly direction in the second concession of Whitby Township, with one branch continuing along Farewell and Harmony creeks, while the second branch extends over to and follows the Oshawa Creek. Over the years the area near the mouth of the Oshawa Creek was more densely settled than Wilson's lot four, and what likely occurred is that the trail shifted to the west in the early 1800s to accommodate settlement in this area. Pedlar continued his description of the trail along the Oshawa Creek as moving north from Joseph Widdifield's homestead:

> At this point it crossed easterly over the Reach Road to the point where it formed a junction with the Trail starting from the Wilson settlement on Lake Ontario. An enterprising Indian trader called [Joseph] Wiley erected a Block House at this junction. This Block House was built of hewed pine logs and while the date of its erection could not be ascertained by any of the pioneers whom the writer met, yet the settlers who first took up lands in the vicinity in 1827, found the house in good condition.[15]

Timothy Fisher, who, as a boy, had come to the area from Fredericksburg (near Napanee, Ontario) with his father George in 1827 and settled on the Seventh Concession of Whitby Township, described the trail to Pedlar. Interestingly, Leslie Frost's trail map shows the Scugog Carrying Place east of the actual route of the trail. He places Wiley's blockhouse on lot nine, when in fact it was on lot twelve next to the trail shown on the 1795 map. Frost's version of the trail north of the Widdifield homestead to the Ninth Concession is also in error.

Pedlar noted that the trail:

> kept west of the present road [Simcoe Street] to Widdifields, in the 4th concession and about from a quarter to a half a mile west of the road from Widdifields to the 8th concession where it crossed the present Reach Road and curved to the Wiley Block House ....[16]

The trail, as marked on the 1795 map, runs east of the Oshawa Creek along lots eleven and twelve, following present-day Simcoe Street within half a lot's width. The trail route moves one lot west in the Fourth Concession and then veers east by three lots in the Ninth Concession — the same route followed by Oshawa's Simcoe Street today. At Wiley's blockhouse the two southern pathways of Scugog Carrying Place merged and continued north over the Oak Ridges Moraine, then called "the Ridges," and down into the Lake Scugog drainage basin. "The long winding Scugog River led into Sturgeon Lake and thence by a short portage over Cameron and Balsam Lakes, thence another portage between the latter lake and Talbot River, thence through Lake Simcoe, and down the Severn River to Matchedash Bay, Lake Huron."[17]

Pedlar also documented eyewitness evidence for the southern part of the trail. John Henry, born in 1820, Harvey Kerr, born in 1810, and Mrs. Hugh Carmichael, daughter of Ambrose Morris, who built a mill at Widdifield's, talked about seeing Natives on the trail near the mouth of the Oshawa Creek as late as 1841.

A view of the trail in 1827 would include a blockhouse along the northern part of Oshawa Creek, another blockhouse at the ridge between Whitby and Reach Townships, and one more at the spot where the trail meets the southern part of Lake Scugog. Except for a few homesteads along the Lake Ontario shoreline and the First Concession there was only Joseph Widdifield's dwelling at the Fourth Concession.

Additional evidence collected by Pedlar indicates that the trail running through Oshawa was used by the Mississauga between 1837 and 1841. By now, Simcoe Street encompassed much of it, and with the ongoing expansion of settlement, the trail would have been blocked in several locations, forcing movement along Simcoe Street and through the centre of the settlement of Oshawa, then called Skae's Corners.

Pedlar described a section of the trail north of the Oak Ridges Moraine as an alternative to the long trip up the Scugog River and over into Lake Simcoe via the Talbot River, north of Beaverton:

> A shorter trail than the one described also started from "Fish Point" on Cedar Creek in the 3rd Concession of Reach Township. This short trail after leaving Fish Point ascended the Nonquon River which flowed into the

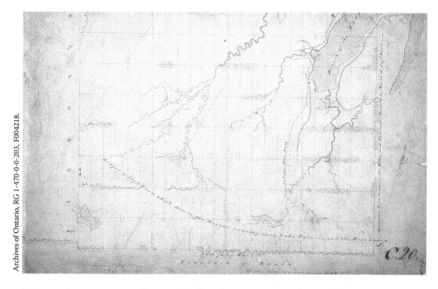

The southern portion of Samuel Wilmot's survey map of 1810 shows that originally Scugog Island was a peninsula. It became an island when a dam was built at Lindsay circa 1829–1830.

Scugog River from the north and went ascending this river a distance. A portage near where Wick now stands led to the Beaver River, thence to Lake Simcoe and down the Severn River to Matchedash Bay, Lake Huron. This shorter trail was used when light supplies were carried.[18]

The northern part of the 1810 Wilmot map shows a trail in the shape of an inverted "U," connecting the Nonquon and Beaver Rivers in the extreme south end of Brock Township. The location of the trail suggests it was a portage between the waterways. After reaching the south end of Lake Scugog, Scugog Carrying Place traversed the lake, then went up the Nonquon River for a short distance where it met the portage extending over to the Beaver River. The shallow Beaver River was either travelled by canoe or on foot, possibly towing canoes to Lake Simcoe.

The portage at Wick is clearly indicated on Samuel Wilmot's map of Reach Township. While the trail mostly followed the Beaver River north of the portage, it veered around the river at the location of

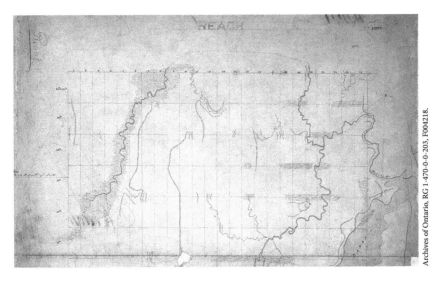

Reach Township Plan, Samuel Wilmot, 1810. *Northern portion. This section of the C20 survey map of 1810 identifies the portage between the Nonquon and Beaver Rivers as shown by the dotted line at the top of the map.*

present-day Cannington to avoid a set of rapids. A short path went around the rapids to the west of Cannington at Saginaw, a site frequented by the Chippewa.

Around 1821, Reuben Crandell, who was born in New York State and then farmed in Prince Edward County, was the first to move north along the trail into Reach Township, where Lake Scugog is situated, and settle just southwest of present-day Port Perry. More and more settlers would soon move into the region. Until 1829 the Mississauga had a camping ground at the head of the trail, which now would be in downtown Port Perry, but as newcomers continued to arrive, the Mississauga moved further north and finally shifted away from Lake Scugog towards Lake Simcoe and Mud Lake, today's Curve Lake.

In 1844, a few Mississauga families returned to Lake Scugog when the government annuity became available to them for the purchase of reserve land, but by this time the new settlement developments at Port Perry prevented them from relocating at their former campground. Today, it is home to seventy people of the Mississauga of Scugog Island

First Nation. At some point in the mid- to late-1840s, the Mississauga travel to Lake Ontario came to an end, but use of the north part of the trail along the Beaver River likely continued.

The year after John Sproule arrived from Fermanagh County, Ireland, in 1823, he settled on lot seventeen, Concession Twelve of Brock. His grandson, Philip Sproule, wrote the following:

> Through the centre of the property from south to north ran an Indian trail used by the Indians for portaging canoes from Lake Scugog to Lake Simcoe. Grandfather said, "I could look from my window and see an Indian in the lead, carrying a rifle. Behind him came the Indian women carrying the canoes on their heads while other Indian men brought up the rear.[19]

All evidence indicates that the Scugog Trail was a Native pathway already in existence when Benjamin Wilson first arrived and in continual use during the first few decades of European settlement, suggesting that the Mississauga and the Chippewa must have had a long tradition of using the Scugog Carrying Place.

JONES'S EASTERN EXTENSION

Four miles east of where the second trail moves into Darlington there existed a trail that extended from Bowmanville to Caesarea on Lake Scugog in Cartwright Township, and another trail ran from Caesarea to the northeast along the Scugog River. The trail Jones depicts heading into Darlington could have connected with the trail in Cartwright and Darlington Townships. As noted, Pedlar describes two paths starting at Lake Ontario, one commencing at the French Block House then travelling north along the west side of Harmony Creek to the north end of Whitby Township, where it merges with the western branch at the Wiley Blockhouse. Augustus Jones's 1795 survey map shows the path along Farewell and Harmony creeks in lots five and six, from the First to the Sixth Concession, where it extends into the neighbouring Township of Darlington. This allows for two possibilities: this branch of the Carrying Place could have continued northeast until it came to the eastern end of Lake Scugog, opposite Washburn Island and Ball Point, or it could have swung east along the Oak Ridges Moraine and possibly extended to Rice Lake.

The 1795 map suggests that the trail started at Wilson's homestead, at the bluff overlooking Lake Ontario, and crossed the baseline that Augustus Jones had surveyed in 1791 where the trail bifurcates into two paths. One path is the already-mentioned trail that travels along Harmony Creek and swings east into Darlington Township, while the other swings west until it reaches the east bank of the Oshawa Creek, near today's King Street. From along the east side of the Oshawa Creek this second trail heads north, crossing the Oak Ridges Moraine, and descends to Cedar Creek and Lake Scugog.

Wilmot's 1810 survey map of Reach Township is in agreement with the Jones map of 1795 in showing a continuation of the trail in a northerly direction. The two maps use the same scale and can be superimposed, one on the other, to examine how the paths line up. Though the Wilmot and Jones maps do not line up exactly (they are separated by the distance of two lots), they do show the continuity of the trail from Whitby into Reach Township and on into Brock.

The second pathway of the Scugog Carrying Place is important because it can be used to demonstrate that the paths changed over time. The eastern branch of the Scugog Trail on the earliest maps extends up the Harmony Creek watershed and turns east, disappearing into neighbouring Darlington Township. After two decades, this eastern branch no longer carried on into Darlington, but instead continued into the northern concessions of Whitby Township where it connected to the western branch of the trail that hugged the east bank of the Oshawa Creek. Another couple of decades later, the eastern branch disappeared and its location was replaced by the Nonquon Road, which in turn became today's Ritson Road.

Sometimes the trails changed as the First Nations moved around the landscape and established temporary camps and villages, only to abandon them after a generation or two to re-establish new settlements in the neighbouring regions. The Scugog Trail was a dynamic structure that evolved over time, and it is, therefore, difficult to pinpoint its exact course over a period of 400 years from the time of occupation by the Iroquois to the first contact with Europeans.

2

Iroquois and Mississauga on the Trail

"Worn smooth like a Buffalo run, caused by the action of countless feet for many generations, many years before white men entered this part of Canada."[1]

The trails that wound their way between Lakes Simcoe and Scugog, then on to Lake Ontario, are shrouded in the prehistoric past. Archaeological records show that immediately after the last glaciers melted and formed the Great Lakes, PaleoIndian hunters followed the caribou here and for the first time humans were trekking into and creating pathways in the region sometime after 10,000 years ago. This story of the trail begins with the first agriculturist Natives and extends to initial contact with Europeans. Between these two historical markers — the immediate post-glacial period and the contact period — the landscape recovered from its frozen epoch and a series of different forest species took root in the Great Lakes region, establishing the basis of the landscape we know today.

Though the Carrying Place's first documented evidence occurs on the 1795 map of Augustus Jones, certainly the Mississauga, who were using the trail at that time, must have been doing so in prior decades. When English settlers first encountered the Mississauga (and Chippewa) in southern Ontario in the 1780s and 1790s, they were spread out along Lake Ontario in a cluster of clans, or *dodems*. One group at the western end of Lake Ontario, the Eagle Clan, pronounced *Ma-se-sau-gee* in the Algonquian language, may have given its name to the Mississauga. Other clans lived at the Bay of Quinte, at the eastern end of Lake Ontario, around Lake Simcoe, and in the Trent River valley. They formed one cultural group, whose members intermarried and traded, and were part of a larger group in the Great Lakes region called the Ojibwa, though they called themselves the *Anishinabe*, meaning "human beings" or "men." Scattered in between Ojibwa settlements were small clusters of several Iroquois tribes at the Grand River and at the eastern end of Lake Ontario. While the Iroquois, loyal to the British, were recent arrivals who had moved from their ancestral home south of Lake Ontario to flee systematic attacks by American troops aimed at starving them off their land in the Mohawk Valley and the Finger Lakes of New York, the Mississauga were not. They had lived there throughout the previous 100 years.

The Scugog Trail was one of several trails connecting Georgian Bay with Lake Ontario. Other carrying places are documented on the 1688 map, developed by Pierre Raffeix (1635–1724), and possibly used for his missionary work with the Algonquians and Iroquois. It depicts four major trails, one of which connected the Humber River with Lake Simcoe; another joined the Rouge River with Lake Simcoe, while a third spanned the distance from the Trent River through the Kawartha lakes into Lake Simcoe. The fourth trail connected the Ganaraska River at Port Hope with Rice Lake to the north, and from there other connections were made to the Trent River and Lake Simcoe. Like the four major trails between Lake Simcoe and Lake Ontario, the Scugog Carrying Place served the same function and probably also existed in the seventeenth century.

The Raffeix map does not show Scugog Carrying Place, perhaps because it was a minor route or one that was not used by the French. The Toronto route via either the Humber or the Rouge River was important during the Seneca occupation of the north shore of Lake Ontario between the 1660s and 1680s and continued in use up to Lieutenant Governor Simcoe's arrival in 1793. The Ganaraska Carrying Place was important to the Mississauga during their conquest of southern Ontario in the 1690s. From the 1770s onward, fur traders used this route to travel to Rice Lake and on into the hinterland. Likewise, the Carrying Place at the mouth of the Trent River remained important because it provided access to a series of lakes in the interior between Lake Simcoe and the Trent.

The Iroquois residing in southern Ontario at the time of contact with European settlers were the last of a series of Iroquoian people who had once occupied the north shores of Lake Ontario dating back to at least the 1200s. The ancestors of the New York Iroquois had also invaded and briefly settled the north shore after causing the expulsion of the Huron, another Iroquoian people, by 1650. The temporary villages set up by these Iroquois are part of the story of how the Mississauga came to occupy the area along the Scugog Carrying Place.

The decline of the Iroquois villages on the north shore of Lake Ontario began during the time that Marquis de Denonville, governor of New France from 1685 to 1689, attacked the Seneca, one of the Iroquois tribes living south of the lake, in 1687, with his 1,600 "Troupes de la Marine" and his First Nations allies. After destroying Seneca villages south of Lake Ontario, Denonville moved north and stopped at the mouth of the Humber River, near Teiaiagon, also a Seneca village, and then on to Gandatskiagon at the mouth of the Rouge River. Whether Denonville's forces also destroyed these last two Seneca villages is not known. However, by 1701 these Iroquois villages had been abandoned and were in the hands of a new group of people, the Mississauga, who had come from a combination of places — some from the Georgian Bay area, some from Nippissing area, and others from around Lake Superior. They now had control of the Toronto Carrying Place.

ARRIVAL OF THE MISSISSAUGA

Peter Jones, son of Augustus Jones, who created the 1795 survey map, was also known by his Mississauga name *Kahkewaquonaby*, meaning "sacred waving feathers." He knew of his people's past history and how they came to southern Ontario. His diaries and his *History of the Ojebway Indians*[2] both record battles between the Mississauga and Iroquois in the late 1690s, with one of the battles taking place around Burlington Bay.

Peter Schmalz recounts the written and oral stories of the Mississauga conquest of southern Ontario and divides the period from the 1651 to

1701 into three stages.[3] The earliest involved the dispersal of the Huron and Algonquians, followed by a second period when the Iroquois from south of Lake Ontario established settlements along the northern shore of the lake in the 1660s to the 1680s. The final stage, which concluded in 1701, witnessed the expulsion of the Iroquois and the return of the Algonquians, this time as the Mississauga (and Chippewa). This period also saw the Algonquians, in partnership with the Wyandot (the remnants of the Huron) and the French, attack the Iroquois living on the north shore of Lake Ontario. After the Iroquois were either killed or fled, the Algonquians attacked them south of Lake Ontario.

Peter Jones's writings and other oral traditions of the Mississauga tell of fierce battles in which they overcame the Iroquois. These stories claim they attacked as two groups: one travelling from Lake Simcoe to

This calotype or early photograph of the Reverend Peter Jones (1802–1856) was taken in Edinburgh in August 1845 while he was visiting Scotland and England to raise money and champion the cause of the Credit River Reserve. This is believed to be the oldest surviving photograph of a First Nations man.

National Galleries of Scotland, Edinburgh, PGP HA 420

ONTARIO IROQUOIAN PREHISTORIC SITES

Scugog Carrying Place is documented as being used by the Mississauga
in 1795, but other evidence is needed to determine prior First Nations'
use of the trail. As noted, Leslie Frost lists a number of archaeological
sites along the Scugog and Kawartha waterways, suggesting that the
Carrying Place had ancient roots. Most of these sites are located in
Victoria County, along the eastern branch of the Scugog Carrying Place.
As for the western branch of the trail, Frost only provides a cursory list
containing one site in Oshawa, two in Reach Township, and four near
Lake Scugog, but with few descriptive details. Since the publication of
Forgotten Pathways in 1973, other sites have been discovered, adding to
our understanding of prehistoric locations near the Scugog Carrying
Place. The archaeological sites described here are found along the western branch of the trail, from Oshawa in the south to Thorah Island in the
north. (See Appendix A for more details.)

Archaeologists have designated an aboriginal settlement that existed
along the east bank of Harmony Creek in the fifteenth century as the
Grandview site because it was discovered near Grandview Street in
Oshawa. This site was within several hundred yards of the eastern branch
of Scugog Carrying Place along Harmony Creek, suggesting that originally this eastern portion of the Carrying Place was more important than
the western branch along the Oshawa Creek. The Grandview site was a
village of the Ontario Iroquoians,[13] who were called the Huron during
the historic period. Before 1500 these people lived in scattered villages
in an area between present-day Orangeville and Bowmanville. Over the
centuries their villages were relocated to the Simcoe County area where
Samuel de Champlain found them in 1615.

A little over eight miles north of the Grandview site, in the headwaters
of the Oshawa Creek, is the Pascoe site. Though not well-studied, Pascoe
is an Iroquoian site, likely the location of a village. Further along the trail
is the Prospect site, north of the Oak Ridges Moraine near the southwest
shore of Lake Scugog and on the Second Concession of Scugog Township
(known as Reach Township until 1856). Ceramics, stone implements, and
bones have been found on the Prospect site, suggesting it too may have

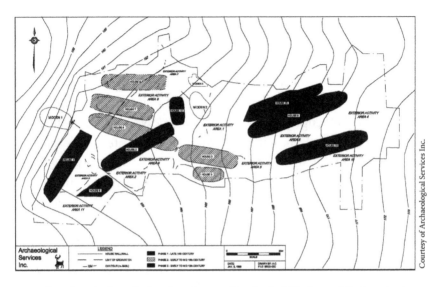

An archaeologist's plan of what Grandview village looked liked as a fully functioning village in the late 1300s and early 1400s. From R.F. Williamson et al., "The Archaeology of the Grandview Site: A Fifteenth Century Iroquoian Community on the North Shore of Lake Ontario." Arch Notes (September/October 2003): 44.

been a village. The site is located on a plateau overlooking two streams, a typical location for an Iroquoian village. Other Iroquoian sites found on the northern edge of Lake Scugog include Seagrave and Washburn.[14] In 2007 a potential First Nations burial site was discovered at Prince Albert, now part of Port Perry. The site, examined by the Mississaugas of Scugog First Nations, revealed evidence suggesting that a minimum of twenty-nine First Nations burials took place at this location.

The Seagrave Ossuary was located near the Nonquon River, close to Scugog Carrying Place. Although the site yielded little information, as an ossurial site it would have represented an Ontario Iroquoian population. The Uxbridge Ossuary, located to the west of Reach Township, is approximately eight miles away and resides southwest of the Beaver River and the Scugog Carrying Place. The ossuary dates from approximately A.D. 1490 and consists of secondary group burials (every so many years the first burials were dug up and reburied in a communal burial plot). These reburials took place once or twice in a generation, during which time an Ontario Iroquoian village would have relocated. It can be reasonably speculated that the Seagrave and Uxbridge Ossuary people were closely related to the Grandview population.

A number of other Ontario Iroquoian sites have been found in the northern townships of Reach, Brock, and Thorah. One Iroquoian site on Lake Scugog is Washburn Island, which has artifacts from both the historic period and Early Iroquoian and dates to around A.D. 1000–1300. However, information on the Washburn Island site is problematic since it was never completely excavated. In 1951, Kenneth Kidd, then a Trent University professor of anthropology and a member of the Ethnology Department at the Royal Ontario Museum, dug some test pits on Washburn Island and discovered two dozen ceramic pieces, but his work was never published. With a crew of eight, Kidd excavated the pits from July 9–24. Before he dug, there had been reports of a burial a few years earlier when a local farmer put up a fence.

Three years before Kidd arrived at the site, Frank Ridley, an avocational archaeologist and a founding member of the Ontario Archaeological Society, excavated on Washburn Island and found various vessels, presumably ceramic, along with a copper awl and a slate bar amulet. Kidd, in his excavation, found much more. Although he found some archaic artifacts, which typically date back over 3,000 years, the majority collected were either of Iroquoian origin or from a later period. Kidd and his crew found over 900 stone flakes, indicating that this was also a manufacturing site for the production of arrowheads and scrapers. Other stone tools were also found, including several adzes, grinding stones, a gorget, and a net sinker used for fishing. The many Iroquoian pottery fragments found at the Washburn site suggest that a large enough Iroquoian population existed there for some time. It certainly was a large campsite, possibly even an Iroquoian village site. In addition, some pottery artifacts dating to the seventeenth and eighteenth centuries point to a time during the era of New France. From the evidence uncovered, Kidd believed some trade goods at the site were of English origin, suggesting a time when the Mississauga of the area were trading with the English south of Lake Ontario.

The Thomas site on lot eighteen, Concession Fourteen of Reach Township near the Nonquon River is a Late Iroquoian village with a reported but un-described ossuary burial nearby. The site also contains some human burials along with 1,516 pottery shards and some pipes. Ontario Iroquoians grew tobacco, and like the historic Huron, used it in ceremonial settings. The pipes from the Thomas site are similar to those found in the Trent Valley, suggesting a link between the two areas.

The Baird site and the Baird ossuary are found near the Thomas site. The Baird site may have been a village, while the ossuary would have contained the human burial remains from nearby locations, such as the Thomas and Baird sites. The site had been dug up some decades past and was reported to contain sixteen to eighteen skeletal remains. The burials were in a circular fashion with the feet pointing toward the centre. In Brock Township, the Markson site is another village site west of the Beaver River near the portage to the Nonquon, as indicated on Samuel Wilmot's survey map of 1810.

Burial sites at Ball Point and Seven Mile Island, or Nonquon Island, on Lake Scugog, are mentioned in early accounts and may date to the time when the Mississauga were at the lake. Another potential Mississauga burial site is located in Port Perry right beside the old Simcoe Road, which replaced the Scugog Carrying Place trail. *The Beaverton Story* describes three Indian sites on Thorah Island off the mouth of the Beaver River and another two sites in the Beaverton area with a population of 200 inhabitants. It further mentions an Indian graveyard in Beaverton and a "little city of the dead" along a creek north of Beaverton.[15]

However, no archaeological evidence is available to document the existence of a Native settlement at Beaverton prior to the coming of the Europeans. On Thorah Island, northeast from the mouth of the Beaver River on Lake Simcoe, there are more archaeological remains. The island contains the Corin and the Bristow sites, both excavated by archaeologist Paul Sweetman during the 1950s and 1960s. Corin is a small fishing camp site dating back 2,000 years, while Bristow is a potential village site with artifacts that date back to the Point Peninsula archaeological period.[16] Both sites also contain proto or early historic Huron material, indicating that they were in use during the contact period with the French. These two sites yielded French axes, iron knives, and copper kettles in close association with Huron sherds. Travellers coming north on the Scugog Carrying Place likely made a stop at Thorah Island if they proceeded to Huron-Wendat territory, which was immediately to the northwest of the island.

The Iroquoian people developed a reliance on agriculture and had several storage procedures for corn, providing a stable food source during the winter. This, in turn, allowed them to live in semi-permanent villages with large structures for accommodations. Each of these structures, called longhouses, accommodated several families, with a separate fireplace and storage area for each family. Corn was stored in interior anterooms in casks, and in exterior vestibules at each end of the longhouse. The ears of corn were harvested, then tied in bundles, hung on racks to dry, shelled, and the kernels put in the casks or bins.

In the fourteenth century, the Iroquoian people who lived in Ontario practised a low-intensity form of agriculture largely based on corn, beans, and squash. A variety of cultivated crops and wild plant food were consumed:

> the inhabitants of the Grandview site cultivated maize, bean, sunflower, cucurbit (a plant in the gourd family), and tobacco. Plant remains also indicate that the settlement benefited from a well-developed anthropogenic plant community made up of locally available forest edge plant species such as bramble, strawberry, and elderberry, and adventive weeds such as chenopod.[17]

Crops were planted between tree stumps in fields near the villages. After exhausting the nutrients in a field, the Iroquoian farmers would move to another nearby virgin area and commence to plant there. In this way, the farmers would exhaust the agricultural potential of an area to the extent that they would have to move. This meant that village sites relocated over the years — a generation or two might live out their lives in one village before their descendants would have to pack up their belongings, move to a new area, build new dwellings, and plant new fields. It is believed that the Iroquoians inhabited the site of Grandview village for approximately forty years.

When Grandview was initially settled in the latter part of the fourteenth century, it consisted of four longhouses closely clustered together on the eastern slope of Harmony Creek, in a village without any wooden palisade or wall. A windbreak or fence connected to a pathway led down the slope towards the creek. On the other side of the stream lay the Scugog Carrying Place. The first structures at Grandview were followed by two additional large longhouses, which suggest permanent residency within kinship groups.

After the initial settlement phase, another two discrete settlements developed at the Grandview site, and have been dated to the first half of the fifteenth century. The last two phases contained eight houses. While the first and second phases were built on the eastern slope of Harmony Creek, the third and last phase was erected on a more level area to the east of the first two areas. Over 11,000 artifacts were found at Grandview with 60 percent of the assemblages covering this later settlement. The site eventually covered about two acres and contained eight semi-subterranean structures, which are interpreted as being sweat lodges. At this later stage of occupation the Grandview site was habitable on a year-round basis.

Grandview would have been related to other villages in the region with which it shared a common kinship and ethnic connections. Ronald Williamson, whose firm, Archaeological Services of Toronto, excavated the Grandview Site, states that:

> the preponderance of available evidence suggests that shortly before A.D. 1400, a group of Iroquoians from the Duffin's Creek or Rouge River watershed in the west came to settle at the Grandview site on Harmony Creek in Oshawa ... the best current indications are that the Grandview villages then moved some 5.5 kilometres to the west and re-established themselves at the MacLeod site near what is now the intersection of Rossland and Thornton Roads.[18]

The nearby MacLeod site dates to around A.D. 1450 with very similar ceramics as the Grandview site, suggesting that the inhabitants of Grandview moved to the MacLeod site after abandoning Grandview.

A display of Grandview pottery and Grandview pipes excavated by Ronald Williamson and his team. Arch Notes *(September/ October 2003): 33, 36*

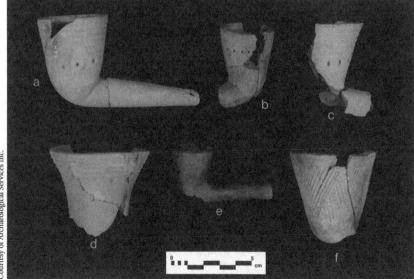

A team of archaeologists (Bill Donaldson, Joyce Holloway, Bruce Drewitt, J.N. Emerson, and Marti Latta) excavated the MacLeod site between 1968 and 1972. The site contained at least two longhouses, though probably not all of the site was excavated, since it appeared that some of it was under the intersection of Rossland and Thornton Roads in Oshawa and therefore not accessible. Some of the structures at the site may have been destroyed prior to its discovery. One of these structures they found measured 190.3 feet by twenty-seven feet, making it larger than any of the structures at the Grandview site. The MacLeod site is contemporary with the last phase of construction at the Grandview site.

A wide assortment of bones from mammals, birds, fish, and reptiles were found, indicating a year-round pattern of hunting and fishing in the area. Plant remains were also found at MacLeod in the form of charred seeds, with maize or corn representing 75 percent of the total and almost 4 percent represented by beans and 7 percent by chenopod, a wild plant belonging to the Goosefoot Family.

An analysis of the remains of ceramic containers used for cooking and storage concluded that the site, and therefore the inhabitants at the MacLeod site, were closely related to the Reesor site on the Rouge River to the west and also showed a strong similarity to sites in Prince Edward County. A ceramic analysis from the Grandview and MacLeod sites also shows close affiliations with the Hardrock site and other Trent Valley archaeological sites. Since Ontario Iroquoian villages often relocated, the Trent Valley population could represent a former southern population that gradually migrated north. MacLeod and Grandview villages existed until about A.D. 1450 while a slightly younger population is represented at the sites of Prospect, Thomas, Washburn Island, and Uxbridge to the north.

James V. Wright, curator emeritus of the Canadian Museum of Civilization, indicates that by about A.D. 1400 the Huron population was divided into a northern and a southern division, occupying the area between Lake Simcoe to Lake Ontario. By approximately A.D. 1550 the southern division moved north, which resulted in a gradual blending of the two groups. Wright speculates that the southern division was composed of the Rock and One-White-Lodge clans that existed among the Huron at the time of first contact with Europeans.[19]

The migration north of the southern Ontario Iroquoian groups from near Lake Ontario fits the prehistoric data that is found at villages and other sites along the Scugog Carrying Place. The oldest sites dating between A.D. 1380 and 1450 are found at Grandview and the MacLeod sites. As one moves north along the Carrying Place the sites become progressively younger in age. The Uxbridge, Thomas, and Baird ossuaries date from around A.D. 1490. Fifty years later, no Iroquoian sites are known in the area where the earlier villages and ossuaries existed. In any case, by the time Champlain visited the Huron, no permanent settlements, with the possible exception of Thorah Island, are known to have existed along the Scugog Carrying Place.

Since the sites are not clustered together but are strung out along the drainage basins of Oshawa and Harmony creeks, Lake Scugog, and the Nonquon and Beaver Rivers, this is the best evidence to suggest that the Scugog Carrying Place may have existed as far back as the latter half of the 1300s.

Iroquois in Southern Ontario

The period between when the Ontario Iroquoians vacated the region where the Scugog Carrying Place was found and the Mississauga moved into the area is poorly understood. After the Ontario Iroquoians moved into Huron-Wendat territory, by the end of the sixteenth century, the area around the Scugog Carrying Place was not occupied by any Native settlements for approximately 100 years. Only after the dispersal of the Huron in 1650 were there new migrants on the major Carrying Places along the north shore of Lake Ontario. The Iroquois, also known as the *Haudenosaunee* in their own language and as the Five Nations to the English, were a group of confederated tribes (Cayuga, Mohawk, Onondaga, Oneida, and Seneca), who were the next to move into the area. Place names identifying two of their villages, Gandatskiagon and Ganaraska, are found in close proximity on French-era maps on either side of the Scugog Carrying Place. Both are identified on the Raffeix map as sites of carrying places. Gandatskiagon was founded around 1650 by the Seneca.

Scugog Carrying Place

By 1673 there were seven new villages settled by the Iroquois along the north shore of Lake Ontario. From east to west they were: Ganneious, on Napanee Bay near the Quinte Peninsula, occupied by the Oneida; Kente on the Bay of Quinte; Kentsio on Rice Lake; and Ganaraska at Port Hope. The last three villages were settled by the Cayuga. The other villages were Quintio, on Rice Lake; Gandatskiagon, near the mouth of the Rouge River; Teyaiagon, or Teiaiagon, near the mouth of the Humber River; and Quinaouatoua, on the portage between the western end of Lake Ontario and the Grand River. The latter three villages were occupied by the Seneca. These settlements controlled the main hunting and trading routes from the north to the Five Nations' homeland in New York.

French maps of the seventeenth century show the carrying places that were used between the north shore of Lake Ontario and the inland waters that led to Georgian Bay on Lake Huron. During this period of Iroquois occupation of the north shore of Lake Ontario, a shift occurs in the importance of the carrying places. Gandatskiagon is well recognized as the primary route from Lake Ontario to Lake Simcoe. The French missionaries Fenelon and Trouvé visited this Seneca town in the winter of 1669. Other French travellers also used the carrying place at Gandatskiagon to get to Lake Huron. However, by the time the French established a fort at Toronto in the early half of the 1700s, the route through Teiaiagon began to take on more importance than the Gandatskiagon route. Speculation would conclude that the importance of the carrying places to Lake Simcoe shifted to the west over a period of several decades or more, from the Scugog Carrying Place to the two Toronto-area carrying places at Teiaiagon and Gandatskiagon.

The Cayuga, Oneida, and Seneca came north because they were continually being harassed by the Andastes, an Iroquoian-speaking tribe located in the Susquehanna Valley during the 1660s. The Cayuga apparently did not stay long, for after the defeat of the Andastes in 1675 they returned to the southern shore of Lake Ontario. The number of Iroquois warriors returning south of the lake increased substantially between 1685 and 1689, when the Seneca and Cayuga increased by 500 warriors. By 1688 the Iroquois settlement again appears to be restricted to the area south of Lake Ontario.

The Search for *Cabane de Plomb*

"forming at once one Grand Highway ... which route has been used from time immemorial by the Indians of every tribe, as well as the Fur Traders, Jesuits and other adventurers."[1]

Specific trees along the trail, usually those on high spots of land, would have been conspicuously marked to indicate the direction of the trail. These trees, designated as signposts by First Nations people, are referred to as "wayfinding" trees and have been found all over eastern North America. A few decades ago, a wayfinding tree bent in an L-shape twenty feet above the ground was located on the trail north of Conlins Road in Oshawa. The Scugog Carrying Place would likely have been marked by distinctive wayfinding trees. With the Huron having their own set of trails within Huron territory, Scugog Carrying Place would have been a natural southeastern extension of their trails. There is also evidence of Ontario Iroquoian villages along the route of the Scugog Carrying Place in the several hundred years prior to historic-era Huron occupation in Simcoe County, but it is not possible to determine which group would have established the trees as trail markers.

As noted, some historians have put forward the thesis that the Scugog Trail was used by the Iroquois to attack the Huron-Wendat. The main proponent of this idea was Leslie Frost, who first publicized the existence of Scugog Carrying Place and gave it its name, having based his claim for the existence of the trail on Samuel Pedlar's historical accounts of early Oshawa. However, Frost's evidence, at best, was circumstantial. He linked the occurrence of *Cabane de Plomb*, the geographical term found on the

1755 d'Anville map of eastern North America, with the French trading post that Pedlar describes near the Benjamin Wilson's homestead.[2]

Frost, who was very familiar with the history of the Lindsay area, collaborated with Thomas Llewellyn Bouckley (1904–1988) on the details of Oshawa history concerning the Scugog Carrying Place. Bouckley had come to Oshawa as a young boy along with his father, Audry, around 1908, a couple of years before Samuel Pedlar died. Bouckley was familiar with the oral history, which suggests that Benjamin Wilson spent his first year in Whitby Township living in an abandoned French trading post. Bouckley speculated that this post was the *Cabane de Plomb* after examining Percy Robinson's 1933 book, *Toronto during the French Régime*, with its reproduction of the d'Anville map identifying the location of *Cabane*.[3]

Samuel Pedlar refers to the trading post as a "French Block House." His manuscript on the Indian trail, combined with the d'Anville map, became the evidence that caused Thomas Bouckley to suggest to Leslie Frost that *Cabane de Plomb* was a French trading post located on the trail about 150 yards east of the Oshawa Harbour Pioneer Cemetery, on lot four, settled by Benjamin Wilson by 1794. Since this collaboration with Leslie Frost, *Cabane* became associated with the Scugog Carrying Place as stipulated in *Forgotten Pathways of the Trent*, and the publication has been cited as proof that *Cabane* and the French-era trading post along the trail are one and the same. However, all the evidence at the disposal of Bouckley and Frost points to their conclusion being mere speculation. With additional information now available, a different picture of the relationship between *Cabane* and the trail is emerging.

A lake similar in appearance to Lake Scugog is suggested on d'Anville's 1755 map. It looks much like the current lake in its surrounding

Facing page (top): Canada Louisiane et terres Angloises. *Northwest section. Jean Baptiste Bourguignon d'Anville, 1755. This early French map displays the location of* Cabane de Plomb. *Facing page (bottom):* Partie Occidentale du Canada et Septentrionale de la Louisiane avec une partie de la Pensilvanie, *Jean Baptiste Bourguignon d'Anville, 1775. A later d'Anville map displaying the location of* Cabane de Plomb.

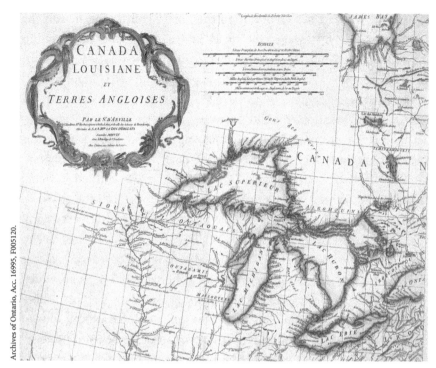

geography, with a river emptying to the north, connecting it with the Trent River valley. However, the small nature of the relief portrayed in the d'Anville map makes an exact identification impossible. A lake similar to Lake Scugog also appears in Giuseppe Bressani's 1657 map, entitled *Novae Franciae Accurata Delineatio*, though no written record from the French period mentions the lake. However, created almost a century earlier than d'Anville's map, Bressani's map suggests that Lake Scugog was known to the early seventeenth-century French explorers in the region.

Jean-Baptiste Bourguignon d'Anville's 1755 map, entitled *Canada, Louisiane, et Terres Angloises*, is presumed to be based on the charts of other mapmakers such as Joseph Gaspard Chaussegros de Léry (père) (1682–1756), who did visit and map Lake Ontario, unlike d'Anville, who never visited North America. D'Anville's previous map of a decade earlier (1745) shows no sign of *Cabane de Plomb*, while on his 1775 map, which is almost identical to his 1755 map, *Cabane* is placed on the north shore of Lake Ontario between Gandatskiagon and Ganaraska, both known Seneca communities colonized in the latter half of the seventeenth century. *Cabane* is shown south of Lake Scugog and Rice Lake, but because of the small scale of the map, its precise location is uncertain. The stream beside *Cabane* on the d'Anville map could be the Oshawa or Farewell Creek, but it could just as easily be Lynde Creek to the west or Soper Creek to the east.

The name *Cabane de Plomb* in French implies a structure of lead, perhaps a trading post where furs were traded for lead shot and other commercially manufactured trade goods such as axes, knives, and kettles. Reports indicate that by 1800 the southern Mississauga had mostly lost their ability to hunt using their traditional weapons and had become fully dependent on European trade goods, including rifles. Lead shot would have been extremely important for hunting. D'Anville, working on his maps in Paris, apparently took the name from the French map-makers who visited the Great Lakes.

In 1726, de Léry created a map of Lake Ontario (*Carte du Lac Ontario*), which shows a *Cabane au Plomb* in the same general location as *Cabane de Plomb* on d'Anville's map. A "post with lead" seems a more appropriate descriptor than a house of lead. De Léry did not see *Cabane*, for he notes on his map that he did not travel the north shore of Lake Ontario, but relied on others for the information. The early map-maker Jean-Baptiste-Louis Franquelin has a *Cabane au Plomb* on his 1699 map of Lake Ontario, which may be the first instance of the use of that term; his earlier map of 1688 did not include a *Cabane au Plomb*. This may indicate that the location came into existence between 1688 and 1699. If so, that would place it in the same time period as its neighbouring villages of Gandatskiagon and Ganaraska. At that time, the Seneca were building villages on the north shore of the lake and *Cabane* could have been an Iroquoian settlement. The use of the French term *Cabane au Plomb* should not imply that it was a French post. Franquelin was a proponent of using French names to replace the various Native names employed on maps of the Great Lakes and he may simply have renamed an Iroquoian village with a French name.

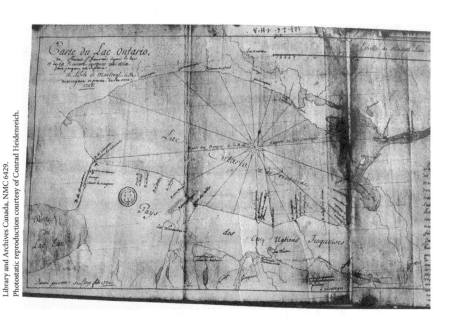

Carte du Lac Ontario et du fleuve St. Laurens depuis le lac Erie jusques au dessus de L'Isle [*sic*] de Montreal. Celle de Niagara en partie du lac erie, 1726. *Gaspard-Joseph Chaussegros de Léry, 1726. De Léry's map illustrates the north shoreline of Lake Ontario of 1726 showing* Cabane au Plomb.

Whatever *Cabane au Plomb* or *Cabane de Plomb* was, it existed by the last decade of the seventeenth century. The data that d'Anville copied was fifty years out of date and did not reflect the actual conditions of the date attached to his maps. D'Anville used the term *Iroquois du Nord* to describe the Iroquois who lived along the north of Lake Ontario only during the period from 1650 to 1700. However, by 1755 the terms *Iroquois du Nord* and *Cabane*, along with place names such as Gandatskiagon, were no longer in existence since the Iroquois had abandoned the north shore of Lake Ontario by 1700.

With the French not having any posts on Lake Ontario in 1699, except at Fort Frontenac (Kingston), *Cabane de Plomb* is not likely to have been a trading post. It is more plausible that *Cabane* was a Native settlement of some type. Frost's expectation that *Cabane* was on the Scugog Carrying Place clouded his judgment when it came to considering alternative sites. Before he published his 1973 book, Frost had correspondence from D.F. McQuat, the archivist of Ontario, who stated that the Oshawa location for *Cabane* was guesswork and that there were no known French-period structures in that area. But Frost did not accept this analysis and persisted with the idea of locating *Cabane* near the east end of the Oshawa Harbour.

As already noted, *Cabane de Plomb* appears on the d'Anville map midway between Gandatskiagon at the mouth of the Rouge River and the mouth of the Ganaraska River. Unfortunately, the d'Anville map is not accurate enough to pinpoint *Cabane* in Whitby Township with any certainty, there being few cartographic landmarks. In fact, no reason exists to exclude neighbouring Darlington Township with its distinctive landmark of Raby Head on Lake Ontario, and which appears in some English maps of the eighteenth century. We owe the location of *Cabane* in Whitby Township to Frost's assumption that it could not be anywhere else.

The Short archaeological site, located in Bowmanville, is a possible candidate for *Cabane de Plomb*. It fits the same general location as is indicated on the d'Anville map, being situated between the Rouge and Ganaraska Rivers. Several burials were discovered near the Short site around 1927 or 1928, but the skeletons were removed or reburied.

A series of historical artifacts were also discovered at the Short site including French and English gun flints and pipes. Actually, such a site with historic artifacts is a better fit for *Cabane* in the years between 1688 and 1699 than the area where Benjamin Wilson settled, which has no archaeological evidence of a Native settlement on the shores of Lake Ontario.

The earliest documentary source for a French trading house comes from the *History of the Early Settlement of Bowmanville*, published in 1875, which quotes a letter written by an early settler, Jessica Burk, who lived east of Benjamin Wilson. The brief quote mentions an "old French trading house, that Wilson got in."[4] It is a matter of speculation whether the post was erected during the French occupation of Lake Ontario prior to 1760, as some have claimed, or whether a French trader built the post during the early years of English administration before 1794. Most likely the latter is true. When Benjamin Wilson came to the area the building was abandoned but still habitable. That is not likely to have been true had it been built during the French period and then abandoned for over thirty years prior to Wilson's arrival.

It's not coincidental that Wilson chose to build his house at the terminus of the Carrying Place. He likely had prior knowledge of the location of the Carrying Place and of the French cabin before arriving there. Thomas Kaiser, a former mayor of Oshawa, suggests that Simcoe knew a French trader had left a cabin on the Scugog Carrying Place.

FRENCH AND ENGLISH TRADERS ON LAKE ONTARIO

We have no records of the early French or English using the Scugog Trail. A photograph of a cross of Lorraine dating from around 1740, found in the Scugog-Kawartha waterway, is the basis of Frost's evidence of trading or missionary activity along the trail in the mid-eighteenth century.[5] Historic-era material discovered at Washburn Island and at the Corin and Bristow sites on Thorah Island demonstrate that French trading goods either came close to or actually did move along the Scugog Carrying Place in the seventeenth and eighteenth centuries.

Scugog Carrying Place

The Bressani map of 1657 shows what is presumably Lake Scugog and also depicts a number of streams along the north shore of Lake Ontario. Since Bressani was a Jesuit who travelled to the Huron lands, his map indicates that the French were familiar with the geography of the region between lower Georgian Bay and Lake Ontario. We know English traders came along the north shore of Lake Ontario to trade with the Mississauga, but they would not have gone up the Scugog Trail, since the Natives traded directly with the English at Albany, New York. Probably the Mississauga were using the Scugog Trail to travel to Lake Ontario to trade, rather than the English traders travelling up the trail to the Mississauga.

Several European traders, however, are found operating along the north shore of Lake Ontario in the 1700s. In his *Toronto during the French Régime*, Percy Robinson provides some information on who was in the region at that time, although he concentrated primarily on fur traders at Toronto. English traders from Albany, New York, travelled along the north shore of Lake Ontario on numerous occasions. Beginning *circa* 1762, Robinson indicates the names of such traders as Schulyer, Stevenson, Everart, and Wendel. That year, Jacques Duperon Baby was trading at Toronto, and by the following year another trader named Knaggs was there. In 1770, St. Jean Rousseau established a trading operation in Toronto near the Humber River.

Another trader, Archibald Thompson, arrived during the American Revolution. "Mr. Thompson, Merch't here, has applied to me for leave to send a Person to Taranto, opposite this, to trade with the Indians."[6] Despite Thompson's initial failure to trade at Toronto, between 1784 and 1786 he moves several times between Niagara and the townships west of Kingston. His name later appears in lists of settlers at Toronto.

Other traders built houses to the east at Ganaraska, which later became Port Hope. Richard Beasley (1761–1842), a fur trader, businessman, and farmer, and Peter Smith (1752–1826), a businessman in Kingston, were trading there by 1783. Even earlier, in 1771, the traders Ferrol Wade and C. Kreuser are recorded at Port Hope. Other traders, who did not settle long in the area, would build a house to facilitate trade with the Mississauga. One such person was John Long, who with a partner from Montreal opened up a trading house at Ganaraska in 1786.

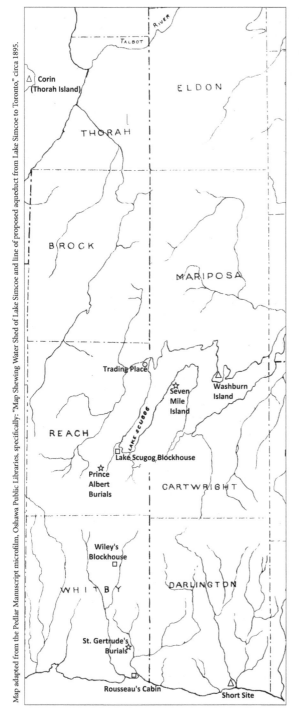

Map adapted from the Pedlar Manuscript microfilm, Oshawa Public Libraries, specifically: "Map Shewing Water Shed of Lake Simcoe and line of proposed aqueduct from Lake Simcoe to Toronto," circa 1895.

Fur Trading Houses; Burial Grounds and First Nation Sites with European Goods (post-1600 to early 1800s).

Map Key:

☐   *Fur Trading Houses*

△   *First Nations Sites*

☆   *Burial Grounds*

○   *Undetermined Trading Place*

William Peak, a Loyalist from the United States, was another early trader along Lake Ontario. His personal account, written in 1837, indicates that he came to Upper Canada in 1783. He first settled near the Don River, but later, by 1793, had moved to a farm in Hope Township in Northumberland County. Later still, in 1798, he moved to Pickering Township where he is credited as being the first settler in the area. Peak claimed that surveyor general D.W. Smith induced him to settle near the mouth of Duffin's Creek at another probable carrying place connecting Lake Ontario with Lake Simcoe. A fur trader and interpreter for the Mississauga, he was known to travel with Chief Wabakischoe along the north shore of Lake Ontario. Peak was one of the individuals Benjamin Wilson met soon after arriving at his new home at the southern terminus of the Scugog Carrying Place.

Although Robinson concentrated on the two main carrying places around Toronto — the Humber and Rouge trails up to the Holland River, and then to Lake Simcoe — he also mentions the other trails that connected Lake Ontario to Lake Simcoe: the Ganaraska and Bay of Quinte Carrying Places. He gives Ganaraska the name of *Pimitiscutiank-Piminiscotyan* and mentions that between 1770 and 1780 a trading house was located there.[7] A portion of the 1755 d'Anville map appears in Robinson's book, showing the region between Toronto and Port Hope where the *Cabane de Plomb* was located. Robinson, however, does not mention *Cabane* in his text; it was others such as Bouckley and Frost who inferred the existence of the *Cabane* at the Scugog Carrying Place from d'Anville's map in Robinson's book.

As noted previously, the real *Cabane au Plomb*, as it was called in the earliest maps, was in existence at some point between 1688 and 1699. This is far too early to be the French trading house that Benjamin Wilson spent his first winter at in Whitby Township.

THE TRADING POST

Assuming the Mississauga used the trail in the 1700s as they did in the 1800s, they would have come down from Lake Scugog in the spring and back down in the autumn while stopping to fish and hunt near Lake Ontario. This would make the log cabin at Wilson's an ideal location for fur traders to barter goods with the Mississauga while they were in the area.

There has been a collective memory of a French trading post, attributed to the early settlers in Whitby Township during the last decade of the eighteenth century, but this should not be construed as proof that this cabin was *Cabane de Plomb*. In fact, in addition to this "remembered" French trading post at Lake Ontario, two other structures existed along the Scugog Carrying Place during the first decades of the 1800s: a blockhouse at Lake Scugog and another near Raglan (between today's Columbus and Port Perry).

Pedlar mentions that the information about the trading post at the lake came from the grandson of Benjamin Wilson, who heard it from his mother (Nancy Wilson), Benjamin's daughter, who was born shortly after the family arrived in the area. Others in the region, such as Jessica Burk, Benjamin's neighbour, are also quoted as having seen the trading post. In his history of Oshawa, Kaiser wrote that, "His first house was the deserted log cabin once used as a trading post by the French previous to the conquest of Quebec. It was located just east of the little burying ground (on top of Gifford Hill), now visible for some distance in almost all directions on the lake front."[8] This is the same spot that Thomas Bouckley gives for *Cabane de Plomb*, though he mistakenly assumed that it and the trading post were one and the same. Lyman Gifford, former mayor of Oshawa from 1958 to 1966, indicated the location of the French trading post as a few hundred feet east of Bouckley's location. Gifford's stipulated location was outlined in a letter recalling his visit to the site in the 1960s with Bob Stephenson, a local scuba diver. Stephenson stated:

> Early one Sunday morning while preparing to dive in Oshawa Harbour, I heard someone calling to me from the East side of the harbour basin (no development there at that time). Putting into shore with my diving pontoon, I recognized Lyman. He suggested that we walk over to the Second marsh, and he would point out the "footings" of the trading post. (We had discussed the *"Cabane de Plomb"*

previously.) As we crossed the field below Cemetery Hill, he explained how he and Lloyd [his brother] had played around the (at that time) "footings" and timbers from the Benjamin Wilson era. Climbing over a wire-fence, approx. 250 ft. from the beach, we crossed a wooded area at the side of the marsh ... Approx. 200 ft. from the wire-fence (East) that Lyman and I had climbed over, he stopped at what appeared to be the South end of a "mound" about 12" high. Despite the small bushes and trees growing inside this clearly defined mounded rectangular area, it was very visible during this period.[9]

In the spring of 2010, Ducks Unlimited were involved in construction work on a canal built along the Second Marsh, where the edges of the canal were dug to a depth of three to four feet along the canal's eastern edge. This work occurred in the vicinity of the trading post site described by Stephenson and its impact on the site is not known. At no time during the initial construction of the canal in 2000, or during additional construction a decade later, was an effort made to undertake an archaeological assessment of this location.

Pinpointing the French trading post with precision has not been possible. Kaiser and Bouckley both place it immediately east of the pioneer cemetery on lot four, while Augustus Jones, as noted earlier, mentions that "St. John lives on the front of this lot." The ploughed area where Bouckley locates the cabin has yielded few if any artifacts and Gifford's suggested location next to the marsh in the adjacent lot three is based only on the eyewitness report quoted above from the previous occupants of the property.

From Augustus Jones we know that the front of Wilson's lot four was inhabited by St. John, also known as Jean Baptiste Rousseau, in August of 1791. One assumption is that he built the French trading house that Wilson discovered on arriving in Whitby Township. It was Rousseau, who, through his contacts with Lieutenant Governor Simcoe, would have passed on the information that his trading cabin on the Scugog Carrying Place was empty and he may have even suggested that someone monitor the Scugog Trail by occupying the log cabin.

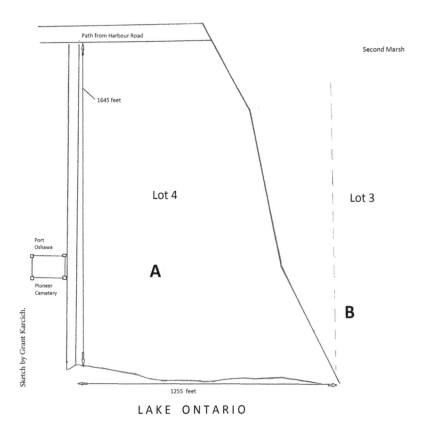

The two documented locations of the French cabin, as indicated by Thomas Bouckley (A) and Lyman Gifford (B), are illustrated above.

Rousseau was born in 1758, and between 1775 and 1779 he served as an interpreter for the British during the American Revolutionary War. After the war he settled in Cataraqui or Kingston in 1783 and continued to live in the Bay of Quinte area where he worked as a trader along the north shore of Lake Ontario. In 1787, he was known to trade "in the bay of Quinte and the regions thereabouts."[10] The trading cabin at the Scugog Carrying Place was likely built during this period. Around 1791 or 1792 Rousseau took his family to Toronto and lived in a house at the mouth of the Humber River, at the terminus of the Toronto Carrying Place where his father had been a trader in 1770.

Robinson notes that in 1770 a Montreal man, St. Jean Rousseau, was given a licence to trade in Toronto for one year. This man was Jean Baptiste's father, Jean Bonaventure Rousseau (1727–1774). A Jean Rousseau, *dit* St. Jean, worked for the French in the Ohio valley in 1735. Jean Baptiste's grandfather, who married in Detroit in 1726, was also called Jean Baptiste. The younger Jean Baptiste, who presumably built the log trading cabin at the head of the Scugog Carrying Place, was a third-generation descendant of a family that frequented the lower Great Lakes from 1735 onwards. As noted, after 1791, Rousseau Jr. settled at the mouth of the Humber River, and in 1793, would help guide Lieutenant Governor Simcoe's ship into Toronto harbour.

As a speaker of the Ojibwa language, Rousseau was called upon to act as interpreter and signer of treaties with the Natives, and his name appears on several signed treaties between 1797 and 1806. Treaties No. 8 (1797), No. 13 (1805), and No. 14 (1806) contain Rousseau's signature, as well as the dodem signature of Wabenose, Augustus Jones's Mississauga father-in-law.[11] The 1806 treaty also contains the signature of Wabakagego. The similarity in name suggests that the latter was the same as Wabakischoe, who helped Benjamin Wilson in his settlement at the head of the Scugog Carrying Place. After leaving the Scugog Trail trading cabin, Jean Baptiste Rousseau went on to establish businesses at the Humber River and later at Ancaster, before participating in the Battle of Queenston Heights in 1812. He died of blood poisoning a month after and was buried with full military honours at Niagara-on-the-Lake in November 1812.[12]

It now becomes apparent that two separate entities existed in the region of the Scugog Carrying Place. *Cabane de Plomb* or *Cabane au Plomb*, as found in the earliest map, is a geographical point on a map dating at least to 1699 in the period when the Iroquois or the Five Nations had established settlements on the north shore of Lake Ontario. Its exact origin or location has not been determined. The other entity is the French cabin, which existed in the century following the Iroquois occupation of the north shore and when French and English fur traders roamed the area. It can be convincingly placed near the mouth of Farewell Creek at the Second Marsh in Oshawa. As for the cabin's association with Jean Baptiste Rousseau, it can now be confirmed by the survey notes of Augustus Jones.

4

YANKEES ON THE TRAIL

"The Indians and their chief all left Lake Scugog and came down their trails to the Annis Creek — the mouth of it (now Port Oshawa) with their canoes on their shoulders and from this place they went in a body up the lake close to shore to York."[1]

After the arrival of the first American settlers, the history of the Scugog Carrying Place is better documented. Within a year of Benjamin Wilson's arrival other settlers, fur traders, and speculators followed him into the township, and within a few more years a small band of Yankee farmers were clearing the forest and finding their way on the Carrying Place.

The early European settlers in Whitby Township, Pedlar reports, thought of the land beyond their farms as the "wilderness." Most of them feared the Native people, as stories of their ferocity in war were rampant. The French and Indian Wars and the American Revolution witnessed mass murder and had spread great terror among these same American settlers. When they came to Whitby Township they brought their fears with them. Though, in this case, the Mississauga had more to fear from the European settlers who brought diseases that killed many of their people. Before Benjamin Wilson arrived on the shores of Lake Ontario, "a smallpox epidemic had swept the First Nations communities of Lake Simcoe and the Niagara Peninsula in 1793. Three years later there were more outbreaks in the province. These epidemics reportedly carried away one-third of the band on the Credit River in present-day Mississauga."[2]

The deadly epidemics and the murder of a prominent Mississauga leader set the Natives on edge. Stories about raids served to exacerbate the tension:

In 1794 three Mississauga raided a farm thirty kilometers north of York, and took all of the farmer's servant's "provisions, and even the Shirt from off his back." Rumors circulated on the Bay of Quinte about a forthcoming attack by the settlement of Rice Lake Mississauga during the summer of 1795. Fortunately for the settlers, once the Rice Lake Indians received their annual presents the threats lessened and the anticipated attack was never made.[3]

WILSON AND HIS NEIGHBOURS

Samuel Pedlar recounts the story of Benjamin Wilson's provisions being stolen by the Mississauga and that Chief Wabakischoe had them returned along with a wampum belt. The belt was hung outside Wilson's log cabin as a sign of protection from any further raids by the Mississauga. Pedlar also notes that Wabakischoe was a frequent visitor to the Wilson homestead.

John E. Farewell (1840–1923), the adopted son of Abram Farewell, also recounts a similar story about Benjamin Wilson but with additional details:

> Shortly after his arrival his place was visited by a band of Indians, who took his tools and provisions which had been furnished to him by the government, and whatever else he had but his boat, and told him to be gone and not to find his way back again. He had come around from Niagara, where the Government was. He went down the lake shore [sic] to Ganaraska, now Port Hope, where he met Wabakischoe, a chief who ruled the Indians from the Humber to the Bay of Quinte. Fortunately for Wilson the chief was accompanied by William Peak, who afterwards settled at Duffin's Creek. Wilson explained to Peak why he was going east instead of west. The chief

learning from Peak what had happened told Wilson to go back with him.[4]

The chief accompanied Wilson and his family back to the head of the Scugog Carrying Place and proceeded to interview the Native men who had taken the family's provisions. What remained of the goods was returned to the Wilson family, along with furs valued at the amount of the provisions not returned. Farewell concludes that "Wilson was not troubled after that. In fact he received much assistance from the Indians in his work."[5]

There is a valid reason explaining why the Mississauga took the Wilson family provisions. According to Ojibwa rules, anyone trespassing on the fishing and hunting grounds of the Mississauga at the mouth of Farewell Creek, as Wilson had done, would have been subject to confiscation of all provisions except for hunting equipment and then forced to leave.[6] The return of provisions and the hanging of a wampum belt on the Wilson house indicates that some type of compromise was concluded whereby the Mississauga fishing grounds were not disturbed, but the Wilson family allowed to remain nearby.

The Jones 1795 map shows the Wilson's homestead on lot four of Broken Front[7] in Whitby Township. When the township was first opened up for settlement registration, Benjamin Wilson applied to the government at York and received a grant of 200 acres. Wilson also farmed on lot five of Broken Front, but because it was set aside as Crown land he leased the lot in 1805 and continued to maintain the lease until his death in 1821.

Benjamin raised a large family, some born in Vermont and some in Whitby Township. After his death his wife Elizabeth lived on lot four with her daughter Nancy Pickell until her death in 1840. The land was sold in 1819 to Benjamin's son-in-law, William Pickell, who likely continued to farm. Today the same land continues to be cultivated.

Various sources have dated the Wilson family's arrival and settlement has been dated between 1790 and 1794. One source claims that Benjamin Wilson came to the area (later known as Gifford Hill) when York (Toronto) was being established by Lieutenant Governor Simcoe, and Simcoe is recorded as having visited the Wilsons on November 21,

The inscription on Benjamin Wilson's gravestone reads "In memory of CAPT. BENJ. WILSON who died March 5th 1821 in the 89 Year of his age." The photo was taken circa 1948, photographer not known.

Oshawa Public Libraries, LH 0257.

1794 while on a trip from Toronto to Kingston.[8] It certainly appears that the Wilsons were living at Gifford Hill in the fall of 1794. However, a plaque at the entrance to the Oshawa Archives and Community Museum gives an earlier arrival date, which had been put forward by the grandson of Benjamin Wilson's grandson, Nelson Pickell, probably between 1894–1895 when Pedlar was interviewing the old settlers, and is therefore somewhat suspect.

Additional evidence also suggests Wilson arrived in Upper Canada in 1793, since a government document for that year lists a Benjamin Willson being granted land at Long Point and Turkey Point on Lake Erie along with two other settlers, Anthony Rummerfield and Roger Conant, both of whom become neighbours of his along the lake. It is to be noted that Benjamin Wilson's surname at times is spelled with two "l"s. In his will he signs as "Willson," but historians writing about him use "Wilson." Though the early Oshawa histories make very few references to Benjamin

Wilson's life prior to his arrival in Upper Canada, they do mention that he was from Putney, Vermont, and came up from Pennsylvania with his new wife, the Widow Lockwood, their two sons, a stepson named Eleazar Lockwood, and a young man named Ransom.

The United States census of 1790 lists a Benjamin Willson as head of a six-person household in Salem, Washington County, New York, across the state line from Vermont. Six family members are also registered with Benjamin Wilson of Whitby in the earliest Whitby census of 1803. Additionally, a land deed dated February 2, 1789, has a Benjamin Wilson from Chono, New York, selling 120 acres in Putney, Vermont, to a Jeremiah Wilson (possibly a brother). Modern day Chono, New York, is within twenty miles of Salem. These documents suggest that Benjamin Wilson's family was still in New York in 1790. It would have been extremely difficult for Benjamin Wilson to travel from Pennsylvania to Whitby Township in that year. However, the route around the west end of Lake Ontario became much easier once York was founded and Simcoe was encouraging incoming settlers. New arrivals received assistance from Simcoe and could now travel around the south shore on Lake Ontario by ship.

Access to new land brought Benjamin Wilson to Whitby Township, as it had previously taken him to Vermont. Benjamin, originally from Rehboth, Massachusetts, had married a local woman, Sarah Sabin (1740–1803). Around 1768, he sought land in Putney, Vermont, and eventually settled there on a disputed lot. Over the course of eighteen years he and Sarah had eight children. During the American Revolution those disputing Wilson's land claim made several attempts to seek title to his land. In 1774, an American Revolution militia corps tried and failed to seize Wilson's land. However, in 1779, when Wilson refused to join the militia, he was fined and his cattle were seized. Following the American Revolution, during the winter of 1784–1785, he left behind his disputed land[9] and his family and moved to New York State where he remarried, presumably Elizabeth Lockwood, with whom he later came to Whitby.

Benjamin Wilson's land ownership issue in Putney, Vermont, was centred on a dispute of jurisdiction between the colonies of New York and Vermont. Many residents of southeastern Vermont, where Wilson lived, remained loyal to New York, while others such as the Green Mountain Boys of western Vermont claimed the land for Vermont. The dispute with New York was ultimately settled in Vermont's favour in 1790. Vermont adopted the constitution of the United States and was admitted as the fourteenth state of the Union in 1791. Because Benjamin had sided with New York, his land claim was not recognized and because the post-revolutionary feelings would have been against supporters of New York State, he was no longer welcome in Vermont.

Where Wilson had been immediately prior to coming to Upper Canada can also be discerned by his contacts. One clue comes from one of his nearest neighbours in Canada, Roger Conant. Benjamin Wilson's birthplace in Rehoboth, Massachusetts, is only eighteen miles from Bridgewater, the birthplace of Roger Conant. Both Conant and Wilson are listed as seeking land on Lake Erie in 1793, and both chose land in the eastern part of the province. Conant settled near Wilson's homestead in the autumn of 1794.

Coincidentally, prior to coming to Upper Canada, Roger Conant had land on the western branch of the Susquehanna River in Pennsylvania, immediately south of New York State near present-day Elmira. Several of Wilson's neighbours in Whitby Township — Charles Annis, Anthony Rummerfield, George Hall, and John Stephens — originally came from this part of Pennsylvania. In addition, the rare surnames Terwilligar and Ransom are found at this time along the western Susquehanna River, and Matthew Terwilligar and Ebenezer Ransom are two of the early settlers who also settled near Wilson. This suggests that Wilson had contact with settlers in this region before he came to Whitby Township.

The Susquehanna settlers travelled a well-worn set of trails to get to Upper Canada. The Iroquois in New York State had a series of east-to-west trails that linked all the sections of the Five Nations territory, with the Mohawks in the east and the Seneca to the west. The Five Nations, who left their settlements in New York State to come to Canada during the American Revolution, would have used these trails, and the Loyalists who came after them also used Native trails to get to Niagara. The Clayton Webb family, who emigrated from New York to Uxbridge in the spring of 1806, left the Susquehanna travelling north to the Genesee River, then west through the Tonawanda Swamp to Queenston.

Some American settlers coming from the Susquehanna followed other trails. The Burk and Trull families came to Darlington Township and settled immediately east of Benjamin Wilson in Whitby Township. Leaving Elmira in the spring of 1794, the Burks travelled north to Seneca Lake and then along the south shore of Lake Ontario to the Niagara River. The Trull family took a similar route going from the Susquehanna to the Mohawk River at Oswego and then along the south shore of Lake Ontario to Niagara. These different journeys indicate that there were at least two main routes from the Susquehanna River area, the original homeland of many of the first settlers to Whitby.

Fur Traders and Farmers

Thomas Conant, the great-grandson of Roger Conant and author of *Life in Canada*, written in 1903, observed that around 1800:

> twice a year, spring and fall, the Indians would come out from the woods to fish in those lakes and marshes and at the outlet of the streams [entering Lakes Ontario and Erie and Simcoe]. So numerous were the Indians at that time that they far outnumbered the whites and when they [the Indians] came for the semi-annual fish they would form a regular village, as they congregated in their tents beside the shore of some marsh or bay upon the great lakes. The settlers' policy was one pre-eminently of conciliation to the Indians.[10]

Conant continued:

> many of these settlers became Indian traders, for the Indians at this time far outnumber the whites; and semi-annually all the Indian tribes came to Lake Ontario to fish. Their trading was done by barter. A party of traders would set out into the woods with their packs of goods

and fire off three guns in succession, which was the signal to the Indians that traders were there. Next morning the Indians would invariably come to the rendezvous to trade their furs for ammunition, blankets and trinkets.[11]

The prospect of buying furs on the Scugog Carrying Place encouraged Acheus Moody Farewell and his brother William to come to Whitby Township in 1802 or 1803. While sailing along Lake Ontario, the Farewells were attracted to the area by the Bluff Point landmark, the one the Mississauga called *Min-ce-nan-quash*. This prominent point of land marked the southern terminus of the Scugog Trail.

Prior to coming to the Whitby area, the Farewell brothers, originally from Vermont, had worked at raising muskrats and beaver on Bond Lake north of Toronto, and for a season A.M. worked for the North West Company. Around 1803 they set out to build a trading house on Ball Point on the northeast end of Lake Scugog. Possibly taking a cue from the earlier trading cabin near Benjamin Wilson's lot, the Farewells decided to use the Scugog Carrying Place and make their living by trading furs with the Mississauga, in particular with the Muskrat group, or totem, and then sell them at York. They too likely had prior contact with the settlers in Whitby Township since the brothers settled near Benjamin Wilson, and on April 3, A.M. Farewell married Elizabeth Annis (sister of David Annis, another fur trader). In June 1804 he bought lot four, First Concession in Whitby Township, immediately north of Wilson's place.

The Farewells were not the only ones to settle down to farm and trade for furs on the Scugog Carrying Place. David Annis had become a fur trader first in Whitby and later branched out to trade as far north as Lake Simcoe. Pedlar recorded:

> David Annis became an Indian trader for furs on his own account in 1808. Besides collecting all the furs about this locality, he made several excursions north to where Port Perry now stands and on to the waters on Lake Simcoe at Beaverton. He and his hired porters drew upon hand sleighs or carried when there was no

According to Thomas Kaiser, this is a photographic image of A.M. Farewell (1789–1869) and his wife Elizabeth Annis (1780–1851). However, it is doubtful if this actually is Elizabeth Annis since she died in 1851, before photography was widely used in Ontario. It may be that of Moody with his second wife, Sarah Haveland Coryell (1803–1880). From T.E. Kaiser, Historic Sketches of Oshawa, *8.*

snow, powder, shot, bullets, guns, blankets, knives and trinkets, such as steel discs for striking fire on the flint. On camping at night they fired off guns in quick succession, which was the signal for the Indians to gather, and next morning all within hearing came with their furs and traded for these goods. David Annis sent these furs to Montreal in Durham boats,[12] and got gold doubloons for them … The returning Durham boats brought back more goods for future trading.[13]

Joseph Wiley, another fur trader, built a log house on the trail in the north end of Whitby Township. The Wiley blockhouse was discovered by George Fisher and his family who had come to the area from Napanee in 1827. Although it was in good condition, it was abandoned and no one knew when it had been erected. Interestingly, a Joseph Wileigh is listed in the 1822 township records and also appears as Joseph Wily in the 1803 township records for the combined townships of Pickering and Whitby. John Carruthers, a Presbyterian pastor, records Wiley as an Indian trader on the Eighth Concession along the Scugog Trail in 1821 and in 1825.[14] Thus it would appear that the Wiley house was erected sometime after 1803 when Joseph Wiley arrived in Whitby Township, but abandoned by 1827.

A Joseph Widdowfield is recorded in G. Brown's *Toronto City and Home District Directory for 1846* as living south of Wiley's house on the Carrying Place. An earlier Joseph Witterfield is listed in county records for 1822. This is likely the Joseph Widdifield whom Pedlar describes as a Quaker. Carruthers records Widdifield as being at Concession Four on Scugog Carry Place in 1821.[15] Historical records for the Whitby area show a variety of spellings for this family. After the Widdifield farm was bought by Ambrose Morris in 1841, the Morris family is noted as having mentioned that a large number of Natives used to camp near their home because of the farm's proximity to the trail.[16]

THE SHARP MURDER

Farewell's fur-trading operation was in its second year when their hired hand, John Sharp, was murdered at their trading house at Ball's Point on Lake Scugog. The exact date for the murder of Sharp is not recorded, but Moody Farewell's obituary[17] mentions that the murder took place at the end of the trading season. In his book about the murder, Brendan O'Brien mentions that it was committed in the spring of 1804, possibly in April or May.[18] However, Moody Farewell married on April 4, 1804, and it was also conceivable that he was trading furs on Lake Scugog that March or earlier when the frozen ground facilitated travel into the interior. According to land registry records he was in York during the first week of June 1804 buying 200 acres from James Givens, the land that would later become his home. Possibly because of lack of money to finalize the deal, Moody took out a £50 mortgage with St. George Quetton, a York merchant and landowner on the fourth of June, which would have allowed him to purchase the property. Sometime in the following year he sold the south half of the same lot to his brother William. He must have paid off the mortgage, for in later years he had title to the north half of lot four. Sharp's murder likely occurred either in March or after the first week of June when the Farewell brothers would have had the next opportunity to spend several weeks fur trading on Lake Scugog.

Chief Wabakischoe, who assisted Benjamin Wilson and worked with Augustus Jones, figures prominently in the story of the murder of John Sharp. He had allegedly been murdered by a Mississauga named Ogetanicut, who apparently killed Sharp in retaliation for the murder of his brother Whistling Duck the previous year. The Farewell brothers, who did not witness the murder, asked Chief Wabakischoe if he knew who had killed Sharp. Wabakischoe had been informed by some eyewitnesses and agreed to assist the brothers in their search. They travelled together on the Scugog Trail from Lake Scugog south to Lake Ontario near Wilson's home. Here the party met Eleazar Lockwood, who had a homestead to the west of Benjamin on the north side of the Oshawa Harbour. Eleazar was aware of a group of Mississauga who had recently camped near his farm. By secretly observing them, he had learned about the murder and noted that the Mississauga, after pulling up camp, departed for the islands at the head of Toronto. Acting on this information, the party went to secure the arrest of Ogetonicut for the murder of John Sharp, with the help of Wabakischoe.

The precise location of the murder site, and therefore the trial location, was yet to be determined. On August 15, 1804, Chief Justice Henry Allcock ordered the surveyor general to determine if the Moody trading house was in the District of Newcastle. The survey party left York two days later and in three days' time they travelled thirty-eight miles and stopped at the northern boundary of Whitby Township, presumably going by way of the Scugog Carrying Place. Over the next three days the survey party ran a line to the location of the Farewell trading post on Lake Scugog. The survey determined that the murder did take place in Newcastle District and John Stegmann, the surveyor in charge, was able to report that:

> in obedience to your request instructions bearing date of the 15th Inst: have the honor to report that the same is complied with, That the exact and position situation of the house of Moody Farewell is seven miles eastward of the division line between the Township of Whitby & Darlington, and that all economy of time and expenses have been made use of __ The protraction of the work will show the real situation. I am with respt.
>
> Signed John Stegmann D.J. Surveyor[19]

A trial was ordered at Presqu'ile within the District of Newcastle, but the land route was in poor shape since the only road, Kingston Road, had suffered heavy rains and was severely damaged and not passable in places. Thus the entire court embarked for Presqu'ile, travelling east from Toronto on the ship the *Speedy*. Though the *Speedy*'s captain considered her unseaworthy, the lieutenant-governor, Peter Hunter, had ordered she be put to sea to take the trial party to Presqu'ile. On board the *Speedy* were John Stegmann and Jacob Herchner, a fur trader from Rice Lake and a merchant at York. He may have been related to Ogetanicut through his Mississauga wife, and his presence on board seems to imply that he was there to act as an interpreter and perhaps as a witness on Ogetanicut's behalf.

One account mentions about the *Speedy*: "on the way down they stopped at Oshawa for two or three Indian men and women, and for some white men who were witnesses in the case."[20] Eleazar Lockwood and the Farewell brothers, who were scheduled to testify at the trial of Ogetonicut, did not travel on the ship, apparently missing it when it stopped at Oshawa. Instead they went to Pres'quile by canoe and were on the lake when a storm hit east of Cobourg on October 8, 1804. The *Speedy* went down in the tempest and all on board drowned.

Stegmann left a daughter behind who had married the surveyor Samuel Wilmot, who six years later surveyed the Scugog Carrying Place in Reach Township. Robert Isaac Dey Gray, the solicitor general of Upper Canada, also perished on the *Speedy*. He left a will that acknowledged that his servants would inherit his property in Whitby Township. On August 7, 1803, he bequeathed that:

> in order that provision may be made for the support of Dorinda "(a black woman servant)" and her children and that she may not want after my decease. My will is & I hereby empower my Executor out of my real estate to raise the sum of twelve hundred pounds Currency and place the same in some solvent & secure fund and the interest arising from the same I give and bequeath to the said Dorinda & her heirs & assigns forever to be paid annually ... I leave all my wearing apparel to my servant Simon & also my silver watch & I give & devise to him & his heirs forever two hundred acres of land that is to say lot number 11 in the first Concession of Whitby.[21]

Unfortunately, Robert Gray's servant and inheritor, Simon Baker, also perished on the *Speedy*. It is unclear who received the Whitby Township inheritance left by Gray. The property willed to Simon (through which the Scugog Trail ran) would become part of downtown Oshawa. In 1990 the relics of the *Speedy*, which included an anchor and chain, cannon shot, a clay pipe, a pair of eyeglasses, and perhaps human skeletal remains, were located on the bottom of Lake Ontario.[22]

The murder of John Sharp was treated more severely than the murder of a Mississauga eight years earlier. In 1796 the Mississauga chief Wakakinine was attacked by a Queen's Ranger in York, resulting in his death. Wakakinine had been a key negotiator in the 1781 purchase of the lands from the Etobicoke River to the Bay of Quinte, which allowed the British to survey Whitby Township. Following his death, the Mississauga in Upper Canada clamoured for revenge against the British government and railed against the proximity of the settlers. Officially, the lack of witnesses led to the trial of Wakakinine's attacker being cancelled. Since the British did next to nothing to punish Wakakinine's alleged attacker the suspicion remained in the minds of the Mississauga that the Crown had different standards of justice for Europeans versus First Nations.

While working at Washburn Island in 1951, archaeologist Kenneth Kidd interviewed an early resident who described having dug up the foundations of a log cabin and a body, along with a leather jacket and a *circa,* 1800 coin. A newspaper account indicated that a shallow grave had been discovered with the remains of a skull with a large gash in it, reported to be that of John Sharp, the fur trader murdered on Washburn Island in 1804. The resident described this burial as having come from a burying ground that had been washed away by the waves of the lake.

Eleazar Lockwood, who overheard Ogetanicut describe the murder of John Sharp at the campsite on the Oshawa Creek, had his own family history of murder and escape. Lockwood's father was murdered by Natives in Pennsylvania, and shortly after Eleazar's birth his mother was taken prisoner. Eleazar's biography, written after his death in 1865, describes how Elizabeth Lockwood endured her captivity and survived the ordeal after being released to a Dutch family. The 1877 Ontario County atlas claims that Elizabeth Lockwood had two previous husbands before marrying Benjamin Wilson, and had lost each to murder by Natives. Eleazar, an expert woodsman, was reputed to go hunting for a week at a time and travel twenty to thirty miles on each excursion. After selling the northern part of his lot on the Broken Front Concession to David Annis in 1815, Eleazar moved to the United States.

A member of the Annis family, Elizabeth, wife of A.M. Farewell, had her own personal story of murder. In July 1778 the Annis family escaped a raid on the Susquehanna River settlement at Wyoming. When Colonel John Butler and his Butlers Rangers and a troop of Seneca and

Ojibwa warriors from southern Ontario attacked, at least 227 American militiamen were killed. The American colonists portrayed the raid on Wyoming as a massacre and used this as their justification for the destruction of forty Iroquoian villages, which ultimately led to the mass migration of the Iroquois from New York State into Upper Canada during the American Revolution.

Later, in 1812, when A.M. Farewell left the fur business, he opened a tavern. By the end of the War of 1812 he had increased his wealth considerably and built a sawmill and gristmill. He later acquired 500 acres in Brock Township, and several more acres in the townships of Reach and Whitby. Interestingly, in their first years in Whitby Township the Farewell brothers had little wealth and had relied on the local environment for sustenance. At that time A.M. Farewell dressed his children in buckskins, hunted game, and, travelling by canoe, fished in the traditional way of the Native people. The settler *cum* fur trader had come up the social ladder.

A powerful hunger for land brought the first American settlers into the townships around the Scugog Carrying Place. After land, furs were a key source of wealth for those incoming settlers, many of

Thomas Conant, *Upper Canada Sketches.* Toronto: W. Briggs, 47.

The Farewell Tavern, photographed circa 1903, was one of the first commercial structures on Danforth Road in Whitby Township.

whom became fur traders on the Scugog Carrying Place. Men like Jean Baptiste Rousseau, the Farewell brothers, John Sharp, David Annis, and Joseph Wiley, all travelled along the Scugog Trail to make a living. They were soon followed by missionaries seeking to save the souls of Natives and settlers.

5

PREACHERS ON THE TRAIL

"Joe Smith preached Mormon doctrine in McGrigor's grove, just where W.H. Thomas' residence now is. Lamoreaux, the MacGahans, and the Seeleys went off with the Mormons from here at that time."[1]

The *Jesuit Relations* refers to the Huron village of Contarea as St. Jean Baptiste and locates it at the north end of Lake Simcoe to the west of Lake Couchiching. This Native centre would have been the last stopping point before travelling to the north end of the Scugog Carrying Place, which began further along the east side of Lake Simcoe. Anyone living or visiting Contarea would likely have come in contact with individuals who used the trail to access the Beaver and Nonquon Rivers. The map, entitled *Novae Franciae*, was published in 1657 by Bressani, a Jesuit missionary who had travelled to Huron country and was familiar with the geography of the region. His map appears to show Lake Scugog and the Scugog River. If the area south of Contarea was familiar to the French Jesuits, it certainly would have been better known to the Huron and the Ojibwa.

During the period from 1650 to 1700 the area became somewhat of a no man's land between the Iroquois living along the north shore of Lake Ontario and the Ojibwa tribes in the interior. The French Sulpician missionaries Fenelon and Trouvé spent one brief winter at Gandatskiagon in 1669 and established a school to teach letters and the gospel to the Iroquois children of the Seneca tribe. However, a food shortage caused them to abandon the mission the following spring.

Over the following century the Mississauga migrated southward and began settling along Lake Scugog and harvesting the abundant wild rice found there. Before long, new missionaries were coming to the Scugog area via the Carrying Place. This time it was Methodists bringing a Protestant faith. Like the Jesuits before them who taught in the Huron language, the Methodists taught their spiritual ideals in the language of the Ojibwa residents.

The Methodist Episcopal Church of America, established in 1784, administered annual conferences in Canada until 1824 when Canada obtained its own separate conference. Conferences were divided into districts and then into circuits operated by one or two itinerant preachers. By 1795 Upper Canada had circuits at Niagara and the Bay of Quinte and ten years later the province had 1,800 Methodist members with ten circuit riders.

One of the earliest travelling Methodist preachers in the Home District, which encompassed Whitby Township, was Nathan Bangs, who was working there as early as 1802. By 1817 a new Methodist circuit was formed at Duffin's Creek, west of Whitby Township. Soon afterwards, the township attained its own circuit, with James Wilson as their minister beginning in 1826. When Robert Corson took over in 1828, he, along with other itinerant preachers, administered to both the European settlers and the Mississauga. In one year, Corson had forty preaching assignments covering Pickering, Whitby, Darlington, Clarke, Brock, and Reach. He would have traversed the Scugog Trail multiple times. In 1829 Corson became the Methodist preacher to the Mississauga at Scugog Island, where the congregation is said to have numbered 200. Other Mississauga missions were established at the Credit River and Rice Lake.

Peter Jones, a Methodist preacher, was part of Corson's mission at Lake Scugog. The son of Augustus Jones, he lived with his extended Mississauga family until he was fifteen years old. Peter's mother was Tubhenahneequay; his grandfather was Wahbonosay, chief of the Eagle clan; and his grandmother was Puhgashkish, who it seems was killed at York during the American invasion of the town in 1813. As noted earlier, Wahbonosay worked for surveyor Augustus Jones, his son-in-law, but he too disappears from the documentary records sometime during the War of 1812.

Peter Jones first appears along the Scugog Carrying Place on January 21, 1827, when he addressed forty Natives at a camp on Mr. Cryderman's place in Darlington Township just east of Whitby. According to his diary, he also came up the trail on his visit to the Mississauga in Scugog in April 1828. Jones would travel along the lakefront from the Credit River where he lived, then access the trail, travelling through the bush on horseback, and continue on to places like Lake Scugog and Rice Lake, ultimately reaching the Bay of Quinte. Usually he was able to make the distance from the Credit to Scugog in a couple of days or so. Travelling back along the Carrying Place to Danforth Road as far as Port Hope, then north on another trail to Rice Lake required a day and a half.

On his 1828 visit, Peter Jones encountered a camp of about 100 Mississauga at Lake Scugog. They were looking for a place to settle at some other location on the lake, since their traditional campsite was no longer available and they were without a reserve recognized by the government. With the ongoing white settlements rapidly taking over the land, they were fearful of finding themselves without a permanent home. Jones travelled with a party of Mississauga to the north end of the lake to examine a new location for the band. To add to the band's difficulties that summer, their community was plagued by an outbreak of disease.

When Jones was back at Scugog on January 20, 1829, he recorded the names of the Mississauga encamped at the site:

> Old Johnson, aged 60; John Goose, aged 40; Sarah, his wife, aged 35; Adam, and Eve his wife, about 30 years old when Quebec was taken; Thomas Pigeon, aged 60; Susan, his wife, aged 40; Jacob, a son, aged 14; Mary, a daughter, 8; David, a son, 8 months; Anna York, aged 50; Mary, her daughter, 18; Anna Nashawash, aged 50; Lydia Pigeon, 6; Phoebe Pigeon, 1, daughters of John and Sarah Pigeon; Rachel Paske, aged 3 months; Sally Queenguish, aged 5 months; Ruth Johnson, aged 4 weeks, daughters of James and Cathy Johnson; Simon Jack, aged 4 years; Martha and Mary Jack, twins, aged 6 months, children of Captain and Mary Jack; Jacob Kechequoke, aged 12 years; Peter Queenguish, aged 1 year, son of widow Queenguish.[2]

If Chief Jacob Crane is counted as well, that makes thirty individuals meeting with Peter Jones. But he mentions that there were 150 individuals at Scugog, so apparently not all attended his religious gatherings.

Jones noted that a church called the Basswood Chapel was in use, and that a school had been set up to educate the Mississauga. Reverend Scott, a Baptist minister sent to the Scugog area by the New England Church Missionary Society to establish the school, had hired Aaron Hurd, son of a local settler, to teach the thirty to fifty students. The school, built at the north end of the Hurd property, was, according to Jones, "built of logs, 22 feet square, hewed in the inside. The floor is laid with split basswood plank, and the roof is covered with basswood troughs."[3] Jones also described the Mississauga's dwellings, "They occupy nine bark wigwams … the fire is made in the centre, and the families sit or lie around it. Each person occupies his or her place in the wigwam without the intrusion of other members of the lodge."[4]

While at Lake Scugog, Jones and Hurd instructed the Mississauga in the techniques of clearing a plot of land and planting crops. An attempt was made to bring hoes, axes, and seeds from Whitby to the Scugog band. A female teacher started sewing and knitting classes for the women at the school. Aaron Hurd continued to teach the Lake Scugog band and moved with them when they relocated to the Rice Lake area in 1830. He went on to study to become a missionary in Connecticut where he died in 1836.

Reverend Scott had tried to secure a land grant of 200 acres along the southwest end of Lake Scugog for the Mississauga to assist the band in staying in the Scugog area. He was not successful and the Scugog mission seems to have been folded into the mission of Rice Lake. Other Mississauga communities, the Narrows at the north end of Lake Simcoe and Alderville at Rice Lake, had been developing for some time.

The Mississauga depended on seasonal vegetation, particularly wild rice, to sustain them throughout the year. The first full survey map of Cartwright Township, completed in 1816 by the deputy provincial surveyor, Samuel Street Wilmot (1774–1856), takes in the eastern part of Lake Scugog and shows extensive wild rice regions in the marshes along the eastern edge of the lake. This would have been a major harvesting area for the Mississauga during the late summer.

Barclay, Clark & Co. Litho, Toronto.

"Indian wigwams of birch bark," by artist: Edward Scrope Shrapnel (1847–1920);
Conant, Thomas, Upper Canada Sketches *(Toronto: Briggs, 1898), facing page 84.*

Typically two individuals harvested the rice, with one using a pole to manoeuvre a canoe while another, equipped with two sticks, would first bend the rice over the edge of the canoe with one stick and then strike the kernels with the other to deposit the rice in the boat. After the rice was collected, it was dried. A mortar and pestle would be used to hull the rice, which was then winnowed by means of birchbark trays and the chaff removed. The rice was stored in bags or baskets of cedar or birch bark, which, if sewn shut or covered, would be preserved for a long time. Wild rice was eaten year round and was critical to their survival during the winter months.

In 1830, William Purdy, a miller originally from Westchester, New York, built a dam and mill on the Scugog River, causing the river to rise by ten feet and flooding part of Lake Scugog. The flooding would have swamped the wild rice fields on the lake and caused a major depletion of game. The resulting loss of food resources would have been a significant factor in the Mississauga leaving northeast Lake Scugog in 1830, thus abandoning Reach Township for more than a decade. Chief Jacob Crane likely guided the Scugog band to Curve Lake in 1830, then on to Balsam Lake in 1836, returning to Lake Scugog in the 1840s. Interestingly, prior to 1790 the bulk of the Mississauga population had lived at Balsam Lake east of Lake Simcoe.[4] Around 1790, the Mississauga moved to Curve Lake.[5] Chief Crane died around 1860.

By 1829 Curve Lake was becoming more of a western-styled community, largely through the efforts of the New England Company, a missionary society that built a village of nineteen houses there in 1830. Forty acres of land were cleared for growing potatoes in addition to the corn they were accustomed to growing when living at Balsam Lake. Squire Marten and Captain John Kawkajewan were leaders of the Mississauga Curve Lake band until 1842 when Marten died and Peter Nogee succeeded both men. He died in 1876.

One of the early missionaries to Whitby Township was Washington Christian, a black Baptist minister who administered to a congregation of both blacks and whites. Sources suggest that he may have been ordained in the Abyssinian Baptist Church in New York. He settled in Toronto in 1825, though his ministry took him eastwards. One person, hearing him speak at Whitby in 1837, described the emotional impact of his sermons: "while truth fell from his lips it reached many hearts and suffused many eyes with tears."[6] Another itinerant preacher in the area was Elizabeth Dart, a Bible Christian.[7] In July of 1833 she travelled throughout Whitby Township preaching in barns wherever she could. She kept a journal and recorded as she travelled west from Cobourg to Whitby:

> I delight to see on the one hand the woods showing forth their beauty in so many shades of green; and on the other, the large Lake runs by Cobourg, shewing [sic] its fulness. These things lead me to reflect on the power of the Creator, and the valuable purposes they serve. The wood to make fire to communicate warmth in this icy climate, and the water for navigation to convey the necessaries of life to the inhabitants in its vicinity.[8]

A well-known local religious figure, Robert Thornton (1806–1875), was a regular traveller on the Scugog Carrying Place. Educated in theology at the Universities of Edinburgh and St. Andrew's in Scotland, Thornton belonged to the Secession Church, a splinter group of the Presbyterian Church of Scotland with a strong focus on missionary work.

John Carruthers, who preceded Robert Thornton in Whitby Township and the northern townships, began the Presbyterian missions along the Carrying Place in 1832. The following year, Thornton came to Cobourg via Rochester, New York, at a time when there was no regular passenger service to the Whitby area. From Cobourg, Thornton and his wife, Margaret Thompson, travelled overland to Whitby. En route, he noted:

> with the exception of a narrow strip, far from continuous, along the southern frontier, Canada was then a vast wilderness.... The clearings were so few and far between

This black and white photo of Reverend Dr. Robert Hill Thornton was taken by William Notman, circa 1870. Thornton was born in 1806 at Calder, near Edinburgh, Scotland, and attended the University of St. Andrews and the Secessionist Church College in Glasgow. From William R. Wood, Past Years in Pickering: Sketches of the History of the Community *(1911).*

as scarcely to interrupt the wilderness monotony. And as for roads, with a few exceptions they were yet in the future. The road was made merely by the cutting and partial clearing of the trees which had covered its surface. To keep these few highways, such as they were, was incompatible with the objects of the missionary and the nature of his work. We had to wend our way through forest paths and from clearing to clearing, where the only mode of location was on foot.[9]

Soon after arriving in Upper Canada, Thornton sought out Presbyterian settlers in Reach Township and began his regular services. While on his travels down the Nonquon River in 1835 he recalled seeing a group of Natives transporting a birchbark canoe along the Carrying Place, heading for Lake Ontario.[10] Thornton built a log church on the Danforth Road, west of Skae's Corners — the future Oshawa. His extensive missionary area, often accessed by horseback over the Scugog Trail, stretched north into Reach Township. Columbus, then known as English Corners and located directly on the Scugog Trail, was on his circuit. Many of the new settlers there, and in the townships north of Whitby, were Scots and Irish, staunch members of the Presbyterian Church. Thornton's arrival led to a log church being built on Harmony Road in Columbus. This church was later replaced by a frame building.

A Methodist missionary, Egerton Ryerson,[11] who also worked with Peter Jones, lived with the Mississauga band at the Credit River. He learned to speak the Ojibwa language and was often in communication with the bands at Lake Scugog, though it appears he never travelled to the lake. But Ryerson did visit the Toronto Carrying Place, travelling to Holland Landing when government provisions were distributed to the Mississauga there. He also travelled further north to an island (possibly Thorah) on the northeast side of Lake Simcoe, across from the northern end of the Scugog Carrying Place. At the Mississauga settlements and meeting places Ryerson encountered French traders, presumably Roman Catholic, who were opposed to any religious conversion of the Mississauga to Protestantism.

There were few Roman Catholics in Whitby Township in the first couple of decades of the nineteenth century. During the 1820s and 1830s they held services in the homes of individuals. Daniel Leonard's home at lot eight, on the south side of Kingston Road, just east of Kerr's Corners (now in downtown Oshawa), was a prominent location for Catholic services. In 1830, Father O'Grady is recorded as having travelled from York to conduct a service there. These Catholic services probably began as early as 1825, a few years after Leonard's arrival from Cork, Ireland. In 1848, the First Roman Catholic church in Whitby Township was built on Simcoe Street, the roadway replacing that stretch of the Scugog Carrying Place. By 1848 a Roman Catholic priest by the name of Jean-Baptiste Proulx was a prominent figure in the township. He had previously been a missionary to the Ojibwa at Wikwemikong on Manitoulin Island where he served for over a decade.

Earlier, in 1829, a log schoolhouse had been built in the downtown area of the village of Kerr's Creek, with Andrew Masson and Fannie Hall as the first teachers. In 1835 the Methodists built the framed Union School House on the corner of Royal and Simcoe Streets. For a short time the schoolhouse also became a centre of worship for all denominations lacking their own places of worship, including Wesleyan Methodists, Roman Catholics, Baptists, Quakers, and Bible Christians. This continued until the Methodists and Roman Catholics began to establish their own churches. The Methodists built their first frame church near Park Road, Oshawa, on what was then called Protestant Hill. The first Anglican Church along the Scugog Trail was at Columbus, a log building constructed in 1835, while the first Anglican Church right in Oshawa was St. George's, built along Park Road sometime during the years of 1847 or 1848.

But the earliest denomination to have a church in Oshawa was the Christian Church, which had spread into Upper Canada from the United States. One of their early congregations was set up in Darlington Township in 1826, only a few miles east of the Scugog Carrying Place along Farewell Creek. In 1831 another congregation formed in Whitby Township and held services in the Coryell schoolhouse on Kingston Road. Pastor Thomas Henry, originally from County Caven, Ireland, became the pastor of the Oshawa Christian Church in 1840. Pastor Henry (or

Elder Henry as he was sometimes known) lived near the mouth of the Oshawa Creek, one of the starting points of the Scugog Carrying Place where he and his family frequently witnessed the Mississauga using the trail in the 1840s.

Perhaps the least known missionaries along the trail were the Mormons, today known as the Latter-Day Saints. Joseph Smith (1805–1844), founder of the Latter-Day Saint movement in the late 1820s, sent followers to York in 1830 to seek copyright funds for the *Book of Mormon*, but the enterprise failed to get recognition in Canada. Smith is known to have made two trips to Upper Canada, one in 1833 to the Brantford area and another to the Toronto area four years later. In 1836 Orson Pratt was preaching for the Mormons in Pickering and Whitby and, a year later in August 1837, Joseph Smith, with Sidney Rigdon, Thomas Marsh, O.P. Rockwell, and Brigham Young entered Canada across the Niagara border. Conferences were held in both Whitby Township and in Scarborough Township. On August 2, 1837, *The Constitution*, a Toronto newspaper, wrote: "We understand that Mr. Smith, a famed chief of the new sect called 'Mormons,' who suffered much persecution in Missouri, and the great preacher, Mr. Rigdon, are in town."

Pedlar describes the Mormon missionary visit of Joseph Smith and his followers when they came to Whitby Township to attend a church meeting that took place south of the village of Skae's Corner's at John McGregor's field (south of Danforth Road, probably near the Union School House). J.T. Coleman also mentions a Mormon delegation visiting in 1839, and once again meeting at McGregor's. The Mormons explained that they were preaching to the Native Americans because the similarity of Native and Hebrew languages led them to believe that Native Americans were descendant of ancient Israelites.[12]

Brigham Roberts's biography on John Taylor, the third president of the Church of Latter-Day Saints, also provides some background on the conference that took place in Whitby in the summer of 1837. He writes about an event taking place in a large barn owned by Edward Lawrence, who is listed in the 1837 Home District Directory as occupying lot seven, Broken Front Concession in Pickering Township.[13] Other sources also confirm that Joseph Smith stayed at the Lawrence residence in Pickering. Mormon missionary work continued in Upper Canada during Joseph Smith's lifetime. John Taylor had been preaching in Whitby Township prior to Joseph Smith's visit of 1837. There are several erroneous accounts of Joseph Smith being in Canada in 1842. Samuel Pedlar describes an additional visit to Whitby by Joseph Smith in 1842, delivering the Mormon doctrine in the same McGregor's grove adjacent to the Carrying Place. Conant, in his *Life in Canada*, also mentions that Joseph Smith came to central Ontario in the summer of 1842, and in his 1898 book he notes the Mormons coming to Butterfield's Corners (present-day Taunton) in 1843. Pedlar and Conant may have confused the later Mormon missions with a return of Joseph Smith to Whitby, since no other record shows Joseph Smith in Canada beyond 1837. Afterwards, he was known to be in Ohio and Illinois until his death in 1844. In all probability the later Mormon missionaries travelled along the secondary trail up from the Kingston Road to the Third Concession on a road that had been cut a few years previously, which roughly corresponds with the Scugog Carrying Place along Harmony Creek.

While in Whitby Township, Joseph Smith informed local converts that they were to travel to the "far west." Two groups of Mormon converts left Canada in 1837 and in 1838, settling in the Mormon community of Nauvoo, Illinois. Edward Lawrence sold his 200-acre farm in Pickering and his Whitby holdings in the summer of 1838 and joined the Mormons in the United States. Pedlar tells of the Seeley and McGahan families, who also sold their farms in Whitby Township and joined the Mormons.[14] Seeley appears in the 1822 census as head of the household of nine individuals, who farmed on lot twenty-two of the Broken Front Concession. The Asa McGahan family farm sold for $4,000 at the time of their leaving. The McGhahan's had arrived in Whitby about 1796 and lived on lot six of Broken Front Concession. Asa McGahan is known to have died in Nauvoo, Illinois, one of the towns founded by the Latter-Day Saints. In *Upper Canada Sketches*, Thomas Conant describes meeting one of the descendants of the McGahan's in Salt Lake City in 1878, who at the time was reported as living twelve miles south of Salt Lake City. Perhaps the Latter-Day Saints were attracted to Whitby because of the New England origins they shared with the early American settlers. Joseph Smith was born in Sharon, Vermont, and when he was ten years old moved to Palmyira, New York, with his family, several miles south of Rochester on the south shore of Lake Ontario. By 1830 Mormon missionaries were working in Kingston, Upper Canada, and Brigham Young (1801–1877) served missions in Canada in 1832 and 1833. Joseph Smith was the president of the Mormon Church until his death in 1844 when Brigham Young took over.

The literal interpretation of the *Book of Mormon* holds that the ancient inhabitants of the Americas had a Middle Eastern origin. The current view of the Latter-Day Saints is that a small portion of Native Americans are derived from a Middle Eastern origin. Certain DNA lineages, in particular the mitochondria DNA X haplogroup, which is found in about 3 percent of North American Native groups, has a common genetic link with people in the Middle East and lends support to the Mormon belief that some of the ancient Hebrews had settled in the Americas.

The *Book of Mormon* calls the early Native Americans *Lamanites*. In 1830 Mormon missionaries preached to the Cattaraugus tribe near

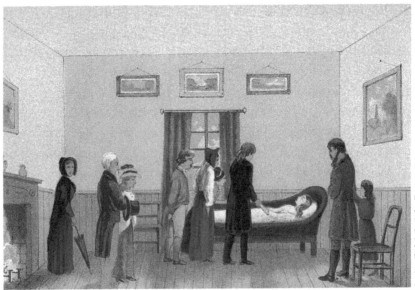

"Mormon attempt to raise the dead," by artist: Edward Scrope Shrapnel (1847–1920); Conant, Thomas, Upper Canada Sketches *(Toronto: Briggs, 1898), facing page 228.*

Barclay, Clark & Co. Litho. Toronto.

Buffalo, New York. Later, Mormon missions went to the Wyandot at Sandusky, Ohio, and to the Shawnee and Delaware in Missouri. The missions generally followed the pattern used by the European settlers. First, the missionaries would seek out the head chiefs of a Native group and then preach to an assembly of people. However, there is no historical record to suggest that the Mormon missions in Upper Canada went to the Mississauga or other Canadian Native groups.

Another religious group that had a connection with Whitby Township is the Millerites or Second Day Adventists. The Millerites were followers of William Miller, a New England preacher who predicted the end of the world to be February 14, 1843. Matthew Terwillegar had come from the Susquehanna River area prior to 1803 as part of the group of American settlers who migrated to Whitby and Darlington Townships after 1793. He settled on lot six of the First Concession in Whitby Township and built his house on the south side of the Kingston or Danforth Road. He and his family were Millerites. As an aside, a number of burials were discovered next to the eastern branch of the Scugog Carrying Place in 2007 on the property that had belonged to the Terwillegar family.

In February 1843, Millerites in the Whitby area held meetings while awaiting the end of the world. Sarah Terwillegar is reported to have made wings of silk and fell and injured herself while attempting to fly from her porch. A farmer near Prince Albert reportedly gave away his farm of 100 acres along with all its contents during the height of the Millerite scare in the winter of 1842–1843. Conant, in *Life in Canada*, describes Millerites as buying flour from John Warren in Oshawa before their anticipated end of the world. Afterwards, in August 1844, William Miller is known to have visited Toronto to attend several meetings. There are also a number of reports of Millerite lectures occurring in Newcastle and Orono (east of Whitby Township) about the same time, although none seemed to have occurred in Oshawa.

According to the 1851 census, after the loss of adherents in 1843 the Second Day Adventist membership dropped to about 663 individuals in Ontario. But these numbers increased considerably in subsequent decades and today they have a strong presence in Oshawa. The Millerites were a branch of the Second Day Adventist movement, and later on the denomination evolved into the Seventh Day Adventists (SDA). Some of the remaining Terwillegar family in Whitby Township were members of this faith. In 1912 Colfax Terwillegar — then the SDA treasurer in Canada — donated his 100-acre farm near Oshawa to his faith, and it has become the location of the Seventh Day Adventist headquarters in Canada today.

In 1842 Charles Terwillegar, son of Matthew, and his family, along with several other local families, left Whitby for the United States. Pedlar mentions that William Pickell and his wife Nancy Wilson, with some of their children, joined the Charles Terwillegar and Nathan Harris families, twenty-five individuals in all, and passed through the newly named village of Oshawa in covered wagons on their way to Wisconsin.[15] Nancy, the daughter of Benjamin Wilson, is recorded as the first settler born in Whitby Township. She lived her remaining adult years near Waterton, Wisconsin, and died there in 1854. Charles Terwillegar became a well-known farmer in Wisconsin, while his son Charles Henry became a landowner in South Dakota.

The Pickells, Terwillegars, and Harrises became part of a "back" migration that had been going on in Whitby Township ever since the first settlers arrived in 1793. Many records show that the children of the first American settlers often relocated to the United States after they came of age, drawn by a combination of religious leanings, remaining ties to relatives south of the border, and new farming opportunities.

The Scugog Carrying Place witnessed a wide range of religious missionaries and ministers along its trails. Some, like the Jesuits, Methodists, and Presbyterians, ventured deep into the trails, while others, like the Mormons, only dreamt of doing so.

6

Expanding European Settlement

"It is a matter of regret, however, that when in 1842, the inhabitants agreed unanimously, to adopt Oshawa as permanent name, that at the same place and hour the meaning of the name was not recorded."[1]

Before the War of 1812 most of the early settlers to Whitby Township were from the American colonies, with the majority of them having come from New England. As late as 1842 the American settlers constituted 20 percent of the township population for that year, the second largest category after the immigrants from England, Scotland, and Ireland. A different settlement profile emerges from the northern townships, where in 1842, 50 percent of the inhabitants of Thorah Township were Scottish, while a large portion of the people settling in Brock Township, about 21 percent of the total, were Irish.

In 1830, there were few places for travellers to stop north of the hamlet of Skae's Corners (Oshawa), located at the junction of the Scugog Trail and Kingston Road. There were no communities in the northern interior and closer to Lake Scugog there were only a few scattered homesteads of settlers who had cleared parcels of land for farming. Between 1830 and 1835 the population of Whitby Township tripled after a peak in migration from Great Britain. As land became scarce along the first two concessions closest to Lake Ontario, settlers began to push into the northern sections of the township and then even further north into the townships of Reach, Brock, and Thorah. The first Thorah settlers were Scots who had emigrated from the Argyll Islands and arrived in Canada in the first half of the 1830s.

The rate of immigration to Upper Canada from Great Britain and Ireland continued to increase substantially during the 1830s. The northern townships of Reach, Brock, and Thorah began attracting large numbers of settlers, as did the northern halves of Whitby and Darlington Townships. The expanding population created a corresponding increase in the demand for the milling of wheat, oats, and barley. For sometime before gristmills were built to the north, the only available mills were one each at Gibbs Mill and Farewell Corners. The exceptional size of Gibbs Mill, originally built in 1821 by Samuel Dearborn, meant that it had practically held a monopoly on the milling industry from the time of its opening. But that was about to change.

As noted, settlers who came to Whitby Township were drawn to the Scugog Carrying Place because of its ready-made access to the interior. It had been a natural choice for Benjamin Wilson to settle at the southern terminus of the Carrying Place, a location that gave him a route north before the advent of any road. He and his stepson Eleazar arrived in 1794 and settled on two adjoining farms, and by the following year a number of his friends from the United States became his neighbours. The Roger Conant, John Burk, and John W. Trull families followed and started farming on the Broken Front Concession along the Lake Ontario shoreline to the east of Wilson. Soon afterward, the George Hall and Charles Annis families came and settled on lots immediately adjoining Wilson's lot, with the Adam Stephen family and others settling to the west of Wilson. (See Appendix C for a list of the first settlers along the Scugog Carrying Place.)

FAREWELL CORNERS AND TOAD HOLLOW

In 1804, Acheus Moody Farewell purchased property one concession north of the lake along the newly-cut Danforth Road. It seems that his brother William had come to the area because of the fur trade, possibly as early as 1802, and was already living close to the marsh at the mouth of Farewell Creek. By 1808 David Annis was passing through the area on a regular basis as he and his porters carried trading items on their way north to Lake Simcoe.

The intersection of the Scugog Carrying Place and the Danforth Road (or Kingston Road, as it was also called) soon became a desirable location for settlement and within twelve years the best land on that concession had been acquired by the ever-increasing number of immigrants. A small settlement soon developed around the tavern and gristmill built by A.M. Farewell during the War of 1812. Five years earlier, he and William had planted cherry trees and established several orchards on their properties, adding further attraction to the area. Farewell frequently referred to the "natural beauty of the little valley by the side of his home before the forest trees were cut away."[2] The clearing of the land continued, and by 1820 the entrepreneurial Farewell brothers had begun operating a potash and pearl ash works. Before long the people were referring to the settlement as Farewell Corners (today's Harmony).

The first main road in the region was Danforth Road. Samuel Wilmot, who began his surveying career by acting as a chain bearer for his father-in-law John Stegmann, was later employed by the government to survey the route for the main east-west road from Kingston to York. This road was cut four rods (sixty-six feet) wide and grubbed two rods on either side by Captain Asa Danforth, who did not complete his work on the road before he left the province, claiming that he was never paid. The road remained impassible during a wet autumn or spring.

Benjamin Wilson wrote to the authorities in 1799 pointing out that the Danforth Road was blocked in certain parts of Whitby and Darlington Townships and needed repair. Despite the many complaints, road conditions remained dismal for several decades. In 1822, Joseph J. Losee and other inhabitants of the Township of Whitby made a formal request to the government for a "sum of money for repair of the highway."[3] However, only when conditions permitted did the mail travel along the road from Kingston to York with a frequency of once every one or two weeks. It would be some time before the Danforth Road was sufficiently repaired to allow traffic to move with reasonable ease.

A small community southeast of Farewell Corners, known as Toad Hollow, developed on lot two of the First Concession at Farewell Creek. When the Farewells built the Toad Hollow gristmill on Black's Creek after their original mill was wrecked in 1838 they added economic potential to the fledgling community, and by the 1840s a cluster of families lived at Toad Hollow, including those of William McQuaid (McWay), Josh Adams, W. Stacey, Miles Luke, and John Quincy.

The Settlement of South Oshawa (The Hollow/Gibbs Mills)

Although full-fledged hamlets and villages do not appear along the Scugog Carrying Place until the 1840s, with the settlements of Sydenham Harbour, Oshawa, Harmony, Columbus, Port Perry, Prince Albert, Cannington, and Beaverton, some concentrations of population had developed in the southern portion during the two previous decades. In the 1820s only South Oshawa contained a large enough cluster of homes and businesses to warrant it being considered a community.

South Oshawa, then the Hollow, was a mile south of Kerr's Creek and two miles north of Lake Ontario on Oshawa Creek, where much of the early development in the southeastern part of Whitby Township was taking place. Since 1821, farmers in both Whitby and Darlington Townships had been taking their grain to Samuel Dearborn's gristmill in the Hollow, so named because of its topography as a large, flat, low-lying section of land. Joseph Gorham built a woollen mill adjacent to Dearborn's mill that year, and Dearborn and his brother-in-law William Cleveland constructed a dam over Oshawa Creek to provide power for both mills. Around 1825 an E. Smith opened a distillery at the Hollow, and in 1836 Miles Luke settled there and started a tannery. By now, the smaller community of Hollow, or Gibbs Mill, was beginning to be known collectively as South Oshawa

When Samuel Dearborn left the mill in 1829, he sold it to John Gibbs. Four years later, his brother Thomas, also a miller, emigrated from Devonshire, England, and joined him in South Oshawa. Within ten years the Gibbs brothers had created the firm of Gibbs and Brother to operate the gristmill and expand their businesses in the community. Later the company developed fulling, oatmeal, and barley mills, a distillery, and a tannery.

Courtesy of Whitby Archives.

The gristmill, originally built in South Oshawa by Samuel Dearborn, was the earliest-known mill constructed along the Oshawa Creek. This illustration is an insert on Tremaine's Map of the County of Ontario, Upper Canada, *1860.*

By 1837 lot eleven in the First Concession, immediately adjoining the Scugog Carrying Place, which encompassed part of today's downtown Oshawa and part of South Oshawa, had one of the highest concentrations of residents in Whitby Township. The *Walton Directory* of that year lists the following nine individuals on the lot: David Dustin, Thomas Gibbs, John McGregor, Joseph Gorham, Ira Hall, Elijah Haight, Andrew McDonald, Charles Payne, and Robert Wilcoxson. Interestingly, W.H. Smith still called the community Gibbs Mills in his 1846 *Canadian Gazetteer*, and described it as, "a settlement one mile south from Oshawa. It contains about 150 inhabitants, grist mill, oatmeal, do., pot barley do., distillery, tannery, and cloth factory (the machinery which is worked by water), where excellent coarse cloth and blankets are made."[4]

During this period of growth there was some speculation regarding various minerals being found in the Oshawa area by some of the

Cornish miners who had recently immigrated to the area. One report mentioned that:

> we received from a resident in the village of Oshawa, a small specimen of gold ore which he received from a farmer from one of the back townships, who state that he obtained it from some stones on his farm, and ... that on reducing it by the aid of the blow-pipe, the globule we obtained was only about the size of the head of a moderate sized pin ... and we have been unable to ascertain the locality from whence it was obtained.[5]

Smith also captured the mining for coal fiasco attempted near Gibbs Mill:

> A large number of the settlers in Whitby are from England, and many of them from Cornwall; some of these were miners, and being misled by the appearance of some shale found near the village [Gibbs Mill], formed a conviction that there must be coal in the neighbourhood; other persons, relying upon the judgment of these miners, and being equally sanguine of success, determined to risk the expense of boring. Subscriptions were raised, and rods made, and the boring commenced, and was continued as long as the funds lasted ... when, no coal making its appearance, those who furnished the funds became tired of the amusement. The locality selected for the operation was the vicinity of Gibbs's Mill, where they commenced boring, close to the bed of the creek; the limestone rock here being exposed at the surface.[6]

Floodwaters from the Oshawa Creek wrecked havoc on the Gibbs mills in 1850. In fact, the mill dam "had been an entire wreck, and we learn too with pleasure that his friends around South Oshawa and between there and Windsor Bay are turning out voluntarily and assisting in repairing the ravages of the flood."[7]

Barclay, Clark & Co. Litho, Toronto.

"Daniel Conant's Lumber Mill," by artist: Edward Scrope Shrapnel (1847–1920); Conant, Thomas, Upper Canada Sketches (Toronto: Briggs, 1898), facing page 135. David Annis's sawmill was an early mill built along the Oshawa Creek.

Earlier, around 1825, David Annis, having dispensed with his fur-trading business, built a sawmill on Scugog Carrying Place along the Oshawa Creek north of where it emptied into the marsh and south of the mill built by Dearborn. The mill supplied lumber for local construction of frame-styled buildings and the excess lumber was transported to markets at Niagara and beyond. When the Irish-born John Warren's gristmill was built in 1837, the year after he purchased a distillery, the timber for its construction was cut at the Annis' sawmill. Since David Annis had no formal education, he had his nephew David Conant take over the mill accounts and the sawmill continued operating until at least 1838.

EARLY DAYS OF OSHAWA (KERR'S CREEK/SKAE'S CORNERS)

The Broken Front and First Concessions were the major settlement points in Whitby Township. However, as arable land became scarce other lots were gradually being taken up in the interior. When settlers moved north of the first couple of concessions they relied on the Carrying Place for access to new farmland yet to be cleared in the forest. Often they settled near the Carrying Place.

Pedlar claims that Jabez Lynde, who had come from Brookville, Massachusetts, made a small clearing on the east bank of the Oshawa Creek around 1810 at what would become part of today's downtown Oshawa. Pedlar also states that Lynde erected a small log house where his family lived for about a year before relocating further west along the Kingston Road, though no other record exists of Lynde building a house in Oshawa. By 1811, Lynde had a tavern licence and was preparing to build his house along the creek that came to bear his name, Lynde Creek, several miles west of the Scugog Carrying Place. It is likely that Lynde had owned the property on the bank of the Oshawa Creek for some time, but sold it before any building took place.

Records indicate that Jabez Lynde concluded the purchase of lot eleven, Concession Two, Whitby, from a Robert Gray of Montreal for £93 and 15 shillings in August 1813. Interestingly, a bill of sale for the property had been concluded in 1809. It appears that this property had been sought earlier as a parcel of land for future development. Lynde held the property as an investment, clearing only a small part of the land near the Kingston Road, enough to meet the legal requirement for land ownership. He is reported to have sold the lot to his brother-in-law, John Kerr, for "a jug of whiskey and a pair of boots."[8] However, Jabez Lynde actually sold his 200 acres of lot number eleven to Kerr for £175 and recorded the sale in the land deeds registry on January 9, 1816. The deed was sworn in during February of that year and signed by Nodiah Woodruff, Lynde's other brother-in-law.

John Kerr and Jabez Lynde had married two sisters (Kerr married Betsy Woodruff and Jabez married Clarissa Woodruff) whose father, Hawkins Woodruff, owned a tavern along Kingston Road, ten miles to the west of Lynde. Nodiah was Hawkins Woodruff's son, who following his father's death in 1812 had inherited his estate. Kerr, originally from New York State, had come to the Oshawa Creek and the Kingston Road area from Duffin's Creek in 1816 and lived at the Nodiah Woodruff's tavern for a short period of time. The following year he built a large-frame tavern on his new lot and a distillery just beside a small spring in the woods, north of the tavern.

Kerr and his wife's relatives appear to have had a monopoly for the dispensing of alcohol in the region. Along from Kerr's tavern there were the Lynde and Woodruff taverns, all three of them strung approximately five to ten miles apart along Kingston Road in the neighbouring townships of Whitby and Pickering.

The year after John Kerr settled on his land he was joined by his brother William, who took up land immediately east of John. Adjoining lots to the south were owned by Charles Arkland and John McGregor. William Kerr settled on lot ten, Concession Two, a lot first registered to their father, Norris Kerr, who is recorded as being a resident of neighbouring Darlington Township in 1801. It is likely that Norris had received this as a land grant. William acquired it from him for £78. Besides farming, William Kerr also sold whisky and is recorded as selling alcohol to the Mississauga at Lake Scugog in the years from 1826 to 1829. This small collection of houses, taverns, and farms dominated by the Kerr brothers soon became known as Kerr's Creek.

Not long afterwards, Charles Arkland added to the collection of taverns in the area by building a fourth one, which later became the Central Hotel. As noted, the lot adjoining Arkland's was farmed by John McGregor, who, like John Kerr, also built a distillery on the east bank of the creek south of Kingston Road. Obviously, the making and selling of whisky was a popular business.

Like Thomas Henry, who had settled on Eleazar Lockwood's farm around 1816, McGregor had worked for the military during the War of 1812, transporting military supplies and guarding prisoners along Kingston Road between Toronto and Kingston. Having seen Whitby Township many times while passing through it during military duty, he decided to settle there after the war was over. McGregor registered his land in 1837, twenty years after having settled there. This property, lot eleven, Concession One, had originally belonged to Robert Isaac Dey Grey, the solicitor general of Upper Canada, who perished when the *Speedy* went down in 1804. Grey had registered the lot in August of

1803 and willed it to his servant, Simon, though no evidence shows that Simon's heirs ever used or sold the land. The land appears to have eventually reverted back to the Crown before McGregor settled there, though there may have been some complications in acquiring a clear title.

One of the earliest documents mentioning the first settlers to Whitby Township describes the marks (such as a cut on the ear, or brand) on cattle, sheep, and hogs, placed there to identify ownership. Reliable fences were a rarity and the animals were prone to wandering. The considerable attention given to the marking indicates the importance of livestock to the early community and demonstrates the wealth attached to livestock.

The first recorded meeting of the early settlers took place at Samuel Munger's farm, when on March 7, 1803, the men came together to choose town officers for the Townships of Pickering and Whitby. They picked a town clerk, two assessors, two wardens, a collector, five pathmasters,[9] a poundkeeper, and two fenceviewers out of a population consisting of only thirty families — a total of 130 individuals. Recognizing their vulnerability as a small number of settlers spread out over two large townships, their first priority was to set up a consistent payment of taxes and establish the enforcement of regulations for the protection of individual property. The settler's view of individual property ownership was completely different from the First Nations' concept of communal property, a reality that frequently created tensions in the area.

Levi Annis, brother of David Annis, had cleared thirty-one acres by burning the trees in the early fall of 1806, then sowed fall wheat between the remaining stumps by "bushing in" the seeding or raking of the ground with a bush to cover the seeds.[10] Levi was settled in Pickering Township by 1804 but returned to Whitby where he registered the sale of Broken Front Concession, lot seventeen in June of 1812. Some years later, he purchased Broken Front, lot six, and settled there in 1823.

J.S. Williamson outlines how the settlers and their livestock lived in an area dominated by wild animals, in Darlington Township near the eastern route of the Scugog Carrying Place:

> Deer were plentiful on the 9th Concession. Pigeons and wild geese came in clouds twice a year, going north in the

Spring and south in the Fall … Bears were plentiful; … the meat was often used in the family. Wolves were killed for two reasons: first because of their prowling disposition and their destruction of sheep; secondly, because of the bounty paid for their capture by the Government. Speckled trout were plentiful in the streams.[11]

Maple sugar making was a craft the settlers learned from the First Nations who used hot stones in birchbark containers to boil the maple sap: "Sugar making was one of the great industries among the settlers …. Sap was gathered with horses and sleighs which conveyed a huge tub which would hold 60 or 70 pails and so the sap was taken to the boiling place."[12]

In 1830, Mrs. Samuel Dearborn, the wife of the miller's son, Samuel Dearborn Jr., recalled that in 1830 Oshawa "bush land exceeded the cleared land."[13] She attended a log school along Danforth Road east of Simcoe Street (Reach Road). This school was in operation between 1829 and 1835 until being replaced by the Union School. She remembered the store operated by Skae and McDonald. Either in 1830 or just a few years before, Skae had built a one-and-a-half-storey brick store on the southeast corner of Simcoe and King Streets. By then, John Kerr had sold his business and moved from the village. The Skae name grew in prominence and Kerr's Creek became known as Skae's Corners.

Martin Shaw from Yorkshire, England, settled here in 1830 and opened a blacksmith's shop. Five years later, Walter Wigg set up a furniture business and Elijah Haight set up his general store on the northeast corner of Simcoe and King Streets. John VanNest, whose family had lived near the mouth of the Oshawa Creek since the early 1830s, hewed the timbers of the Skae's first store in 1837. In 1838, Richard Woon from Cornwall, England, built the Oshawa House, soon to be acclaimed as the best tavern between Kingston and Toronto.

In addition to Edward Skae and his general store, the 1837 *Walton Directory* lists several other residents on the two-hundred-acre lot ten, Concession One of Whitby Township, including John Butler, Dennis Daley, Philip Reader, and Daniel Williams. Adjacent on the west and

Oshawa Daily-Times Gazette, January 24, 1948.

This sketch of Simcoe Street facing south shows Skae's General Store and the Munro Hotel and was drawn by Edward Carswell, circa 1848.[14]

to the north of this concentration of residences, was John Kerr's tavern and distillery.

Kerr sold his property to a James Hall in 1829, who in turn sold the lot to Irish-born John Warren in October of 1836. Warren had lived on Danforth Road, west of Skae's Corners, since 1821, and he, along with his brother William, had operated several stores at Hamer's Corners (today's town of Whitby). John and William Warren were also the first postmasters in the Township of Whitby.

The Naming of Oshawa

In 1842, the residents of Skae's Corners solicited the provincial government for a post office in the village. Since the authorities required a name to be picked by the local residents, a process was set up that ultimately led to a choice between Skae's Corners and Sydenham, the latter name recognizing a former lieutenant governor, Lord Sydenham, who had recently died. Since there were not enough votes for either the name of Skae or Sydenham, another alternative was needed.

A story handed down over time mentions that A.M. Farewell was travelling through the village with a couple of First Nations men and they stopped while the meeting was underway. One of the Natives was asked for his opinion for a name and he suggested "Oshawa."

The most common meaning of the word "Oshawa" given by most local historians is "crossing of the waters," indicating a sort of portage. Pedlar, however, could not be sure of the meaning of the name "Oshawa," so he listed other possibilities — it could mean either "Whitefish Creek," "the village crossing of the creek," or the Indian trail itself. But he was not satisfied until he could solicit more opinions on what the word "Oshawa" meant. One of his sources suggests that "Oshawa" comes from the Algonquian word *Ashawee* meaning, "he crosses a river, lake, etc." From the Mississauga on Georgina Island on Lake Simcoe he received information that the name *Oshuhwahnoo* implies a southern tribe, and therefore Oshawa might have come from it. From the Scugog Mississauga, he was told that the derivation was from *Oshwae* or *Osh-wa-e* meaning "over the Big Lake."[15]

According to others, the name "Oshawa" seems first to have been given to the locality around present-day Oshawa by the Scugog Misssissauga. W.H. Higgins, in recounting the story of Joseph Gould of Uxbridge, suggested that the name Oshawa was a familiar "old" term used by the early settlers and Natives. He wrote that, "Oshawa was formerly known as Skae's Corners, after Mr. Edward Skae had opened a store there. Before that time several other names, after those of the old settlers, were given the locality. But it had retained the old Indian appellation of Oshawa. The Indian meaning of the word signifies Salmon Creek."[16] The *Historical Atlas of the County of Ontario* from 1877 claims the meaning for Oshawa is "Salmon Creek," while Elder Thomas Henry states that Oshawa means "whitefish" or "Whitefish Creek" in the language spoken by the Mississauga.[17]

The possible definitions of the name "Oshawa" seem almost limitless. Author Thomas Kaiser, a former Oshawa mayor and doctor, mentions that when A.M. Farewell and the two First Nations people interviewed at the meeting to find a new name for the post office, that the Natives suggested the name Oshawa meaning the "crossing of a stream."[18] George Hamilton Grierson, according to Pedlar, believed Oshawa was the name for the Scugog Trail running north to the Ridges (Oak Ridges Moraine). This same interpretation is given more recently by Percy Fletcher.[19]

Whatever the actual source or meaning, the name Oshawa took hold, and in 1842 the first post office in the village was opened with Edward Skae as postmaster.

7

Settlers Migrate Northward

"In the year 1828, Pioneer Hinkson underbrushed and blazed the Reach Road from the settlement on the 2nd concession (now Oshawa) to the Widdifield Creek in the 4th concession."[1]

Prior to the arrival of settlers the only cleared land north of the Danforth Road was at the Wiley blockhouse and another blockhouse at the south end of Lake Scugog where Joseph Wyle, an Indian trader, was operating on Concession Eight, a mile southeast of Raglan and about eight miles north of Danforth Road. In 1821, several settlers began pushing northward from Kerr's Creek (and Farewell Corners) along the Scugog Carrying Place.

Three miles north of the Danforth Road, Joseph Widdifield settled on lot ten, Concession Four of Whitby Township. Reuben Crandell went into Reach Township and John Fralick settled between them. On the eastern side of the Carrying Place Charles Terwillegar, under a government contract, cut and cleared a road allowance two rod (thirty-three feet) wide from the first concession to the Sixth Concession. On the western branch the Scugog Carrying Place was west of the road to Widdifield's and separated from it by a quarter- to as much as a half-mile.

George Hinkson, who had come to Whitby Township from Vermont in 1823, was responsible for opening up the Scugog Carrying Place to settler traffic. In 1828 he cut away the trail's underbrush from Concession Two to the Fourth Concession at the Widdifield farm. Between 1833 and 1835, once he was awarded the contract for the work, he had his sons cut a more permanent route there. This cleared-out stretch would become Reach Road.

It is believed that one of Hinkson's sons was buried in the Farewell Cemetery at Harmony. When Harmony Road was being widened in 1995, excavations underway near the cemetery discovered a grave that was identified as that of George W. Hinkson. Judging by the skeletal remains he had died between 1875 and 1900. His father had died in 1857 and was also buried at Farewell Cemetery. When DNA samples were analyzed for both sets of remains, the results confirmed that the unearthed remains were indeed that of a relative, likely his son.

THE NORTHERN PART OF WHITBY TOWNSHIP

With the arrival of more and more prospective settlers, the shift northward continued. Around 1825 Chester Webster (from Massachusetts) and Jacob Smith from Fredericksburg (near Napanee, Ontario) settled in the vicinity of what became English Corners, later renamed Columbus. When Timothy Fisher — also from Fredericksburg, but born in New York State — moved his family to Concession Seven of Whitby Township in 1827, he had to transport them and all of his goods over the Scugog Trail since there was no other way north from Kerr's Creek. Samuel Dearborn, having sold his gristmill at South Oshawa, moved north along the Scugog Trail in 1829 and resumed farming on lot eleven of Concession Three. The lumber for the new Dearborn house was cut at the nearby Widdifield sawmill.

During the clearing of the forest, cut timber not used for lumber was burned:

> They would cut the underbrush down and pile it up in small heaps then they would cut down the oak and other large trees. They next cut the bodies of the trees into logs; took the tops and chopped them up fine, and piled them up in separate heaps. Next they set fire to the brush and burned up the heaps. In this way, it would take a good hand from eight to ten days to chop an acre. Then it would take five men and a yoke of oxen a day to clear up from one-half to an acre, logging; and it would

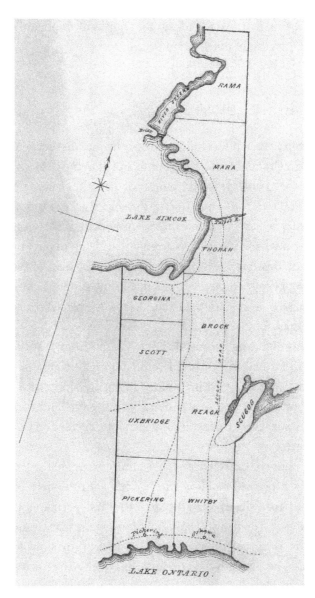

This Ontario County map, developed in 1853, shows the locations of the townships of Whitby, Reach, Brock, and Thorah, cartographer, Thomas Devine. From the Atlas containing Maps of the Counties of Upper and Lower Canada laid before the legislature of the Province of Canada in the year 1853, *produced by the Crown Lands Department.*

take a man or two to pick up the chunks of wood and do the burning of the logs.[2]

SETTLING REACH TOWNSHIP

The Township of Reach was inhabited only by the Mississauga until 1821 when Reuben Crandell moved his family north to the clearing at Wiley's, a move that took two days from Columbus.[3] Later he cleared a path fifteen miles long and two rods wide (thirty-three feet) from Dayton's Corners (today's Prince Albert) to about three miles north of Harmony, creating just width enough for his team of oxen and a sleigh to pass through. He accomplished this feat in over a summer with the help of two axemen. The trees were dropped on each side of the cut and logs cut in the centre were dragged away with the oxen. Poles were placed over streams to make them passable.

After immigrating from Saratoga County, New York, in 1812, Crandell had farmed in Prince Edward County for nine years and then moved to the southern part of Whitby Township along with a group of Fredericksburg farmers. He had been scouting for land further north in the newly surveyed Township of Brock, but decided to purchase 400 acres in Reach.

When Reuben Crandell and his family struggled over the ridge (Oak Ridges Moraine), hauling their goods with the help of a yoke of oxen hitched to a sleigh, they became the first permanent European settlers in Reach Township. Their isolation meant that Crandell had to travel back to Harmony on a regular basis to get provisions for his family and to haul his grain to the gristmills in Whitby Township, a distance of about ten miles.

In 1823, Crandell was joined by John Rae (or Ray), who settled on lot eleven, Concession Two, Reach Township. Rae, who became Crandell's closest neighbour, had previously been renting land at Wiley's block house. A William Wade is recorded as having cleared land on the front of Concession Five that year, though it appears he did not remain there for long. Two other unidentified families are also noted as having come to the area the next year. Before Rae's death in 1825, he and Crandell enlarged the Scugog Trail thus creating even better access from their farms to Wiley's in Whitby Township.

According to local folklore, Crandell distilled his own whisky and had introduced the local Mississauga to its effects. One day when he was at Harmony selling his potash along the eastern trail of the Carrying Place, a group of Mississauga came to the Crandell homestead demanding some whisky. Eventually the family bartered whisky for the weapons the Natives were carrying and managed to provide the spirits while locking out the group. When Rueben returned home, the men had left, but returned a few days later at which time their guns and knives were returned.

After ten years of farming his land, which later became the community of Prince Albert, the Crandell family again moved further north along the Carrying Place, this time to settle at what became known as Crandell's Corners. The name of the community would later be changed to Borelia, now part of Port Perry.

In 1824, Abner Hurd and Daniel Dayton, originally from Massachusetts, settled in Reach Township and began building their own houses near Crandell's farm, today's Prince Albert. The following year, these few Reach settlers laid out an improved ox-cart road near the Carrying Place, running from Dayton's location down to Wiley's blockhouse, and providing them with a much easier route for transporting their grain to the mill at the south end of Oshawa.

Samuel Farmer's book confirms that one of the very early settlers in the developing community of Prince Albert was Abner Hurd Sr. and that the first settler in Port Perry was Elias Williams, about 1830.[4] In 1828, new settlers built a log school for the Mississauga on land donated by Hurd and another schoolhouse for themselves west of Prince Albert. As settlement expanded, three separate communities would develop in close proximity to each other: Prince Albert, Port Perry, and Borelia. Shortly after 1872, when the railway came through, they were incorporated into Port Perry.

By 1831 the following people are recorded as having moved to the Prince Albert area: Abram Ewers, Donald Christie, Robert Munroe, Archie

McDermid, Peter Christie, John McKercher, Mr. Thompson, Charles Stevens, John Vernon, and William Ashton. The census for that year shows 134 individuals living in the township. Other settlers, such as Jeremiah Orser, who arrived in 1837, continued to move into the township, and by 1842 the population had grown to 1,052 individuals, with five sawmills and two gristmills operating in the area. For the record, the first European settler on Scugog Island appears to have been a Joseph Graxton, who settled there in 1834.[5]

ON TO BROCK TOWNSHIP

The first group of Scottish settlers arrived in Brock Township during the 1820s, however, over the following decades many of them resettled in Bruce and Grey Counties. Samuel Wilmot started surveying Brock Township in between March and May 1817, but the brutal weather and boggy terrain defeated him. He returned to complete the survey on November 12, 1817, working his way north along the Scugog Carrying Place from Whitby with a team and wagon. His journal notes describe the hardships he and his crew endured: "Day after day he was forced to turn back to Reach Township, driven there by the rain, the snow and the impassable swamps."[6] In conducting the survey, Wilmot travelled as far north as Lake Simcoe twice, on both occasions in May and November. He completed the survey by the end of 1817.

William Bagshaw, who brought his family from Suffolk, England, was reported as looking for arable land in Brock Township around 1817. Two years would pass before he could bring his wife and eight children and settle in the southwest portion of the township. His house, built of hewn round logs, was completed on December 25, 1819. Interestingly, Bagshaw arrived in Brock by way of Yonge Street having determined not to use the Scugog Carrying Place, which then could not be used for the transport of farm animals and heavy provisions. Several other early settlers also came to this corner of Brock Township via Yonge Street, north to Holland Landing, and on to Lake Simcoe and then across the lake. However, since the story of the Scugog Trail is the focus here, attention is given to those families who settled in the centre of Brock Township along the Carrying Place and who travelled north using this trail.

J.E. Farewell credits the first European settler in Brock Township as being James Reekie who arrived in October 10, 1818.[7] J.E.'s ancestor, Moody Farewell, also bought 500 acres in Brock, as noted in the Ontario assembly journals for 1828.[8]

Irvine Johnston, born in County Fermanagh, Ireland, came to Brock no later than October 1829 and is recorded as having settled on Concession Twelve, lot nineteen. Initially, he had settled in Nova Scotia in 1819 and later moved to Hallowell Township (in today's Prince Edward County) in Upper Canada. It is said that Johnston had received correspondence from Robert Sproul, also from Fermanagh, asking him to leave Hallowell Township and resettle in Brock. Around 1823 Robert and his wife Margaret Junkin acted on that advice. That same year another cluster of Sprouls (John, William, and Christopher), who had also been farming in Hallowell Township, joined them in Brock.

Homesteader John Brandon's log house, measuring twenty-four by twenty feet, was built in Brock Township, lot eighteen, Concession Thirteen, sometime between 1825 and 1835. Miraculously, the cabin, with its stone fireplace three feet high and six feet long and sleeping loft up top, has survived. It was donated to the Cannington Historical Society and has since been relocated to the Historical Museum in MacLeod Park, Cannington, where it is open to the public at seasonable times.

As discussed earlier, religion followed the settlers. Itinerant ministers began riding the Methodist circuit in the area in the 1830s and impromptu services were held in the homes and barns of John Brandon and Robert Sproul. Throughout 1834 and 1835 Adam Elliot held Anglican services for both Mississauga and white setters. Two years later an Anglican church was constructed in Cannington in 1837 at a cost of $600.

The Brandon Cabin, one of the earliest structures in Brock Township, is still standing and now part of the Cannington Historical Society's Centennial Museum.

SETTLING THORAH TOWNSHIP

John Edward White began surveying the Thorah Township in 1821 and was rewarded with a land grant of 1,700 acres within the township. He would complete the survey of the township with surveyor David Gibson.[9] White eventually settled at Lake Simcoe, immediately north of today's Beaverton, and his son James is listed as the first white male child born in the township. During that same year, William Turner, an Irishman, came to Thorah and also settled on Lake Simcoe. He arrived by way of Lake Simcoe after having travelled north along the Toronto Carrying Place at the Humber River.

During the 1820s, Scottish immigrants were the main newcomers, including the Campbell, Cameron, and McRae families, who settled in the south part of Thorah. One of the first residents of the community of Beaverton was John Bruce and his wife Roberta Fraser, who arrived there in 1828 after having emigrated from Isle of Islay. Throughout the 1820s and 1830s many of the settlers originated from the Argyll Islands of Tiree, Mull, and Islay, off the west coast of Scotland. The Islay settlers are noted as having come in four different ships, the *Albion* in 1832, *Stirling Castle* in 1834, the *Hector* in 1835, and the *Deveron* in 1836.[10]

In her 1952 book on Thorah Township, Mary Houston Ritchie mentions several early settlers, including William Turner, Corporal Crawford, and Donald Cameron. Turner must have been a veteran of the Napoleonic War since his tombstone reads, "Ensign William Turner, of Sicilian Regiment, native of Bandon Co., Cork, Ireland, died Oct. 2, 1867, aged 83 years."[11] Turner is credited with building the first European-style house in Thorah Township in 1822. The lumber for the doors and windows for his log home were shipped from Holland Landing on the south shore of Lake Simcoe. Turner's daughter Elizabeth was the first white female born in the township.

Corporal Crawford, a Scotsman, who had lost an eye in battle during the Napoleonic Wars, was discharged from the British Army and ultimately settled in Thorah Township. Crawford built a hut next to a stream on Lake Simcoe, reported to be near the site of Beaverton and along a trail that led to a Native village at the north side of the lake. His family, which moved to the hut, was decimated one evening, as recounted by W. H. Higgins in the *Life and Times of Joseph Gould*.

> He [Corporal Crawford] was in the habit of making short excursions, in order to get supplies of fresh venison, which he was always able to fetch to the hut before night to the expectant family.... Far into the night, the howling of the [wolf] pack, at first distant, came nearer and nearer to the hut; the watching woman heard a rush past, and believing that her husband was pursed, in her fond eagerness to give him succour opened the door. Fatal step! The ferocious brutes rushed in, tumbling over each other in their bloody eagerness; the savage animals fought and tore each other in glutting on their defenceless prey.... With the first streak of daylight he

made his way home, where, frantic and heartbroken in
his agony, he encountered the tragic scene.[12]

The family had been killed with the exception of the seven year-old
daughter who was taken away to live with her mother's relatives. Higgins
goes on to say that Corporal Crawford was adopted and cared for by the
Mississauga, but since this took place along Lake Simcoe, it is more likely
that the native group was the Chippewa.

Once he was settled, Donald Cameron encouraged friends in
Scotland to settle in Thorah. Some of these families were from the Isle of
Islay, while others came from the Highland districts. By 1830 the Scottish
family names of Calder, McFadyen, Bruce, Gunn, Gordon, Fraser, and
Murray appear in the land registries for Thorah. Archibald McMillan
came to Canada and he too linked up with Donald Cameron, who
encouraged him to take up land in Thorah.

Other Scottish settlers arrived from Sutherlandshire. They include
the Gordon family, who made their way to Thorah via the Carrying
Place at Holland Landing in 1831. James Gordon is recorded as being
the first blacksmith in Beaverton. He died in 1846. However, the first
permanent family in what is today's Beaverton was the Alex Calder
family, who arrived in 1828. The Calders were part of a group of Islay
settlers, who had previously settled in North Carolina, but, not liking
the climate and politics in the United States, they sent agents to Canada
to seek out new land. After relocating to Thorah, Calder built the first
gristmill in the township.

John Carruthers a Presbyterian minister who came from Whitby in
1832 to administer to the Scottish Highlanders north of Reach Township,
conducted a religious gathering in Thorah on October 31, 1832. He
wrote that, Thorah was settled by "Highland Scotch, and had a promis-
ing appearance for the support of a Minister of the Kirk."[13] In 1840, the
Scots in Thorah built a stone church in Beaverton where services were
conducted in English and in Gaelic, their mother tongue.

Other settlers arrived in Thorah from communities further south.
The family of Artemas Thompson was one of those who came from
Prince Edward County in 1831. He bought 200 acres on lot thirteen,

Photograph by Grant Karcich.

Today, the grave marker for Lachlin and Ann Cameron can still be viewed at St. Andrew's Presbyterian Cemetery in Beaverton, near the Stone Church. Their tombstone inscription reads, "In memory of, Lachlin Cameron, native of Inverness-shire, Scotland, who departed this life, Feb. 16, 1838, aged 93 y'rs, Ann Cameron, who departed this life, Sep. 16, 1842 ag'd 80 y'rs, being also a native of Inverness-shire."

Concession Six along the Scugog Trail and also purchased several lots in what became the village of Beaverton, one plot of which was given to the Wesleyan Methodists to serve as a site for a church. Over the next couple of decades his Thompson family spread out through Thorah and other adjacent townships.

By 1830, Thorah Township had thirty-five houses. By the time of a local 1848 census, the data collected shows a considerable growth: 146 farmers, twenty-six labourers, one merchant, one physician, one surgeon, one innkeeper, one fuller, two churches, four schools and one inn in the township. Two years later, the population, totalled 1,062 inhabitants.

Initially, Thorah Township residents had no direct link to the rest of the province in the south — their only connections were either along Lake Simcoe to the Toronto Carrying Place or up the Beaver River and onto the Scugog Carrying Place. Naturally, they requested road links with the south. Arad Smalley of Newmarket (sometimes recorded as Smelly) was contracted to survey a road in 1827, which he called the Whitby Road, later called the Cameron Road. The road followed along the west bank of the Beaver River, parallel to the Scugog Carrying Place down to where Cannington is today. From there, his survey ran due east to the Brock and Mariposa town line, following it for six to seven miles down to the Nonquon River. In 1829, Smalley surveyed another road in Thorah along the coastline of Lake Simcoe from the Township's southwest perimeter, north to the Talbot River.

His route, along with the other road Smalley surveyed down through Reach Township to Columbus in Whitby Township, was the first settler route linking Lake Simcoe to Lake Ontario and passing through these townships. However, the route was not a modern road by any means and travel remained an arduous task.

8

MARGINALIZATION OF THE FIRST NATIONS

"It was thought that as the present Indians on Scugog Island is a remnant of the Mississaugas, the tribe of Indians who at one time claimed the site of the present town of Oshawa and neighbourhood as their hunting ground."[1]

The Scugog Carrying Place at the Oshawa Creek became a staging ground for the Mississauga, who while at the south end of the trail would camp near Wilson's homestead. John Henry, who grew up on the farm where the Thomas Henry House now stands as part of the museum in Oshawa, recalled seeing the Mississauga there:

> He saw, a large number of Indians camped in their wigwams on his father's farm, overlooking the mouth of the creek (now the marsh at Port Oshawa). At that time the woods next to the marsh had not been cleared away, and, as there were no harbour improvements, wharfs, etc. etc. at the Port prior to 1841, the neighbours along the Lake Shore came up the marsh to a little launching place on the front of their farm. The Indians found this marsh a safe place to bring their fleet of canoes.[2]

Both John Henry and another longtime resident of Whitby Township, Harvey Kerr, claimed that the trail began on the Henry farm.

George Hinkson also describes the Mississauga in the Oshawa Creek valley where, according to Samuel Pedlar:

many times Indians encamped in flats of the creek below the present track of the Grand Trunk Railway [later the Canadian National Railway]. Their wigwams, upright poles stuck in the ground and covered with cedar boughs were frequently to be seen in the place. The valley of the creek down to the marsh was a favourite trapping place. The Indians catched large numbers of muskrat and minks there the hind quarter of which when skinned made a dainty meal, of which the Indians appeared to be very fond.[3]

While camped at these annual gatherings the Mississauga were able to hunt for small game and harvest wild rice or other crops they had planted.

The fishing season, which started in August when the salmon came to spawn, was a time for families to come together in large encampments. This first run of fish was followed by lake trout at the beginning of October and then whitefish into November. In the spring, the Mississauga concentrated on other species, such as pickerel, maskinonge, suckers, black bass, and sturgeon. In the treaties with the British Crown, the Mississauga retained the fishery rights along the shorelines of Lakes Ontario and Simcoe, which originally included ownership of the river and creek mouths. Their fishing rights were protected by a series of laws called the *Act for the Preservation of Salmon* that were enacted between 1807 and 1823.[4]

Although the Mississauga had not had a settlement on Lake Scugog for over a decade from 1830 to 1844, they continued to use the Scugog Carrying Place well into the 1840s. By that time a series of related Mississauga bands were occupying lands at Rice Lake and Lakes Scugog and Simcoe. They had been introduced to European-style farming and were beginning to abandon their former nomadic lifestyle. However, some, like Chief Waubakosh, continued the nomadic life style by travelling the trail from Lake Scugog to Lake Ontario every fall from 1808 to 1847.

John VanNest, who had been in Skae's Corners from 1830 when he hewed the timber for the settlement's first store, occasionally travelled up to Lake Scugog. He first went there to troll for fish in Lake Scugog in 1830 with his stepfather Jason Bates. A West Durham history written in 1894 claimed that their troll line had been made by a blacksmith at Thornton's Corners near Kingston Road. VanNest noted that when he was at the lake, there were only two Mississauga families in the area. By this time, most of the Mississauga had left Lake Scugog and relocated further north.

When the Mississauga returned to resettle at Lake Scugog in 1844, they found plans underway for the creation of the village of Port Perry on the site of their former campsite. Consequently, they had to settle for a few lots on Scugog Island and Chief Jacob Crane, who had been at Scugog in the 1820s, brought his family back to the new location. Using their annual payment funds, the band purchased land for a reserve on Scugog Island in 1844, the land they currently occupy. Smith's *Gazetteer* describes this group in 1846 as follows: "another party of the same tribe [Mississauga] is settled near Scugog Lake, in the township of Cartwright. This party consists of one chief, 22 warriors, and 19 women, with 14 children who receive presents and 12 who do not."[5] The 1851 census for Scugog Township, which at that time covered only Scugog Island, lists a Chief Jacob Crane and other possible First Nations names including Star Crane, Jacob Crane, and several families with the Johnson surname, sometimes spelled "Jonson," all of whom are presumed to be Native people. The 1851 census also indicates that the Scugog band had constructed a church of hewed logs, measuring eighteen by twenty-four feet, to replace the one built near Port Perry over twenty-five years earlier.

Smith also recorded the location and size of other Mississauga bands:

> There are other Indian settlements in this section of the country; one of Messesagas [*sic*], in the township of Smith, at Mud Lake, consisting of one chief, nineteen warriors, twenty-four women, and eight children, who receive presents, and sixteen children who, having the misfortune to be born since the first day of January, 1846 do not receive presents ... A third party of the same tribe is settled in the township of Otonabee, on Rice

Lake; it consists of four chiefs, 31 warriors, 43 women, and 33 children who receive presents, and twenty-five who do not.[6]

The group at Mud Lake, today known as Curve Lake, developed into a well-established community. By 1857 it had ninety-six residents with seventy acres of cleared land growing wheat, corn, and potatoes. This settlement had seventeen log houses and six barns or sheds, along with a log church.[7] Peter Nogee continued to lead the band at Curve Lake into the 1840s and 1850s along with John Bigman.

In his writings about the Native peoples, Smith continued by describing a fourth group. Along with the Mississauga, the Chippewa formed another branch of the Ojibwa people. Each had separate hunting and fishing areas, with the Chippewa on Lake Simcoe inhabiting that lake and using the Beaver River on the east of the lake where they tapped maples for sugar. They also used the east side of Lake Simcoe for their spring fishing and the islands of Thorah, Georgina, and Snake for their autumn fishing sites. The Mississauga of Curve Lake carried out their annual fall fishing at the Ganaraska River, while the dodem at Rice Lake would fish at the Trent River, and the Scugog band fished annually near the mouth of the Oshawa Creek.

In 1833, the Presbyterian missionary John Carruthers described the Chippewa as coming from the Narrows on the northern end of Lake Simcoe to Georgina and along the east end of Lake Simcoe to camp and hunt in the area. While there they would often visit with the incoming settlers. One of the Chippewa bands on Lake Simcoe was headed by William Yellowhead, known to the Ojibwa as Musquakie, a name that, as some authors suggest, is the origin of the name for Muskoka, the area north of Orillia.

Carruthers also described Thomas Anderson, appointed Indian superintendent by the Indian Department, and in 1830 ordered to build mills, schools, and houses for the Chippewa at Coldwater and the Narrows, today's Orillia. Before his appointment Anderson had been a trader with the First Nations in Michigan and Wisconsin. As was the norm for the times, Carruthers's writings clearly reveal a negative bias towards Native

Courtesy of Gordon Dibb, York North Archaeological Services.

The illustration of a sugar-making camp on lot seventeen, Brock Township, was drawn by Robert Holmes, a Cannington-born artist and drawing master at Upper Canada College. It shows the boiling of maple sap and a Native structure of a conical design.

people and significantly downplay the impact that the arrival of the Europeans had on Native lifestyle:

> The tribe under the chief Yellowhead, now settled at Rama, was located at the narrows of Lake Simcoe, where the village of Orillia now stands ... They were in the constant habit of drinking spirituous liquors to excess; not one of them could read or write; and they scarcely knew anything of religion. Their hunting grounds were exhausted; the Government presents were exchanged for whisky. They were in debt to all the traders, and unable to obtain more credit; and thus were constantly in a state bordering on starvation ... By studious attention to their habits and prejudices, they were at length brought to acquiesce, and the general result has been

that each Indian with a family, has now a little farm under cultivation, on which he raises not only potatoes and Indian Corn, but also wheat, oats, peas, &c.; his wigwam is exchanged for the log house; hunting has in many cases, been abandoned altogether.[8]

This band at Rama had previously lived and hunted in the Lake Simcoe area until 1830 when they were concentrated at the Narrows (today's Orilla), an ancient fishing location for the Native people. Once there, the band had help with the building of a chapel and a church from Methodist missionaries, however, the lack of government and missionary funds led to the closure of these settlements in Coldwater and the Narrows in 1837.

Yellowhead and his band, as a result of increasing pressure from incoming settlers, moved from the Narrows to the eastern side of Lake Cochiching at Rama in 1838–1839. They purchased 1,600 acres by using their annuities as payment and proceeded to clear some of the land. Another Chippewa band led by Chief Snake resettled on their traditional land on the islands in Lake Simcoe. Georgina Island is still a reserve. The missionaries working there reported that, by 1841, the Rama band was able to sell four hundred to five hundred bushels of potatoes beyond their own needs. However, it turned out that the claims were exaggerated and though some Chippewa took up farming, others clung to their customary ways.

Chief William Yellowhead and family are reported to have used the Scugog Carrying Place along the Beaver River, often frequenting the area immediately west of Cannington on the Robert Sproul property. The 1851 census lists several possible family members of Chief William, including his wife Eliza, age fifty, an Augustus Yellowhead aged twenty-six, and Eliza Yellowhead age nineteen. The Yellowhead family had winter hunting grounds in Muskoka and Algonquin Park area at Lake of Bays, Ox-Tongue, Canoe, and Trout Lakes.[9] They apparently continued to use the Beaver River trail over the next three decades.

Regional Aboriginal Population 1818–1850[10]

Aboriginal Groups	1818–19	1825	1830	1842–46	1850
Lake Scugog		150	0	64	68
The Narrows of Rama	540		250		184
Rice Lake	348				136
Mud Lake (Chemung Lake)				189	69
Alnwick and Grape Island	218		200	233	190
Snake Island (Lake Simcoe)					109
Georgina Island (Lake Simcoe)					2 families

The Scugog Carrying Place gradually disappeared. Samuel Pedlar's eyewitnesses tell of the Mississauga camping on the upper part of the Scugog Carrying Place on lot ten of the Fourth Concession of Whitby around the year 1841. Chief Waubakosh travelled from Lake Scugog to Lake Ontario annually in the years 1808 to 1847 according to Thomas Conant. The stretch of the trail from Lake Scugog to Lake Ontario was likely not used by any Native group after 1850, though the trail continues to be in use along the Beaver River. The mills in the hamlets of Cannington, Port Perry, and Columbus would have been obstacles to travel and the village of Oshawa would have presented a formidable barrier. As well, the small settlement with a wharf and shipping traffic at the mouth of the Oshawa Creek would have dissuaded travel and camping on that part of the trail where the Mississauga traditionally fished in the autumn. However, the northern part of the trail along the Beaver River was used well into the 1880s by the descendants of Chief Yellowhead and his family. They continued to frequent a bend in the river called Saginaw, immediately west of Cannington.[11]

The Scugog Carrying Place had been a viable part of the Huron-Wendat and Mississauga world for hundreds of years. It allowed them to practise their culture and economic way of life by linking them to their fishing and hunting sites at Lakes Simcoe, Scugog, and Ontario. With the coming of traders, missionaries, and settlers, the First Nations connections to the land were first disrupted then gradually diminished to the

This photograph of a First Nations camp was taken by an unidentified photographer near the Robert Carpenter family property on lots seventeen and eighteen, Concession Twelve, Brock Township, sometime between 1880 and 1900. The Carpenter family has traditionally attributed it to the Yellowhead family from Rama.

point that they could no longer sustain their traditional way of life. The Scugog Carrying Place was abandoned and slowly taken over by either the forest or by farmers' fields.

Today, the descendants of the Mississauga and the Huron are spread out over several communities. On Scugog Island the Mississauga of Scugog Island First Nation operate as one of the smallest First Nations communities in Canada, with less than 100 residents. Two other bands are related to the Scugog group: one is at Curve Lake and the other is in Rama Township, with the latter numbering about 1,500 individuals. The Huron also have distinct communities, though they are scattered across North America. The Huron-Wendat Nation of 3,000 residents is located in Wendake, Quebec, while several Wyandot communities numbering 4,000 individuals can be found in Michigan, Kansas, and Oklahoma.

Canadian 2006 Census of Aboriginal Population for
Oshawa, Clarington, Whitby, Scugog, Brock
and Neighbouring Areas[12]

Community	Total Population	Aboriginal Population	First Nations (Mississauga/ Chippewa)	Métis Population
Oshawa	140,240	2,515	1,530	775
Clarington	77,370	1,095	625	410
Whitby	110,455		1,175	
Scugog Twp.	21,155		180	
Brock Twp.	11,760		120	
Mississauga of Scugog Island First Nation			217	
Curve Lake			1,060	
Chippewas of Rama First Nation			1,500	
Chippewas of Georgina Island			754	
Hiawatha First Nation			514	
Alderville First Nation			1,046	

The aboriginal population in Durham Region, which corresponds to the Scugog Carrying Place, is spread out through the communities of Oshawa, Whitby, Clarington, Scugog, and Brock. Though small in number, aboriginal people make up 1.8 percent of the population of Oshawa, 1.4 percent of Clarington, and 1 percent in Whitby and Brock Township. These population figures include the modern descendants of the First Nations as well as the Métis.

For the past fifteen years the Great Blue Heron Charity Casino has been operating on Scugog Island. The Baagwating Community Association, the charitable arm of the Mississauga's of Scugog Island, has provided over $6.7 million to various charities, agencies, and various elementary and post-secondary educational institutions as well as contributing to other First Nations communities.

9

GROWTH OF COMMUNITIES IN WHITBY TOWNSHIP

"In the valley of the creek off Union and Queen Street, there were a number of old time industries prior to 1842 … an oldtime foundry was in operation at the same place."[1]

As a result of the ongoing influx of European settlers, new communities began to form along the route of the Scugog Carrying Place. Oshawa and the communities to the south, such as South Oshawa and Syndenham Harbour, grew up on the western branch of the Carrying Place, while Harmony developed on its eastern branch. North of Oshawa and Harmony, in the townships of Reach, Brock, and Thorah, the evolving communities of Columbus, Prince Albert, Port Perry, Seagrave, Cannington, and Beaverton, all developed along the route of the Scugog Carrying Place. Clearly, the aboriginal trail was instrumental in defining where most of the communities would develop in these townships.

It was apparent that these future hamlets and towns were already experiencing growth by the late 1830s. *Walton's Directory* of 1837 shows five main clusters of settlements with a density of over six families. These were located on the First Concession on lots two, four, eleven, twenty-two, and twenty-seven. Today, lot twenty-seven is the downtown section of the town of Whitby, while lot twenty-two is near the location of Hammer's Corners, which had a general store and the only post office in the township. Lots two and four define the area where the Farewell brothers originally settled (Farewell Corners) and which evolved into the hamlet of Harmony. Lot eleven is now part of downtown Oshawa. In 1837, a concentration of settlements also existed along the Kingston Road where additional future towns and hamlets would develop. Hammer's Corners was absorbed into the growing town of Whitby, while Harmony was eventually amalgamated with Oshawa.

PORT OSHAWA (SYDENHAM HARBOUR)

The low-lying area around Benjamin Wilson and Eleazar Lockwood's homesteads bordered Lake Ontario and contained several marshes. It was here that the Scugog Trail started. As noted in 1795, its southern starting point initially was on Wilson's lot near the mouth of Farewell Creek, but in later decades it shifted west to Thomas Henry's lot along Annis (later Oshawa) Creek. What became known as Port Oshawa, first known as Sydenham Harbour, was located at the mouth of the Oshawa Creek and its accompanying marsh. When Lockwood left the area after the War of 1812, John Henry, Thomas's father, took over the Lockwood homestead in 1816, and James Hall, possibly of the Halls of Susquehanna, acquired the Lockwood lease on lot eight in 1823, but proceeded to settle on lots one and two around what today is known as the Second Marsh.

Benjamin Wilson, who lived just east of the Oshawa Creek, died in 1821 and was buried near his home in a small pioneer cemetery on the top of Gifford Hill, so-named for the landowner Lyman Gifford (1903–1970) who was born on the family farm north of the Oshawa Harbour and was mayor of Oshawa during the 1960s. Wilson's neighbour to the west of the creek, Thomas Henry, had already buried several family members there.

Henry became the pastor of the Christian Church in Oshawa, as well as harbourmaster and a shareholder in the Sydenham Harbour Company. He travelled the province as a minister of the Christian Church in Canada and was a leading proponent for establishing the *Christian Luminary*, the newspaper that began publishing in Oshawa in 1844. Henry acted as both a publishing agent and financial benefactor for the paper, but, five years later, when the cost of publishing a hymn book exceeded what Henry could afford, the *Luminary* ceased publishing in 1849.

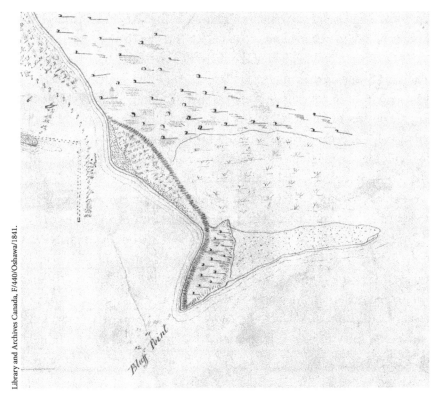

Library and Archives Canada, F/440/Oshawa/1841.

Black's and Annis's Creek map — insert showing Bluff Point.

landmark frequently referred to by early settlers. The point would later be eroded away by the persistent wave action of the lake.

A curious place name, *Presqu'ile petit ecort*, occurs on Labroquerie's 1757 map of Lake Ontario, a name that may be translated into English as "small bluff point." Few such landmarks of this description were ever shown on early maps of the north shore of Lake Ontario between Ganaraska and Toronto. However, that is exactly where *Presqu'ile petit ecort* occurs on Labroquerie's map. It may have been Bluff Point.

Pedlar states that, on January 18, 1841, when preliminary steps were taken prior to petitioning Parliament for a charter, it was "resolved that all interested in the rising prosperity of this village and vicinity, be requested to become shareholders in a joint Stock Company for the purpose of making a good road and erecting a wharf and storehouse in the most eligible and convenient situation on the lake shore,"[4] moved by Joseph Wood, merchant, and seconded by Thomas Henry.

At a subsequent meeting of the promoters, held in Charles Arkland's Tavern at Skae's Corners on the January 22, 1841, the tenders, which previously had been advertised, were opened as follows: Mr. David Annis for 15,000 feet of three-inch plank at $12 per thousand delivered at the mouth of the creek; Mr. D. Camstock for the wharf; and William Fisher for building the piers for the proposed wharf and filling the same with 300 "cords of stone."[5] These tenders were all accepted.

Pedlar continued the story of how the Sydenham Harbour Company was formed: "At another meeting held on the 18th of September 1841 … an application for a charter 'The Sydenham Harbour Company' was duly drawn and signed by the following petitioners: J.B. Warren, E. Skae, P.M. Nicol, Joseph Wood, David Annis, Thomas Henry, Thomas Gibbs, Samuel Hall, Malcolm Wright, Hugh Munroe, Jas. D. Hoitt, Ethan Card, Robert Wilcockson, Elijah Haight, John McGregor, John Amsberry, John Robsons, John McGill."[6] Names of all the prominent individuals at Skae's Corners appear listed as petitioners for the new harbour company.

However, the double piers as outlined on the 1841 map never materialized. Instead, a single long pier was constructed immediately west of the opening from Annis (Oshawa) Creek. Nor was the proposed road to Farewell Corners built on the east side of the creek, thus rescuing the lower part of the Scugog Trail from imminent destruction at least for the immediate future.

The Sydenham Harbour Company was incorporated as a company soon after and a pier and breakwater were built at the marshy mouth of the Oshawa Creek. Before long the harbour was bustling with activity, exporting oatmeal, flour, whisky, and lumber to Montreal and Kingston, as well as the United States. The first harbourmaster was George A. Mothersill, from 1841 to1848, followed by Joseph Wood in 1849. When both Mothersill and Wood contracted cholera and died after assisting disease-stricken immigrants at the port, Thomas (Elder) Henry took over from 1849 to 1854. Henry was one of the founders and the first president of the Sydenham Harbour Company.

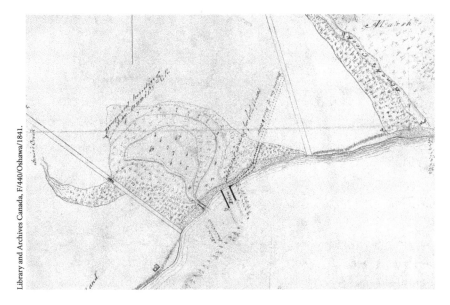

Black's and Annis's Creek map — insert showing Oshawa Piers

Initially, the harbour had only a few residents, and, not surprisingly, most of the growth occurred after the harbour pier was constructed. Samuel Hall, son of James Hall, built several storehouses and an elevator near the pier. The enterprising Samuel garnered considerable wealth through his construction contracts and would go on to build factories and mills in other parts of Whitby Township, as well the storehouse and elevator at Oshawa Harbour and several factories in downtown Oshawa. The first customs officer at Sydenham Harbour, a Mr. Ritchie, maintained an office there. After the pier was built, the steamboat *America* began regular service at the Harbour three times a week between Rochester and Toronto. Smith describes the Oshawa Harbour in his 1846 *Gazetteer* as, "a small shipping place on Lake Ontario, three miles from the village of Oshawa. There are storehouses for storing produce, one tavern, and houses for the wharfinger and deputy customs-house officer."[7] In his *County of Ontario*, Farewell mentions that later there would be several piers along the harbour and a breakwater, but that over time they were washed away and only one pier remained.[8]

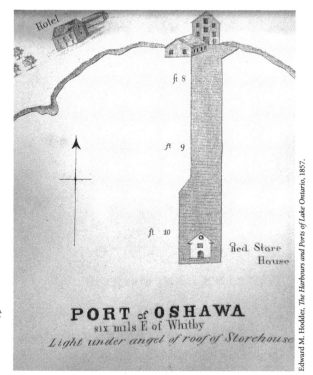

Hotel

ft 8

ft 9

ft 10

Red Store
House

PORT of OSHAWA
six mils E of Whitby
Light under angel of roof of Storehouse

Edward M. Hodder, *The Harbours and Ports of Lake Ontario*, 1857.

This 1857 sketch of the early pier and other nearby buildings at Port Oshawa, artist unknown, is the earliest known representation of the harbour.

Three buildings, the Guy, Henry, and Robinson Houses, which make up today's Oshawa Community Museum and Archives, date back to the early development at the harbour. The Guy House was home to James Guy who emigrated from Cornwall in 1842 and acquired it around 1865, during the period he was harbourmaster from 1853–1892. The original builder is not known, but the house is believed to date from about 1845. The Henry House is believed to have been built *circa* 1840. The Robinson House was originally built by a local man, John Robinson, *circa* 1857, to serve as both a hotel and a residence. These three heritage houses form the current museum on Simcoe Street South, next door to the harbour.

HARMONY (FAREWELL CORNERS)

One of the first schools in Whitby Township appears to have been built in 1812 along Kingston Road on the stretch that was later to become Wilson Street. In his 1970 book on education in Oshawa, Douglas Ross mentions that "various letters and manuscripts describe it as being 'near the Rogers' homestead' and 'a few minutes' walk from the Pickell's farm.'" A school was built in Harmony (then Farewell Corners) in 1829, with the first teacher reported to be a John Ritson (today's Ritson Road is named after him) and the second one being Abram Farewell, son of A.M. Farewell. Another school, later known as S.S. No. 1 East Whitby, was constructed in brick in 1871. The school still standing on the original site today dates to 1924 and is not currently in use.

The Farewell's gristmill that began functioning during the War of 1812 operated until being destroyed in a fire in 1834. William Farewell's son Cornwall built another mill just east of the first one on Farewell Creek. He had operated a sawmill business to the south of Harmony before moving to Oshawa in 1843.

The Farewells were very active in a multitude of commercial enterprises. Around 1835 the family built the schooner *Caledonia*, the first of their fleet of ships. Abram Farewell, the fifth son of A.M. Farewell and older brother of William, joined his father's commercial businesses at Harmony in 1830. Seven years later he opened a general mercantile business in Harmony and is recorded as going to Montreal semi-annually to purchase goods.

Abram later went into the grain-export business and became part owner of the schooners *Lord Durham* and *Emerald*, both of which sailed out of Port Oshawa, then known as Sydenham Harbour. He, along with a business partner, was responsible for shipping some of the first Canadian crude oil (the source of which is not recorded) to Europe on the brig *Snow Bird*. In 1843 Abram was elected to the Home District Council, where he remained until his defeat at the polls in 1849. Later he would run for other public offices.

J.W. Fowke, another merchant, is noted as having set up his business at Harmony where he lived from 1840 to 1861. The 1851 census shows that, by then, Harmony also had a turning lathe and a stave machine works powered by the nearby stream. Farewell Corners was experiencing encouraging growth.

J.E. Farewell, when describing the waters of the Farewell Creek and the Second Marsh in his *County of Ontario*, states that "the waters in its bay were deep enough for large sized vessels, as was the river entering into it, the western branch of which was large enough to drive saw mills, flouring mills, brewery, a distillery, furniture factory, at Farewell Corners, now Harmony."[10] However, after this high point in the early 1850s the community began to decline. Pedlar, writing in 1895, states that "Harmony now without a single mechanic had at one time two blacksmiths shops, two shoemaker shops, two cooper shops, three carpenter shops, two tailor shops, a saw mill and a manufactory of furniture employing twenty men."[11]

Farewell also noted that the industrial development at Farewell Corners could not be sustained, for he went on to write:

> had the head of these streams [Harmony and Farewell Creeks] been examined the adventurers would have found that a half-mile and 1 1/4 miles away was the source of the supply, which would cease as soon as the clearing of the lands along side them was done. The Oshawa creek had its source west of Raglan, ten miles away, and its volume and continuance was the cause of Oshawa's prosperity.[12]

The loss of water power was, as J.E. Farewell noted, the key reason that Harmony's growth stopped. The communities of both Harmony and Toad Hollow began to decline while Oshawa grew. In 1837, the Farewells closed their tavern business. William Farewell died in 1845, while his brother Acheus Moody lived more than two decades longer. By the 1840s the village of Oshawa had begun to attract settlers from both hamlets. With the stream that powered the gristmill drying up, Cornwall Farewell closed the sawmill on the same stream and moved to Oshawa to open a hotel. A flood in April 1850 that damaged or destroyed several dams along the Creek near Harmony hastened the demise.[13] In 1861, J.W. Fowke also moved his business to Oshawa.

Located only a few miles to the west, the now rapidly expanding village of Oshawa soon had several mills and a variety of businesses. Harmony was finished as a commercial location. Only the Robinson gristmill survived there until 1865 when it also closed.

The settlement of Skae's Corners (Oshawa) had 150 residents in 1837. In 1837, John Borlase Warren (1798–1879), who had emigrated from Ireland, built a large gristmill on the land that John Kerr had owned, on the east side of the Oshawa Creek along the Scugog Carrying Place, immediately north of the Kingston Road. This property had been sold by Kerr to the construction mogul Samuel Hall, who in turn sold it to Warren. Interestingly, Warren was married to Louisa Lynde, a daughter of Jabez Lynde, who had previously owned this property before Kerr acquired it. Besides the mill, Warren, like John Kerr before him, operated a distillery and maintained a large general store on the northwest corner of Simcoe and King Streets. In 1842, the number of inhabitants had grown to 850, and by 1850 the population was over 1,100.

INDUSTRIALIZATION OF OSHAWA

Warren's Oshawa Flour Mill became a major factor in the development of modern Oshawa and also served as a magnet for future industries. The establishment of the mill, which coincided with an increase in immigration, led to the employment of a number of individuals and provided a good source of income for Warren. The ever-expanding settlement led to an even greater demand for milling — a demand that his mill couldn't always meet — but one that greatly enhanced Warren's profitability.

The same year that Warren built his mill, two wagon and carriage makers, J.D. Hoitt and Hiram Taplin, arrived in Skae's Corners and set up businesses as carriage-makers. Five years later, Ethan Card would build a carding and woollen mill north of Warren's enterprise. He later moved up the Scugog Trail to Cannington to start another business. However, his influence in the new town was short-lived since he died in Oshawa in 1854 at the age of sixty-two. Hugh and Alexander Munroe, who

When John Borlase Warren (1798–1879) opened the large Oshawa Flour Mill in 1837, he initiated an industrial surge in the town. A successful businessman, Warren would also open a general store at the intersection of King and Simcoe Streets. He amassed a small fortune, only to lose much of it after suffering financial problems in the wheat market. The mill went to William Gibbs in 1865 as did his residence, Prospect Park, (later known as Parkwood, the home of Samuel McLaughlin of General Motors fame). From Tremaine's Map of the County of Ontario, Upper Canada, *1860.*

had been working as millwrights, operated a factory in Oshawa. Hugh and his family, along with his bachelor brother Alexander, had arrived in Canada in 1831 from Tullochue in Knockancuirn, Scotland. Later, Hugh would establish a new enterprise in Cannington and his brother Alexander would join him, but only for a short while as he is reported as having died in Oshawa in 1851.

Business opportunities continued to increase. John Warren added a distillery and general store to his operations in 1837, the same year Thomas Fuller built a furniture factory in a small frame building at the corner of

Bond and Simcoe Streets. In 1838, Richard Woon began operating his tavern, the Oshawa House, on Kingston Road (later King Street) right in the centre of the booming village. Soon afterwards, Patrick Wall built a cooperage in 1839 and S.B. Fairbanks opened a solicitor's office, soon to be followed in 1840 by the Oshawa Cabinet Company operated by the Gibbs brothers. The next year saw the arrival of Henry Pedlar's blacksmith shop, Thomas Bryout's boot-and-shoe store, and Moscrip's foundry. As more and more specialized manufacturing was drawn into town to produce the goods required by the typical farm worker, there was a shift from small enterprises to the introduction of large businesses requiring trained individuals, all made possible by the availability of money. As Leo Johnson noted:

> In 1840 a markedly different kind of industry, a cabinet works, requiring high level of skills and a disciplined, stable labour force, appeared for the first time … Since cabinet-making and foundry work were highly skilled and specialized, their products were costly and required both a large market area and a largely cash economy to survive. Their introduction shows that by 1840 there had been a major development away from pioneer production methods towards a "mature" economy with good transportation, more advanced technology, and high levels of craftsmanship.[14]

The years 1840–1841 can be considered the transition to a much more advanced form of industrial production.

Interestingly, however, when William Glenney arrived in Oshawa in 1840 from Bailieborough in Cavan, Ireland, he described the village as "not more than a dozen houses on King Street, and on both sides of Simcoe Street South from the Methodist Church to the lake, there was nothing but woods to the lake except a few small clearings on both sides of the road. North on Simcoe Street from the piano works [William Street] was also woods."[15]

When the first mail arrived in the newly named Oshawa in 1842, it was delivered by Weller's stagecoach. William Glenney, initially a clerk in the store owned by Edward Skae (the first postmaster), later became the second postmaster for the town. He was the first to open the mailbags destined for the village. By 1849, the year after Skae died, he would be operating his own general store and the post office on the same site, having either purchased or leased the business from the Skae family.

New settlers came to the newly named Oshawa in droves to get their grain milled. Samuel Pedlar noted: "the winter scenes when between 1845 and years later the Scotch farmers came in immense numbers with their wheat and pork laden sleighs to the Oshawa of Old. These sleighs came from Elden, Opps, Brock, Mara, Rama, Mariposa, Reach and other northern townships."[16] Business at the mills would lead to an increasingly vibrant economy where money was available and local merchants experienced increasing sales. Some businesses developed specifically to cater to those farmers bringing their grain to Skae's Corners.

The influx of people and money continued to attract other businesses to the area. Immediately south of the Warren property, along the creek where John McGregor had built a distillery and brewery, new enterprises were taking root. By 1842, Robert Moscrip's foundry was already smelting pig iron, which was used to produce mill-machinery castings. This, in turn, allowed a large number of mills to flourish on the tributaries near the Scugog Carrying Place.

One of the first publications in Oshawa, the *Literary News Letter*, dated August 23, 1849, contains an advertisement for Robert Moscrip's foundry and claims it "will at all times hold his self in readiness to make or mend anything about the mills on the shortest notice."[17] Businessmen seem to have responded to this type of encouragement. David Spaulding operated a brewery near the Moscrip foundry. Peter M. Nichol purchased McGregor's distillery and brewery and then erected a small gristmill on the same site while also operating a general store called the "City Cash Store" on King and Union Streets. For a list of mills, distilleries, factories, and tanneries on tributaries near the Scugog Carrying Place, see Appendix D.

By 1846 Skae's Corner's, now Oshawa, had the look of a progressive settlement. Smith wrote in his *Canadian Gazetteer* that:

Oshawa is a place of considerable business, having a good farming country behind it; it contains about 1000 inhabitants. Churches and chapels three viz., Catholic, Methodist and Christian. Post Office, post every day. Three physicians and surgeons, two lawyers, two grist-mills (one containing five run of stones), one foundry, one brewery, one carding machine and fulling mill, two distilleries, one ashery, eleven stores, one machine shop, one trip hammer driven by water, one bookseller, one chemist and druggist, one auctioneer, three hatters, seven blacksmiths, four taverns, two watchmakers, five tailors, five shoemakers, one grocery and bakery, one chair factory, four cabinet makers, three wagon makers, one bank agency.[18]

In his 1847 edition of the *Gazetteer*, Smith published a street scene depicting King Street East. This, the first illustration of Oshawa to be published, depicts a number of new businesses along King Street. A list of stores and their owners shows: Simpson and Burk; *Luminary* (printing) office (newspaper started in 1844 by a Mr. Oliphant and a Mr. White); All Nations market — Pork White; Egerton Ryerson's (law) office; Miss Payne's millinery; Sons Hall (Grand Division Sons of Temperance); John McMahen's store (dry goods and general merchant); Russell's watch shop; post office, postmaster Gavin Burns (emigrated from Scotland to Oshawa in 1844); J. Whitelaw (harness-maker that came to Oshawa around 1840); Keddie, Boyd, and Luxmore saddlers (John Keddie was a saddler who emigrated from Scotland about 1846); Hyland's store (general store); William May's store; Walter Sutton's drugstore (he came around 1847); Henry Carswell's bakery (came to Oshawa in 1846); Edward French (came to Oshawa before 1836); L. Van Camp; and Wood's store (possibly Joseph Wood). Many of these businesses were new to the village, as can be seen by the identification of their proprietors, many of whom had come to Oshawa in the few years prior to the publication of the illustration.[19]

The *Christian Luminary*, promoted by Elder Thomas Henry of the Christian Church (became part of the United Church in 1924), was

The first image of Oshawa to be published was released in 1847, artist unknown. It illustrates the transformation of Oshawa in the early to mid-1840s from a small farming community into a commercial centre with a newspaper, stores, tradespeople, a post office, and a temperance hall. From Smith's *Canadian* Gazetteer *(1846–47), First edition, facing page 136.*

published between 1844 and 1849 by the firm of Oliphant and White in Oshawa. Before the *Luminary* folded, the same publishers started another newspaper called the *Literary Newsletter* in 1848. A few years later this newspaper was renamed the *Oshawa Reformer*. Another rival newspaper started by Thomas Gibbs and Abram Farewell commenced publishing under the name of the *Oshawa Freeman*, and in 1856 it was renamed the *Oshawa Vindicator*.

In 1948, another sketch appeared in the *Oshawa Times*, another paper in the community, showing Skae's general store and Munroe's hotel along with a view of Simcoe Street South. This sketch was drawn by Edward Carswell, then a young man of seventeen, who in 1835 had immigrated to Canada from Ware, England, with his parents. He studied ornamental painting in Toronto, and by 1849 was settled in Oshawa. He drew several sketches of the town, some of which appeared in Thomas Kaiser's 1921 book on Oshawa, *Upper Canada Sketches*. Edward Carswell had an illustrious career. When he was twelve years old, he moved to live with a Colonel Dixon and the Methodist minister Peter Jones for several years before becoming a painter. Two of Jones's sons were painters and this likely influenced Carswell in his choice of career. He also became a circuit lecturer for the Temperance Movement and had regular speaking engagements across the United States.

Growth continued to accelerate, and by 1857 Oshawa was being described as a:

> flourishing incorporated village in the Township of Whitby and County of Ontario, miles from Sydenham Harbour, on Lake Ontario. A large business is done in the produce of the country, and the place is especially celebrated for flour of a very superior brand. Several large factories also have been established, particularly the Oshawa Manufacturing Company, the most extensive in the country engaged in the fabrication of agricultural implements, and Fuller & Co.'s furniture factory, which establishments make extensive shipments of their goods to different parts of Canada. The Grand Trunk Railway has a station here, at which all trains stop. Distant from Toronto 33 miles, and from Montreal 300 miles. A daily stage, carrying the mail, runs north from Oshawa through Columbus, Raglan, Prince Albert, Borelia, and Port Perry, to Beaverton, on Lake Simcoe, distance 50 miles.[20]

The industrial development of Oshawa proceeded into the following decades. Oshawa was incorporated as a village by the Municipal Act of 1849, which passed on January 1, 1850.[21] The first village council consisted of Thomas N. Gibbs, John B. Warren, Silas B. Fairbanks, Patrick Wall, and George Monroe[22] — all leading figures in the development of the community.

EMERGENCE OF COLUMBUS (ENGLISH CORNERS)

The settlement began to develop as farmers began to shift north from Skae's Corners along the Scugog Carrying Place. Initially it was known as English Corners because many of the early settlers were from Cornwall and Devon, including Joseph Adams and Robert Ashton, all having emigrated from England during a period of peak migration from the British Isles.

As noted earlier, after the fur trader Joseph Wiley left the area on the trail north of Kerr's Creek sometime around 1825, the only new settler was Joseph Widdifield, a Quaker who had come to his farm by means of the Scugog Carrying Place in 1821 and established a mill. Widdifield later left for Norwich, Ontario, in about 1856. George McGill from Paisley, Scotland, settled on lot seven, Concession Three. In 1821, "at which time there were but a few, if any settlements north of him. The settlers of the 1st and Second Concession referred to this region as the wilderness at the time McGill settled there and for some time thereafter."[23] John Dickie, from Paisley, Scotland, settled next door on lot 8, that same year.

Six years later, in 1827, George Fisher, who had come from Fredericksburg, Ontario, but had been born in New York State, settled lot twelve, Concession Seven. Since there was no road at the time, Fisher also had to use the Scugog Carrying Place to access his lot. The trail was to the west of the present road, Simcoe Street, to Widdifield's place. The much-needed improvement to aid settlers in transporting their goods, however meagre, was slow to come. As discussed earlier, in 1828, George Hinkson underbrushed and blazed a portion of the trail leading to the Fourth Concession, Whitby Township — the section that became known as Read Road and is now Simcoe Street. In 1831, Charles Terwillegar, from New York State, had secured a contract from the government to cut and clear the two rod (about six miles) road north from Harmony on the north side of Concession Six of Whitby Township. Between 1833 and 1835, when Hinckson obtained a contract for removing undergrowth from the roadway, his two sons and Ira Hall did the work.

Henry Hicks, from Luxillian, Cornwall, settled in English Corners around 1828. Shortly after 1831, William H. Gibbs, also Cornish, built a gristmill, a half mile to the west on a branch of the Oshawa Creek. He also operated a general store in Oshawa. William was the brother of T.N. Gibbs, who would later acquire the Oshawa Mill from John Warren. Miller Ambrose Morris purchased Widdifield's mill in 1841 and would later erect another gristmill.

In 1835, a woollen mill, the Empire Mills, was built on a branch of Oshawa Creek by a company owned by William Matheson and John Ratcliffe. The creek was dammed and a raceway created to harness the waterpower. When word went out to recruit experienced workers from England, a number of mill workers emigrated from Yorkshire and Lancashire to work at Empire Mills. They built cottages in the new settlement and English Corners began to experience a boom.

Smith's *Gazetteer* referred to the settlement as:

> A village in the township of Whitby, situated on the plank road to Scugog, six miles north from Windsor [Whitby]. It has been settled about eight years, and contains nearly 300 inhabitants. There is a Methodist church in the village, and an Episcopal church a short distance west of it. There are grist mills in the neighbourhood. Professions and Trades — One ashery, four stores, two taverns, two wagon makers, two tailors, two blacksmiths, four shoemakers.[24]

The first Episcopal or Anglican church in Whitby Township was established in the Columbus area as St. Paul's and opened in 1835 when Adam Elliot delivered the inaugural sermon.

When the village acquired a post office in August 1847, the name was changed to Columbus. In his 1850 book, Smith describes Columbus:

> as ... about three hundred inhabitants, it is a tolerably thriving settlement, although it is too near Oshawa to do a large business, indeed it appears to have remained nearly stationary for the last three or four years. It contains a grist mill, with two run of stones, a saw mill, tannery, ashery, and soap and candle factory, Post Office

and three churches; United Presbyterian, Wesleyan Methodist, and Bible Christian; and there is a Episcopal Church about one mile west from the village.[25]

More than a decade after Columbus is recorded by Smith, Lovell's directory records that its population had increased by fifty inhabitants and that one additional shoemaker and blacksmith were added to the hamlet along with a mason, ploughmaker, and saddlemaker, indicating that the community was continuing to prosper.

RAGLAN (O'BOYLE'S CORNERS/NEWTOWN)

Another hamlet did emerge slightly to the north, still in Whitby Township. This small settlement, known as O'Boyle's Corners, formed along the Trail about two-and-a-half miles north of Columbus, then called English Corners. It would later become known as Newtown and then as Raglan. Some years earlier, Joseph Wiley had built a blockhouse to support his work in the fur trade, just south of O'Boyle's Corners, and lived there from 1821 to 1825.

The following advertisement was printed in the *Globe* newspaper in Toronto in 1849, indicating that land was for sale in the hamlet:

> All that highly valuable Tavern, Stables, Sheds and Outbuildings, together with One Acre and a half of excellent land, on which there is a fine Orchard, situated at the North-east angle of Lot No. 13 in the 8th Concession of the Township of Whitby, in the flourishing Village of Newtown, (formerly O'Boyle's Corners), on the great Simcoe Street Road, nearly midway between Oshawa and Prince Albert, being two and a half North of Columbus.[26]

The property stayed on the market throughout the fall and winter of 1849–1850, possibly because other cheaper land could be purchased in the townships to the north. Many of the newcomers in this area north of Columbus would relocate to the northern townships in the desire to seek out new and less expensive land. There is still a settlement there today, now known as Raglan.

The main road through Columbus would become a toll road named Simcoe Street. Just a couple of lots to the east was the Nonquon Road, which did not have tolls. Known as the poor man's road, it extended over the ridge to Seagrave near the mouth of Nonquon River. Today, the remnants of this road are incorporated into Ritson Road. Simcoe Street was the settler's version of the main branch of the Scugog Carrying Place, and the Nonquon Road probably developed from the eastern branch of the Carrying Place.

Thomas Bouckley, photographic historian and an early member of the Oshawa Historical Society, preferred the Nonquon Road route as having been the Scugog Trail since he states: "my feeling is that the Nonquon Road followed the trail rather than Simcoe Street or Reach Road. It would be more accessible to both the Oshawa Creek and the Farewell or Harmony Creek to the east. It apparently was the shortest way to Scugog and with the most gradual incline."[27] Bessie Gagnon, a long-time Oshawa genealogist, however, remembers the trail in the 1930s roughly following the route of Ritson Road as a crooked path, unlike the street today. Both Bouckley and Gagnon have now passed away, but their memories of the old roads helps keep alive the indebtedness the roads had to the previously existing Scugog Carrying Place.

10

Villages Further North Along the Trail

"Many years ago Mr. Card left Oshawa. He set up business at Cannington ... Mr. William Thomas, Senior, who many years ago passed away, owned the line of stages running from Oshawa to Columbus, Raglan, Prince Albert and other northern villages."[1]

Prince Albert (Dayton's Corners)

The families of Abner Hurd and Daniel Dayton were the first to settle around Prince Albert in 1824. A crude road, following the pathway of the Scugog Carrying Place, provided the route between Prince Albert and Wiley's place in Whitby Township. In 1828, Hurd and his neighbours, the Daniel Dayton and Reuben Crandell families, came together to build the first schoolhouse in Dayton's Corners in Reach Township. The first schoolteacher was a Scotsman by the name of Cull, who was billeted in the settlers' homes. Since Hurd settled just east of Prince Albert and Dayton settled right in what later became the town, the fledgling community took on Dayton's name. When the Presbyterian minister John Carruthers visited the area in 1832, he observed that there were only one or two houses in the village. By the next year, Messers P. Hurd (possibly related to Abner Hurd) and Co. began operating the first general store in the community. In 1836, a second store was opened by a George Leach, and four years later he included a post office in his store and became the first postmaster of the village.

Six years later in his 1846 *Gazetteer*, Smith adds that its, "population [is] about 200. There is in the village, a Methodist church, five stores, two taverns, two asheries, one blacksmith, one waggon maker, two shoemakers, two tailors."[2] But the community was attracting notice. That year, George Currie came to Prince Albert as a recruiting agent for John Warren, his mission to encourage more farmers to patronize the Warren Mill in Oshawa. Soon afterwards, Dr. Jonathan Foote began a medical practice in Prince Albert.

By 1852, Smith is describing Prince Albert as:

> contains about three hundred inhabitants, appears to be a busy little place, being at a sufficient distance from Oshawa and Whitby to enable it to command a tolerable trade of its own. It is pleasantly situated, and will probably become a thriving little town; it has been settled about eight years, and contains two tanneries and three asheries, and a Post Office.[3]

The first houses in nearby Borelia, situated between Scugog Village and Prince Albert, were built in 1847. Eventually, the three communities — Prince Albert, Borelia, and Scugog Village — would merge, becoming Port Perry. During the latter 1840s and into the 1850s, during the Crimean War, grain temporarily became a highly priced commodity, bringing considerable prosperity to the area. The merchants in Prince Albert bought grain from farmers of the northern townships to resell in the markets of Montreal and elsewhere. When the war ended in 1856, the economy entered a period of economic depression.

PORT PERRY (SCUGOG VILLAGE)

Up until 1829 the Mississauga, who from pre-European times had settlements along Lake Scugog, occupied land in the location of today's Port Perry. During his 1809–1810 survey, Samuel Wilmot noted a burial ground found there along the Scugog Carrying Place, and Peter Jones, the Methodist missionary, mentioned sicknesses and death among the Scugog Mississauga. The two findings may be connected. The Mississauga left the lake only to return in 1844, but because their former location was owned by various white settlers, they relocated to Scugog Island where they purchased land for a reserve, as discussed earlier, and where their descendants are found today.

A small log storehouse was in existence on Lake Scugog before the first permanent settler, Elias Williams, arrived to settle within the current boundaries of Port Perry. He is recorded as having built a house on his lot in 1830 or 1831, but the village owes its existence to Peter Perry,[4] a politician and land speculator from Whitby (then known as Perry's Corners). In 1845, he drew up a street plan for what he called the "Village of Scugog." Prior to this, to initiate his venture, Perry had purchased Williams's lot. But before he could develop plans for his venture, a S.E. Crandell built the first hotel in 1842 on what would become Queen Street, while it was still a heavily wooded property. Perry, however, proceeded to purchase eighty acres in April 1843 in what he envisioned would become the heart of his village, and then proceeded to sell off small lots.

By the following year the fledgling community had a wharf on Lake Scugog, a warehouse, and temporary housing along the lakeshore for workmen, and the ambitious Perry was busily hiring men interested in transporting lumber over land to Whitby.

To encourage prospective settlers, Perry, who also had a store in the town of Whitby, also opened another general store and a grain outlet in his Scugog village. The store, opened in 1845 under the management of C. Draper & Co. (Chester Draper), was located at the lakeshore on Water Street. During the next year, John W. Davis and John Nott opened a furniture factory that used horses to drive the machinery. Perry also sold lots to Daniel Way who built a sawmill, and a quarter-lot to a John Davis. Two years later another three lots were sold to a Samuel Hill.

By 1847 Anglican Church services had begun at Davis's shop and were taking place every two weeks. That year Harrison Haight established another hotel in the village. He may have been the same Harrison Haight who had opened a general store in Oshawa a decade earlier. In the early 1840s, the (Harrison) Paxton and Way sawmill cut lumber for the building of a plank road between the town of Whitby and Scugog Village, a distance of about eighteen miles.

Peter Perry had advocated for the planked Central Line from Whitby Harbour to Port Perry and planned to connect it to the south end of the Beaver River in Reach Township. The portion between Whitby and Port Perry was completed in 1846 after Perry used his influence to obtain provincial funding, a sum of 9,510 pounds. However, by 1850, the planks were wearing out and were being replaced with gravel. Perry, with the backing of the Port Whitby and Lake Scugog and Huron Road

Home & Simcoe Districts Canada. Compiled from the Township Maps in the Surveyor General's Office *by C. Rankin Esq. of the Surveyor General's Department, shows the Reach Road in 1841 stretching from Danforth Road in Whitby Township through to Beaverton in Thorah Township.*

Extracted from Library and Archives Canada, H1/409/Home/1841, NMC17638.

companies, bought the Central Line from the province that year at half the cost of its construction. To make the roadway economical, tolls were charged for its use. However, farmers, who were forced to use the new road in the summer, did not use it in the winter, preferring to drive their sleighs over parallel concession roads such as the Nonquon Road, and thus avoid paying the tolls. The road never made a profit.

Merchants in Oshawa opposed the Central Line as it would divert business to the village of Whitby. Competition between Whitby and Oshawa began in the early 1840s when both communities saw the potential for building harbours and connecting them with roads to the northern townships. The businessmen of Oshawa formed the Nonquon Road Company, which included some of the richest residents of Oshawa, such as a Mr. McGill, A. Farewell, T.N. Gibbs, G.H. Grierson, and Colonel Fairbanks. The Nonquon Road Company spent 5,000–7,000 pounds, almost half the construction cost for the Central Line, and ran the new Simcoe Street to the east of the old street where flatter terrain would reduce construction costs. In 1852, a new road was built by the Oshawa Road and Harbour Company to improve a two-mile stretch of roadway passing through Port Perry.

By the autumn of 1848, three sawmills had been erected on the waterfront of Scugog Village. Samuel Hill built a mill in the village in 1850, and three years later, John Cameron, representing the Port Perry Land Co. erected another sawmill and a gristmill. This gristmill was first run by Harrison Paxton, and later by a Mr. Johnston, before it burnt to the ground in 1856. Hurd's mill at Borelia was destroyed by a tornado in 1850.

Scugog Village developed rapidly once a mail stage began running in Reach Township in 1848, and a post office, with Joseph Bigelow as postmaster, opened in 1852, and the village name was changed to Port Perry. In 1853, C.S. Jewell began operating another daily stage between Port Perry and Whitby. The competition between the two stagecoach companies reduced the cost of travel to 20 cents for a trip between Lake Scugog to Lake Ontario.

John Lovell, in his 1857 *Directory*, describes Port Perry as:

> a flourishing village in the Township of Reach and County
> of Ontario. It is built on an eminence and commands

an extensive view of the waters of Lake Scugog and is connected with Scugog Island by a floating bridge three quarters of a mile in length. It has daily steam communication with Lindsay, Fenelon Falls, and ports on the Lake. Manufactories of considerable size exist in the village, which has also extensive business in wheat and lumber. Population about 400. Prince Albert next door to Port Perry is listed with a population of 600. Columbus a village of 350 inhabitants between Port Perry and Oshawa is listed with businesses of a hotel, mill, grocery and hardware store, and five shoemakers.[5]

Chester Draper went bankrupt about 1853 while managing Peter Perry's stores in the region. But, by this time, Peter Perry, once again elected to the provincial legislature, had acquired government funding to develop a harbour in Whitby, plus additional money for the construction of a new road from Whitby to Port Perry, as noted earlier. He had predicted that the Whitby Road would allow farmers to bring their wheat to Whitby and also bring the lumber down from the northern townships. However, he died in 1851 before the road could be fully completed into

Anglo-American Magazine, January 1854. Toronto Reference Library.

PORT PERRY.

This woodcut, one of a set of three, shows the northeast side of Queen Street. It is believed to be the earliest illustration of Port Perry.

Brock and Thorah Townships. His son, John Ham Perry, carried on his father's businesses until 1853 when he gave up the commercial enterprises to become the county registrar for the newly created County of Ontario, which incorporated the townships of Whitby and Reach.

Chester Draper returned to Whitby in 1853 and went on to prosper there, having acquired the grain elevators at Port Whitby. He also benefited from the construction of the Whitby Road to Scugog Village, now known as Port Perry.

Other Whitby associates of Peter Perry, contractors James Rowe and James Cotton, had constructed warehouses mainly for the storage of grain at the Port of Whitby, then known as Windsor Harbour. They also built a steamship, the *Woodman*, on Lake Scugog, which was launched on the lake on August 29, 1850. Powered by a steam engine manufactured by the Gartshore and Company of Dundas, Ontario, it began a regularly scheduled three-times-a-week connection on the Scugog River between Port Perry and Lindsay. The stagecoach companies coordinated their stage runs with the departure of the steamship.

Before the advent of the railway, travellers from Port Perry could venture into the north either via the new Nonquon Road to the north end of Lake Simcoe or into the northeast by steamship. Those travelling south to Oshawa and Whitby could take steamships from there to other areas including Kingston and Rochester, New York, and continue their travels to Montreal or New York City. The Scugog Carrying Place was no longer needed as a transportation route.

SEAGRAVE (NONQUON)

A bridge across the Nonquon River, which empties into Lake Scugog, existed before 1849. Originally, the village that grew around the bridge was named Nonquon, but had its name changed to Seagrave when a post office opened. Some entrepreneurial settlers, such as Moody Farewell (who continued to live in Harmony) and Ben Pickle, had migrated northward from Whitby Township in search of new opportunities, while other early settlers, including a Palmer, James Carr, and Arthur Miller came to open new homesteads. A sawmill was in operation before 1850, using water power from the river, and the first store in the village was set up by a Mr. Snooks. He was soon followed by a grocer, a cobbler, and two blacksmiths, John Tax and Lorne Starr.

The village developed an industrial core with Palmer Carr manufacturing grain handles, wooden forks, and scythes in a small factory; John Allen turning out brushes; Thomas Couch, a cooper, making barrels, churns, and butter tubs; and Joseph Stephenson manufacturing wagons and sleighs. In 1850, Abraham Correll built the Nonquon Tavern using two-inch planks that had been supplied by the Farewell sawmill. Pedlar mentions an Abraham Coryell as an early settler on lot seven, Concession Two, of Whitby Township in 1816, who left for the United States, only to return later. He died in 1851 at the age of seventy-eight. He may be the same person who built the Nonquon Tavern.

Solomon Orser settled between Port Perry and the Nonquon River, driving a yoke of steers up the Scugog Carrying Place after having travelled all the way from Kingston. Soon after James Moon arrived and built the Nonquon House south of the river, while Charles Black opened another tavern on the north part of the river. Around 1846 Edward Asling built a gristmill that later would be powered by steam.

An interest in damming the Nonquon River to increase its depth to six feet, thus permitting the transport of lumber down the river, led to many discussions regarding its commercial payoff. In June 1854, the Nonquon River Navigation Improvement Company incorporated in the village of Harmony in June 1854. The company, whose members included Abram and Charles Farewell, claimed to have capital for the project, but a dam never materialized.

Moody Farewell built Reach Township's first steam sawmill at Seagrave at the mouth of the Nonquon River in 1854. As the story goes, there was some difficulty in getting the construction underway since workmen could not be found. Farewell noted that, "the mill was not raised on the day appointed because he refused to supply intoxicating liquors for the 'raisin.' It was subsequently raised by Sons of Temperance from Oshawa, Raglan, and Port Perry, and other temperance men from the Township of Reach. Reach now is and for years has been the only Local Option municipality in the county, except Scugog and Pickering."[6]

SUNDERLAND (JONES'S CORNERS)

Although Sunderland is along the Scugog Carrying Place, it did not develop as a community of any substance until the railway came through in the 1870s. It is noted here since John Baker built a schoolhouse near there in 1849 on lot eleven, Concession Eleven, of Reach Township. Lorenzo Jones opened up a blacksmith shop on the adjoining lot twelve and Archibald Jones put up a tavern.[7]

CANNINGTON (MCCASKILL'S MILLS)

After the McCaskill brothers took over Joel Horner's mills in 1833, the village was known as McCaskill's Mills. When this settlement in Brock Township had grown sufficiently enough to warrant a post office, the town officials met to select an official name. The name "Cannington" was chosen in recognition of George Cannington (1770–1827), former foreign secretary and British prime minister. In 1847, mail service began with William Donald, carrying mail from Cannington to Whitby on horseback. Two years later, Charles Gibbs, a local merchant, was named Cannington's first postmaster.

Irvine Johnston, from Fermanagh County, Ireland, is known to have been in Brock Township by 1829, although he had petitioned the government for 200 acres in 1825. Ultimately, he did receive a free grant of the acreage requested on lot nineteen, Concession Twelve. Six years later, he purchased an additional 200 acres on an adjoining lot. That year, 1836, Johnston was appointed as a Methodist steward with authority to register the baptisms and marriages in the township.

Irvine's father, Charles Johnston, brought other members of his family to Brock Township and settled on 200 acres near his son in 1833. He became a leader for the Methodist classes taught in Brock Township in

1837, and also a trustee of the Brock Methodist church in 1843 when a log chapel was built near his home. Charles died there in March 1845 and was buried in the Methodist cemetery near Cannington.

An early Methodist obituary notice for a Thomas Graham of Limerick, Ireland, claims his family settled in Brock Township in 1831. Joel Horner is said to have arrived in 1827, followed by Lachlin Davidson four years later. Horner built both a gristmill and sawmill in Cannington in 1830 near the stretch of the Beaver River where the rapids occur. His nephew, Joseph Davidson, also settled along the Carrying Place and opened the first store for the young village across from the mill. Irvine Johnston would also start a general store in partnership with John Sharpe in the 1850s.

Horner's gristmill was located on the southwest corner of the village on property owned by Richard and George Morden, who had been granted the property in the late 1820s. The mill was much smaller than Warren's mill, which had been operating in Oshawa since 1837, but it could accommodate the needs of most of the local farmers. Irvine Johnston farmed the northeast corner and a German immigrant by the name of William Reitze had cleared the northeast corner of the village.

The area continued to attract settlers. Joseph Thompson, arriving in 1834 or 1835, settled on the Eleventh Concession of Brock, a mile south of town. In 1840, Sam Baird operated a livery stable in the village, and in 1846 witnessed the arrival of Alfred Wyatt who opened up a chemist shop. In 1848, William Gibbs's son, Charles, opened another general store, where, with the coming of the postal service, he would also serve as postmaster. William Gibbs had previously homesteaded north of Cannington in Thorah Township. Robert Munroe, son of Hugh Munroe, a miller from Oshawa, started the first silversmith in the village.

When William Donald arrived in Cannington in 1845, having walked from Oshawa to join his uncle, a carpenter named Lachlin Davidson, the area was still quite heavily forested, but farming was gradually replacing the trees. Two years later, he was transporting the mail. "In an interview on his eightieth birthday, Mr. Donald recalled that there had been but few houses in Cannington at the time of his arrival."[8]

By 1848, the millwrights, Alex and Hugh Munroe, had acquired the McCaskill's Mill. After having operated a mill in Oshawa, they decided to try their fortune further north along the Carrying Place. They were soon followed by another Oshawa businessman, Ethan Card, who began a woollen mill that same year. Ethan also operated a clothing store and sold fine china. In 1849, Alex Munroe began a distillery on the Beaver River and a Mr. McTaggart started a liquor store, and a tannery and brewery sprang up near the distillery. A few years later, Thomas Cleft opened a carriage-making shop in the village, and in 1858 Christopher and Wesley Brandon opened a bakery. The Brandon brothers were part of John Brandon's family who had settled in Brock, north of Cannington. A Mr. Breathwaite was the village's first blacksmith. In 1853, he was joined by another blacksmith, John Holmes, who set up a second smithy.

Still others came to Cannington to work as carpenters building homes and other structures. Lachlan Davidson is known to have built a house and store. A few years after his nephew William joined him, the brothers, Alexander and Daniel Ross, of Portmahomack, Scotland, are recorded as coming to Cannington to work as carpenters. During the 1840s two other men worked as building contractors in Cannington: Allan Cavanagh and J.T.V. May.

Mention is made of a log schoolhouse existing in the village as early as 1836. It was replaced by a new frame school building in 1849.

Farewell, County of Ontario, Whitby, Gazette-Chronicle Press, 1907, 86.

This very early photograph of Cannington, circa 1864, photographer unidentified, shows Cameron Street facing west from St. John Street.

In 1846 a Presbyterian Church was built in Cannington, while Robert Sproul donated land for a cemetery and log chapel for the Methodists in 1844. By 1846 a Presbyterian Church was serving the community, and, as noted, the post office was in place with Charles Gibbs as postmaster.

W. H. Smith described Brock Township and the village of Cannington:

> ... as a good township of land, which is improving rapidly and becoming well settled. It is watered by the Black or Beaver River, numerous branches of which intersect the township. The village of Cannington is situated on the river, twenty-three miles from Prince Albert. It contains a gristmill and saw mill, woollen factory and distillery ... In eighteen hundred and forty-two Brock contained fifteen hundred and forty-one inhabitants, two grist and three saw mills; and in eighteen hundred and fifty the number had increased to three thousand one hundred and seventy-four inhabitants, two grist and seven saw mills.[9]

In 1971, while laying a sewer, workmen unearthed timbers from an old corduroy road that had spanned Brock Township during the settlement years. Back then, Irvine Johnston had been an overseer of highways later became a road commissioner for Brock Township. By the 1840s the residents of Cannington recognized the need to connect their community with the Reach/Simcoe Road to the south of them, with links to the Nonquon Road stretching from Beaverton to Oshawa.

The residents of Brock and Thorah Townships petitioned the province to build a road from Reach through their townships to Lake Simcoe. Settlers in other adjacent townships such as Mariposa, Ops, and Emily would also benefit by the construction of such a road along the Carrying Place. In 1842, a roadway was surveyed from the town of Whitby north to Manchester, immediately west of Prince Albert on to the Couchiching Narrows at Lake Simcoe. By 1846 the construction of a plank road between the town of Whitby and Port Perry was underway. Even though the planks were three inches thick by twelve feet in length, they were not sufficient for road building through the swamps in the Seventh and Eighth Concessions of Reach Township. It wasn't until some decades later that this Centre Line became a viable road. Between 1846 and 1848 the Thorah Road, an extension of Simcoe Street, was constructed north of Beaverton, from the Talbot River to the Narrows at Atherley on the north end of Lake Simcoe. The Bouchette map of 1846 shows that Simcoe Street stretched from Lake Ontario to the north end of Lake Simcoe.

Improvements to the new road system were ongoing during the 1840s. In May 1843 the local council passed a bylaw to construct a road on what is now Cameron Street in Cannington. The 1847 council minutes recorded a motion to have, "Duncan Brown to commence at Town Line from thence to Lot 21 in clearing off old timber and cutting a drain between two creeks on Lot No. 22 — 12th Concession."[10] In 1849, a bylaw was passed to spend eight pounds for the construction of a bridge over the Beaver River.

However, even by 1866, Cannington was still typically rural, as can be concluded when Hugh Munroe brought in a petition for a bylaw banning sheep from running at large in the village.

BEAVERTON (MILTON)

The first European family to settle in the Beaverton area was the Calders, who arrived there around 1828, having emigrated from the Isle of Islay, Scotland. Duncan Calder built the first gristmill in the town and distilled whisky. His brother, Alexander Calder, operated a sawmill and became a cabinet maker. In 1830 the Gordon family, also from Scotland, arrived and settled the township not too far from the mills. James Gordon would become the town's first blacksmith. Three years later, Kenneth Cameron followed them from Scotland to open the hamlet's first store, where he also became the first postmaster. The Proctor family also came in 1833 and opened another store, and in 1845 the Proctor family built a mill on the Beaver River, half a mile south of the Calder mill.

When Arad Smalley was surveying the Township of Thorah in 1830, he found only two heads of households in what later became Beaverton: that of Donald Calder and Samuel Fransworth. "In 1834 Beaverton was only a bush, store and a few shanties in a clearance on the Beaverton River."[11] Smith, in his 1846 *Gazetteer*, describes the community as follows: "a village in the township of Thorah, on the bank of Lake Simcoe, contains about half a dozen houses,"[12] with a post office with mail delivery twice a week. By 1851 two dozen families are recorded in the Assessment Roll for Beaverton.[13]

The hamlet had good water transportation links. The "Paddlewheel steamboat, the *Sir John Colborne* was launched in 1832 and sailed between the Holland River on Lake Simcoe and Orillia. Twice a week she would coast along the east side of Lake Simcoe past Beaverton."[14] Smith mentions that "the steamboat 'Beaver' touches here, but cannot approach the shore, the water on the bank being too shallow."[15]

Signs of a new community taking permanent root were evident in the schools and mail service from Beaverton. The first school in the hamlet was opened in 1835, followed by a second in 1844, a log building, twenty feet by eighteen feet. The first schoolteacher, David Ross, received an annual teacher's pay of £75.

In 1827, Donald Cameron obtained a permit to have mail delivered between Thorah and Whitby Townships. Kenneth Campbell took on the job of mailman. Since there were no postage stamps in use at this time, his payment consisted of subscriptions and the amount that the senders would pay for the delivery of their mail, based on the distance. In the late 1820s, the nearest post office was at Hamer's Corners in Whitby Township, operated by the Warren brothers. Campbell travelled back and forth on foot from Beaverton to the Whitby post office on Kingston Road every two weeks. By 1835 Beaverton had its own post office with James Ellis as the second postmaster.

Though Thorah Township developed more slowly than its neighbouring townships to its south, it still followed the same patterns as those townships did. Smith describes Thorah as:

> a rather small township; the land generally is tolerably good, and considering its remote situation it had made

pretty fair progress. It is watered by the Black or Beaver River, near the mouth of which is situated the village of Beaverton, where is a grist and saw mill, two distilleries, two asheries, and a tannery. There is also a Presbyterian Church. In eighteen hundred and forty-two the township contained six hundred and seventy inhabitants, one grist and two saw mills. In eighteen hundred and fifty the population had increased to one thousand and sixty-two, it contained two grist and two saw mills.[16]

The Scottish Presbyterians built the Stone Church in Beaverton beginning in 1840,[17] and another Presbyterian church was erected in 1847, followed by a frame Roman Catholic Church in 1855. Other buildings in the village included a schoolhouse, a flour mill, a sawmill, a woollen mill, two tanneries, and a furniture factory. A town hall was constructed in 1846. The *County of Ontario Directory* (1869–1870) lists a population of 700 inhabitants.[18]

Photograph by Grant Karcich

The construction of St. Andrew's Presbyterian Church in Beaverton, also known as the Stone Church, covered the period of 1840 to 1853. Services were delivered in the Gaelic language. The church still stands on its original site and is used for special occasions.

Population for Whitby, Reach, Brock, Thorah, Townships 1804–1850[19]

	1804	1809	1811	1817	1820	1825	1830	1837	1840	1842	1850
Townships											
Whitby	88	193	279	289	505	1,135	1,659	3,808	5,013	5,714	6,900
Reach						57	93	444	771	1,052	2,492
Brock						242	450	1,240	1,330	1,541	3,174
Thorah							184	599	514	670	1,062
Communities											
Oshawa								150		850	1,100
South Oshawa										150	
Columbus									300		400
Port Perry											150
Borelia											100
Prince Albert											300
Beaverton											177
Lindsay											200

By 1851 Beaverton had four general stores, and two years later a library and reading room was established in the community. Daily stage-coach service was in operation that year linking it to Whitby. Within four years, Beaverton had its first newspaper, the *Packet*, published by William Hillam.

Whitby Road, later called the Cameron Road, which was surveyed by Arad Smalley in 1827, saw extensive use in the 1840s. It connected Beaverton by way of Cannington, six to seven miles south to the Nonquon River. The Cameron Road, which skirted the west bank of the Beaver River, remained in use up to the 1870s. The northern section of the Cameron Road appears to follow the older Scugog Trail. As in the other townships, the roads in Thorah were maintained by local landowners.

11

DEATH AND TEMPERANCE ON THE TRAIL

"Declared to be a 'Stout pamphlet' which did much to set on foot that prohibition sentiment which has done so much to retard the liquor traffic."[1]

LIFE EXPECTANCY AND DISEASE

The Ontario Iroquoians who inhabited the communities along the Scugog Carrying Place gradually adapted to a less migratory lifestyle and a more European-based form of agriculture for growing food staples like corn and squash. With increased crop production, they now had greater food supplies to draw upon in times of drought or hunting shortages. An indication of an improvement in living standards would be reflected in an increase in the average life expectancy of the Iroquoian population. Such information is available from the excavated burials of pre-Mississaugan communities.

A multitude of burials and ossuaries are found along the Scugog Carrying Place, but, except for the Uxbridge Ossuary, they have not been studied in detail. Human remains, consisting of several teeth and some cranial and post-cranial bones, eleven elements in all, were discovered at the McLeod site. Since the remains were found in three scattered locations, they likely represent three to five individuals and may have been isolated burials. A thermally-altered phalanx or finger bone that had sustained fire damage was also discovered. Initially, it was speculated that the burnt finger was evidence of cannibalism, but later conclusions point to ritualistic cremation to preserve a body for a later burial.

Map Key:

O Ossuaries

△ Village Sites

A map showing the ossuary and village sites (A.D. 1380–1500) of the Ontario Iroquoians along the Carrying Place.

Map adapted from the Pedlar Manuscript microfilm, Oshawa Public Libraries, specifically: "Map Shewing Water Shed of Lake Simcoe and line of proposed aqueduct from Lake Simcoe to Toronto," circa 1895.

A single molar tooth discovered at the MacLeod site had a very deep cavity that had belonged to an individual who, while alive, would have been in quite some pain. Cavities are routinely found on the teeth of Ontario Iroquoians of this period. The heavy dependence on starchy foods such as corn would likely have contributed to poor dental condition. Though no large number of human burials was found at MacLeod, and none evident at Grandview, it is possible to get a glimpse of human health by studying the nearby population north of these sites, at the Seagrave and Uxbridge ossuary sites.

The Uxbridge Ossuary, a mass burial in the Township of Uxbridge, excavated in the late 1970s by Patsy Cook and members of the Ontario Archaeological Society, is located within twelve miles from the Scugog Carrying Place. It provides information on the health of the Native people along the Scugog Carrying Place during the fifteenth century through the study of the life expectancy of the populations. The ossuary burials there consist of a minimum 487 individuals, and from these skeletal remains a population estimate and life expectancies were calculated. Though no village site has been discovered for the Uxbridge Ossuary population, such a village would have been located somewhere within a few tens of miles or less. Anthropologists that studied the site estimated a village population size of 1,188 individuals.

Additionally, the skeletal sample from the Uxbridge Ossuary was analyzed for age of individuals based on dental and pelvic bones. This analysis estimates the number of individuals alive in discrete age categories from infants through to old age. The data is placed in a table, called a life table, which estimates the life expectancy in each age category. A life table for the Uxbridge Ossuary population indicates a life expectancy at birth to be twenty-five years. This means that infants less than one year in age, on average, were expected to live up to their twenty-fifth year. Life expectancy increases with age, so those who lived beyond their first year had an increased chance of living beyond their twenty-fifth year. The Uxbridge Ossuary people were estimated to live into their early sixties.[2]

For a comparison between the Ontario Iroquoians of the fourteenth and fifteenth centuries and the nineteenth-century European settlers, the tombstones at the Port Oshawa Pioneer Cemetery and the Methodist

Cemetery in Oshawa were examined to determine life expectancy for the newly-arriving Europeans using the age of the individual based on the birth and death dates. A forty-person sample from the burials between 1860 and 1900 in the Port Oshawa Cemetery was examined, which yielded life expectancy based on deaths at the time of burial of an estimated 37.1 years for the one- to six-year-old age range. A lower first year life expectancy was observed when examining the Methodist Pioneer Cemetery in Oshawa for 1840 to 1880, indicating that the health conditions were similar in the village of Oshawa or Skae's Corners as they were at Port Oshawa. At least 10 percent of the individuals from these two cemeteries lived to about seventy-eight years of age.

The life expectancy method of the Uxbridge Ossuary and the Methodist and Port Oshawa Cemeteries are directly comparable, as they are all developed through the same methodology. The life expectancy of European settlers was greater than the Ontario Iroquoian population along the Scugog Carrying Place. More sustainable agricultural methods and better storage facilities probably account for the longer life expectancy in Europeans and may help explain why the Mississauga adopted the European mode of agriculture in the 1830s and 1840s.

However, life expectancy is not an indicator of risk to diseases, which impact the longevity of life. Diseases were a major contributor to the quality of health in prehistoric and pioneer days. The Uxbridge population showed some diseases, particularly tuberculosis, which was found in thirty individuals and indicated that tuberculosis affected about 10 to 15 percent of the population. In addition, the smallpox epidemics that engulfed the Huron-Wendat from 1639–1640 and the Mississauga in 1793 and 1796, took a large toll on the Native populations.

The Native populations were highly susceptible to diseases such as smallpox, for which they had no natural immunity. The arriving Europeans and American settlers, though they fared better against smallpox, were also very vulnerable to diseases such as cholera, which was caused by poor sanitation in overcrowded conditions. In Upper Canada, cholera struck most severely during the warm summer months of 1832 and later in the summer of 1849. The deadly disease is reported to have arrived in Canada in June 1832 aboard an Irish immigrant ship, the *Carrick*, spreading first

Life Expectancy for Iroquoian and Nineteenth Century Populations

Age Ranges	Port Oshawa	Methodist Oshawa	Uxbridge Ossuary*
0–1	37.1	30.8	25.0
1–6	38.3	34.6	26.8
6–12	36.1	38	24.9
12–18	33.1	33.4	19.7
18–24	30	28.7	15.9
24–30	30.5	26.6	12
30–36	26.9	23.9	10.4
36–42	29.4	23.2	8.8
42–48	25.1	20.5	9.1
48–54	20.6	16.1	6.1
54–60	17.3	13	2.5
60–66	13.9	9	
66–72	10.3	5.9	
72–78	8	3.4	
78–84	3	3	

*The Uxbridge Ossuary data is approximate to conform to the slightly dissimilar age ranges used for the two European populations

to Montreal and then into Upper Canada. The occurrences of cholera reached epidemic proportions as the number of deaths increased over the months of July and August and continued into September.

In 1832 cholera was reported in nearby Pickering, Cobourg, and Toronto, but no cases were recorded in Whitby or Reach Townships. An outbreak of cholera was reported at George Post's tavern on lot four, Concession One, in Pickering Township. Since most cholera deaths were confined to highly concentrated locations, such as in more populated towns and overcrowded, unsanitary ships, it is not surprising that the area around the Scugog Carrying Place escaped the epidemic.

An almost identical situation of unsanitary conditions in parts of Europe brought cholera back to Canada in 1849. Heavy immigration from the British Isles, particularly from Ireland after the potato famine, brought a flood of new settlers and another cholera epidemic to the country. Both the 1832 and 1849 epidemics had come on the heels of two peaks in immigration. In both years cases were first reported in the eastern part of British North America before spreading to Upper Canada, starting in the months of June, with the number of deaths from cholera progressively increasing until August when they trailed off and ended in the last few weeks of September or the beginning of October.

The cholera epidemic in Upper Canada, affecting Whitby Township in 1849, but not in 1832, is explained by the growth in population and services between the two years. In 1832, population in Whitby was quite small and European immigrants were only beginning to arrive. Also, there was no port in Oshawa at the time and no regularly scheduled shipping route connecting the township to larger centres. However, by 1849 a thrice-weekly boat service from Rochester, New York, to Cobourg, Port Hope, and Oshawa Harbour was in place. In 1833 the only boat service connected Rochester, New York, to Cobourg, which could explain why Cobourg suffered during the 1832 cholera outbreak and why Whitby did not.

Toronto's first case of cholera for 1849 was reported on July 6, when a woman traveller arrived from Hamilton. The woman died within ten hours while five or six others in Toronto contracted the disease. By the time the last case was reported on September 18, 452 persons had died of the disease.[3] The daily cholera deaths being reported in the *Globe* showed a spike in numbers during the last week of August.

The 1849 epidemic had a major impact in Whitby Township, particularly the area around Oshawa Harbour, and this time it was felt along the Scugog Carrying Place, killing both settlers and newly arriving immigrants. Pedlar points out that two harbourmasters, George Mothersill and Joseph Wood, died on August 29 while assisting immigrants at the harbour.[4] An unknown number of people did die of cholera at Oshawa Harbour that year and a number of other deaths there in August, attributed to an unidentified disease, may well have been caused by cholera. A William Townsend of Oshawa died of what was believed to be an apoplectic fit at the end of July in 1849, as reported in the *Globe*.[5] Samuel Pedlar's uncle, Josiah Pedlar, died in August, though he had otherwise been in good health, and Samuel mentions that in addition to his uncle "that the same year a number of good citizens passed away."[6]

The Literary News Letter, published in Oshawa on August 23, 1849, recorded: "the cholera has made its appearance in the vicinity of Oshawa. About 200 emigrants, principally Highland Scotch, were landed at our harbour a day or two since, some of whom on landing were attacked by cholera and one person has already died."[7] The immigrants were on the way to Thorah Township. A number of Scottish immigrants died at the harbour and according to Pedlar, a total of three immigrants perished from the disease.

There were reports of fifteen Catholic Irish dying at the Oshawa Harbour in 1849. The group, travelling by ship from Montreal to Niagara, were left at Oshawa when they became sick. All died and were buried in one large grave in the southwest corner of the Port Oshawa Pioneer Cemetery. During that period there were some reports of ships dropping off immigrants at the nearest port when cholera struck the passengers.

Thomas Conant reports on the story in some detail, though he wrongly places the incident as occurring in 1855:

> One midsummer day Captain Kerr came into Port Oshawa, about 1855, at 9 o'clock in the morning, with a boatload of Highland Scotchmen as passengers. At this port about 150 of them landed, and their goods and baggage were placed in the general storehouse upon the wharf. In the presence of Mr. [Joseph] Wood, the port wharfinger, and Mr. [George] Mothersill, a gentleman, who was looking on, many of these packages, for the first time since leaving the ocean ship, were opened out in the storehouse. In a very few hours from the time when they say these goods unpacked, strange to relate, both these gentlemen died, while the landed emigrants started to walk northward from Port Oshawa to get to the homes of their relatives in Mariposa in the county of Victoria. To rest over night they entered a large cooper

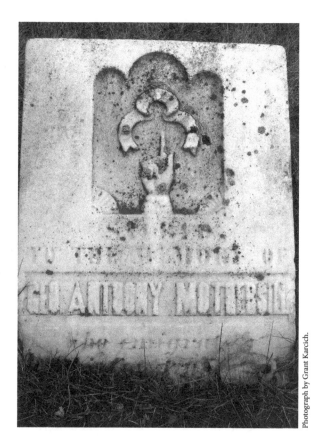

The gravestone for George Mothersill, who died of cholera at Oshawa Harbour in 1849, stands in St. George's Anglican Cemetery in Oshawa. The tombstone inscription says, "Sacred to the memory of Geo. Anthony Mothersill, who emigrated to this country in 1833, and died Aug. 29, 1849, AE 53 yrs."

Photograph by Grant Karcich.

shop then standing on the south side of Oshawa, and remained for the night. Next morning early they left, and the cooper on coming into the shop was horrified to find a dead man lying upon his shavings.[8]

Since Harmony was the nearest location to the harbour, the stricken Scotsmen may have walked up the Scugog Carrying Place into the hamlet only to die soon afterwards.

Later reports also mention up to fourteen people dying at the harbour and being quickly buried in mass graves in Port Oshawa Pioneer Cemetery. This is confirmed in an article written on the centenary of the 1849 burials, published in the *Oshawa Daily Times-Gazette* of March 12, 1949. It mentioning that fourteen victims were buried in unmarked graves in the southwest corner of the cemetery, while other graves were near the edge of the cliff at the south of the cemetery.[9]

Burials outside of the perimeter were described by Gordon Conant's book, *Life in Canada*, published in 1903:

> during the years 1847–49 ... cholera victims were landed at the Oshawa Pier and it is said 14 victims were landed in one night. There were all dead the next day and were buried in the Potter's field at the south west corner of the cemetery overlooking the ship yard and the pier. The graves were unmarked as far as I have ever known or seen. There is, however, evidence that some of the victims were buried near the edge of the cliff south of the cemetery, parts of the remains having been exposed through the erosion of the bank from year to year.[10]

Records indicate that the pioneer cemetery was in regular use up to the internment of William Maynard in 1926. However, by 1966, when a chain-link fence was erected around the site, no further burials were taking place there. Most of the burials in the original cemetery were moved in 1975 when a Toronto cemetery firm was hired to disinter 195 burials at the Port Oshawa Pioneer Cemetery and reburied them at Bonnie Brae Point Cemetery on the west side of Oshawa harbour. But, of those disinterred, no mention is made as to whether or not the cholera victims or others that were outside the perimeter of the cemetery were part of the relocation.

THE TEMPERANCE MOVEMENT

The interaction between the Mississauga and the incoming European settlers led to social problems that beset both communities. Both had to adapt to new conditions that resulted from the interaction of two diverse cultures. Natives adopted the material culture of the Europeans while retaining their own spiritual and traditional culture. The Europeans adapted by borrowing the names of places and items from Algonquian and Iroquoian languages and by relying heavily on Native food products and on the existing Native pathways and communication links around the Great Lakes.

A not-so-positive example resulting from their interaction is found in the introduction of alcohol to Native communities. Peter Jones had experienced several incidents of alcohol abuse as a young boy. He saw his uncle, Joseph Sawyer, sell his son for nine litres of whisky and Peter himself was adopted by Chief James Jajetance, who often became inebriated. One winter day the chief left Peter outside in the cold for several days without food causing him to become temporarily lame. His mother, Tuhbenahneequay, nursed him from his injury so that he regained the use of his legs. Peter referred to drunkenness as *Keushquabee* meaning that the "head turns round and the man is crazy."[11] He was strong-willed enough as an adult not to drink alcohol.

In the early years of contact with European settlers, the Mississauga were often preyed on by unscrupulous whisky dealers. Peter Jones commented on his visit to the Mississauga at Lake Scugog in 1828:

> of the Indians about Schoogog Lake a friend informed me of the following particulars respecting these Indians: Two white men went out to traffic with them for furs, taking with them two barrels of whiskey, hoping when they got the Indians into the bush they would be induced to drink, when they would be able to get their furs from them; but in this they were sadly disappointed, for after making one or two of them drunk, the Christian Indians went to them in a body and demanded the liquor, telling them they would not trade with them any more unless they gave it up; so the white men, sooner than lose their trade, gave up the whiskey to the Indians, who immediately took the barrels to the middle of the lake, cut a hole through the ice, tied weights to them and sunk them to the bottom.[12]

Egerton Ryerson, a Methodist missionary in the area, told a similar story of a trader enticing the Scugog band with whisky. Ryerson names the individual as Carr, "an old Methodist back-slider."[13] The surname Carr is often written as Kerr, and an early settler family named Kerr lived in Whitby Township.

The idea of temperance began in the United States and became pronounced in Ontario in the 1830s through the teachings of itinerant preachers of all denominations from New York. One such early advocate was a T. Turner of New York, who addressed several Ontario communities on the subject in 1835. The teachings of Methodists ministers such as William Case also greatly influenced the temperance movement. By 1832 there were approximately 100 temperance organizations in Ontario, one of them being in Whitby. At its third anniversary meeting in 1834, the Whitby Temperance Society claimed to have 320 members.[14]

Generally these early temperance meetings were held annually, but a few met more frequently. Usually a prayer was held, minutes of previous meetings were read, and an address was given on temperance issues. Proponents of these early temperance groups were split between those who allowed some drinking and those who were for total abstinence. Some of the societies allowed partial use of alcohol such as beer and wine, while others did not tolerate any alcohol. By the 1840s, however, they had evolved into the latter type — total abstinence from all drinking.

Presbyterian minister Robert Thornton and Methodist Egerton Ryerson must have been troubled by the fact that there were several distilleries at Skae's Corners in Whitby Township. Ryerson is credited with the creation of the first temperance society at York in 1830, while Thornton became a local leader of the temperance movement in Whitby Township. Church historian Walter Jackson states:

> that when Robert Thornton arrived in Whitby it was a part of 'the wild west'! ... a frontier community. Whiskey was sold by the gallon ... 25 cents a gallon was considered expensive! By 1840 the new settlers began to battle the danger they saw in drunkenness. Robert Thornton was a leader in this fight. The first demonstration, a march from Oshawa to Whitby was organized at his home at Thornton Corners.[15]

Because of his empathy for the temperance movement, Acheus Moody Farewell closed his tavern in 1838 after having operated it for over twenty-five years.

Due to the isolation and social conditions of the early settlements, consumption of alcohol was widely practised in Whitby and the northern townships. Since there were few religious leaders in the early period, the influence of the church was correspondingly weak, however, as more churches became established more pressure was placed on abolishing the sale of alcohol. Not surprisingly, businesses, which relied on alcohol sales, were much opposed to the temperance. The economic significance of whisky sales is outlined in the *History of the County of Ontario*:

> In the early periods when grain was cheap and difficult to transport, whiskey produced from wheat paid for many early farms. Moreover, in an era when travel was slow and difficult, frequent inns were necessary for the comfort and well-being of travellers and the sale of alcohol was a mainstay of the innkeepers' incomes. Without the sale of whiskey there is little double that many, if not most, inns would have been forced to close. Indeed, not only was the latter argument used to defend the sale of whiskey, but in periods of strong temperance agitation the dependency of the public on the inns was exploited to prevent the effective introduction of anti-liquor legislation.[16]

Much of the early history of Ontario is tied to the selling of spirits and other commercial transactions. Alcohol and other trade goods attracted the Mississauga to settle in southern Ontario and it also attracted the English traders who would seek them out to exchange commodities, often alcohol. After petitions from the Native reserves at Muncey and the Grand River, the province passed an Act in 1840 forbidding the sale of liquor to the Mississauga and other Native groups.

However, whisky sales to European settlers continued. Early settlers were quite accustomed to alcohol, and at times would not assist other settlers who were raising a barn unless spirits were provided. John

Kerr built a distillery on the Carrying Place after he arrived in 1816, and several others following him did the same. Thus their business interests ensured alcohol as part of the culture on the Carrying Place.

S. Farmer, in writing *On the Shores of Lake Scugog*, noted that:

> whiskey used to be sold for twenty-five cents per gallon and all who profess to know say that it was purer and better liquor than you can get to-day for twenty times the money. That was the retail price. Wholesale it was ten cents, and the commission man sold it to the hotelkeepers for 15c. per gallon ... Within sixty year past there were twenty-four places where you could buy liquor in the Township of Reach ... It is estimated that there were twenty-five hotels on the road between Manilla and Oshawa, not including the latter place.[17]

Abram Farewell, son of A.M. Farewell, was a strong advocate for the temperance movement. He visited several American states, studying their prohibition legislation, and published his results in a pamphlet that he distributed throughout the area. He also became a leading member of the Oshawa Sons of Temperance.

Edward Carswell, the artist who illustrated many of Oshawa's buildings, was another proponent of temperance and became a member of the Oshawa Division No. 35 of the Sons of Temperance, the year it was formed. Having been born in England in 1831, and living beyond the turn of the century, he is one of those figures whose lifespan connects the nineteenth-century settlers with the early twentieth-century generation. In his youth he had spent three years with Peter Jones in western Ontario. After leaving Jones, Edward trained as a painter in Toronto before moving to Oshawa where his brother operated a bakery. Once there, Edward established a business selling books and stationary in addition to pursuing his artwork. His various sketches of Oshawa have appeared in a number of publications.

Carswell became a lifelong abstainer after going out with the village band one evening, drinking beer at a neighbouring town. He became sick to the point that he swore off liquor. In 1849, Carswell became prominent in the Oshawa Sons of Temperance and was elected grand conductor in 1857 and grand worthy associate in 1860. Later, when he was elected to the National Division, he lectured across Canada and the United States and is said to have spoken in most of the American states, particularly those in the South. As G.W. Bungay described in his book on illustrious abstainers, "his lectures have a literary as well as a moral value, and men of letters who may not care a fig for 'the cause' will find his eloquence a source of entertainment and instruction."[18]

Momentum for the temperance cause increased in Oshawa with the incorporation of the Oshawa chapter of the Sons of Temperance. Pedlar described its founding:

> Oshawa Division No. 35 was organized on the 6th of November 1849, by Revd. Robert Dick of Toronto … The first meeting took place in the Public Hall, corner Centre and Athol St. at 4 o'clock in the afternoon. The following meetings were held in the Public meeting Hall of the Commercial Hotel which stood on the corner of Centre and King Streets.[19]

A building called the Sons Hall, constructed that same year, became the headquarters of the temperance movement in Oshawa. For over fifty years this facility functioned as a meeting place for the Sons of Temperance and as a school.

For a time, Oshawa became the focal point for the temperance movement. Pedlar described a meeting of the provincial Grand Division of the Sons of Temperance:

> In the month of October 1852 Oshawa was honoured by the Sons of Temperance of Canada by their holding the Grand Division of the Order here. The Sons' Hall was completed in time for this gathering. The meeting lasted several days. The representatives were a fine body of men including J.B. Gough,[20] Samuel Carey, the distinguished

Ohio Senator, and others. The people of Oshawa and surrounding districts crowded at the Public Meetings to hear the orations of J.B. Gough and Carey and others. It was the most memorable assemblage of prominent men and witnesses in this part of Canada.[21]

Courtesy of Oshawa Community Archives, A982.54.1.

A circa 1900 image of the Sons of Temperance Building, built on Simcoe Street in the spring of 1852, still retains the look of the original hall, constructed almost half a century earlier.

It seemed, at least for a time, that the forces of sobriety might not achieve their goal. Even before the settlers arrived, fur traders were already subjecting the Mississauga to the influence of liquor. The First Nations people along the Carrying Place tried to shake off this influence with the help of Christian missionaries, such as Egerton Ryerson and Peter Jones, but had limited success. The powerful commercial interests of some settlers saw to it that distilleries and breweries were among the first businesses to be established in the fledgling settlements along the Carrying Place. In time, however, the temperance work of men like Robert Thornton and Edward Carswell did reduce the influence of liquor along the Scugog Trail, so that by the time the trail fell into disuse, the forces of moderation were prevailing.

12

THE LEGACY OF THE TRAIL

*"In the month of October 1894, the writer walked to the
Lake shore, to see the mere remnant, of what at one time
was one of the beautiful spots, on the north shore of Lake
Ontario."*[1]

MIN-CE-NAN-QUASH

In 1796, Augustus Jones' survey notes describe *Min-ce-nan-quash*, a peninsula east of Wilson's and the terminus of the Scugog Carrying Place, which he calls a "Peninsula, almost an Island."[2] Shortly afterwards, this landmark caught the attention of the Farewell brothers as they were paddling along the Lake Ontario shoreline and they decided to settle in the area. By 1840, *Min-ce-nan-quash*, now known by its English name, Bluff Point, had been eroded to forty acres, down from the hundred acres recorded years earlier. J.E. Farewell states that a fisherman by the name of Terrill lived on Bluff Point while, "native Indian potatoes were growing on it" and that "Bluff point, now contains 3 or 4 acres."[3] Bluff Point continued to shrink, and by 1895 Samuel Pedlar is noting that "the present small bluff with its chisel point appears to defy the angry waters of Lake Ontario, but it is clear, the resistance cannot last many years."[4] Soon afterwards, in 1907, Farewell described Bluff Point as having disappeared under the waves of Lake Ontario. Much later, in the 1960s, Bob Stephenson, an Oshawa diver, reconnoitered the submerged remains of boats that had floundered on the underwater remains of Bluff Point.

Though the Scugog Carrying Place no longer exists and Bluff Point has been claimed by Lake Ontario, those remaining sections of the trail, such as the Port Oshawa cemetery, the Wilson homestead, and Rousseau's trading cabin, described in chapter three, are a part of our historical record and remain in our collective memories. Over the years, several Oshawa mayors have promoted awareness of these sites between Oshawa Harbour and the Second Marsh and along the trail route. Thomas E. Kaiser (mayor of Oshawa from 1907–1908), wrote about the settlement of Benjamin Wilson and the trading post. Gordon D. Conant (mayor of Oshawa from 1916–1917) kept the location of the Wilson homestead alive through his articles in the local newspaper, and Lyman Gifford (mayor of Oshawa from 1957–1960 and 1963–1966) told everyone who would listen about where the trading post stood. This collective knowledge was passed down from the Wilson family, to the Conants, to the Giffords, and now on to us.

The story of the Scugog Trail opened with an Oshawa newspaper headline involving the dredging at the Oshawa Harbour and its impact on Gifford Hill, named for a previous owner, Lyman Gifford, who farmed the Broken Front lots four and five of Whitby Township — the same lots that Benjamin Wilson farmed as the first settler in the region. In 1960, the City of Oshawa purchased the property from Lyman Gifford. Through legal action in 2006, completed in 2010, the city retrieved forty-eight acres of the original property, but the Gifford Hill lands were not part of the deal with the Oshawa Harbour Commission.

The Sydenham Harbour Company, which was founded by private enterprise in 1841, became the federally controlled Oshawa Harbour Company sometime between 1878 and 1907 and was responsible for the creation of the existing harbour basin in the 1930s. Between 1841 and the 1930s a pier on the west side of the harbour had accommodated both passenger boat traffic and commercial operations, such as coal imported for the local market. The harbour also serviced the shipping of local products to external markets, particularly exporting grain and lumber. On June 9, 1960, federal legislation transferred responsibility for Oshawa Harbour operations from the Federal Department of Transport to the Oshawa Harbour Commission. Six years later, the City of Oshawa transferred sixty-one acres of land around the harbour, including Gifford Hill, to the Harbour Commission. Beginning in the 1960s, improvements to

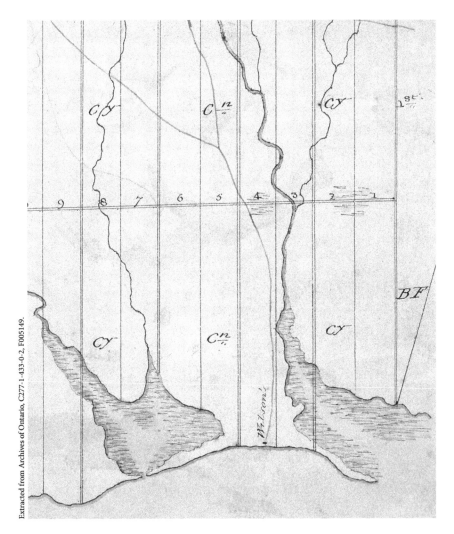

Detail from the 1795 Whitby Township Plan developed by surveyor Augustus Jones, showing Benjamin Wilson's homestead.

southeast corner of lot four, the lot Benjamin Wilson inhabited, which may be depicting an abandoned dwelling. Another clue comes from Blanche Meeker, who in her book on Benjamin Wilson, suggests that the Wilson cabin was 150 yards inland from Lake Ontario.[12]

When Thomas Conant owned Gifford Hill, he claimed that the hill contained First Nations burials, but at the time there was little evidence

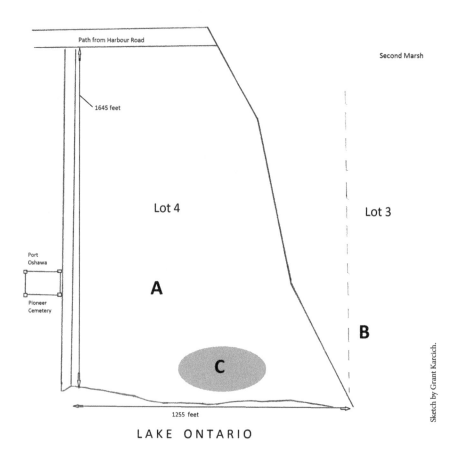

Path from Harbour Road

Second Marsh

1645 feet

Lot 4

Lot 3

Port
Oshawa

A

Pioneer
Cemetery

B

C

1255 feet

LAKE ONTARIO

Sketch by Grant Karcich.

The location of Wilson (C) and Rousseau (A or B) cabins on Gifford Hill.

of prehistoric occupation. However, in 1976, a local student found a stone artifact, which may have been a tool. Since 1978 artifacts have been found on the lot, and, in 1980, a surface search was carried out by the author and a concentration of artifacts found at the south end of the site near the bluff suggests this may have been the location of the site of Wilson cabin. The following year more surface material was collected. These items included mostly ceramic and bone with small amounts of metal, glass, and stone. Most were found within seventy-three feet from the lakeshore.

The ceramic pieces at the Wilson site were identified as nineteenth century ceramics by Donald Brown, the lead archaeologist in the excavation of Fort Rouillé, the French fort at Toronto, which dated to the 1750s. The bone consisted of twenty-one pieces of faunal material, mostly bovid long bones or teeth along with some bird bones. While the ceramics could have come from the period that the Wilson homestead was in use, the bone and teeth could not be dated.

Better indicators of the Wilson time period were two ceramic pipe stems, one with the letters "RRY" etched on one side and "GIASE" etched on the other. These may have been the last three letters of "Murray," the name of a Montreal pipe company operating in the 1840s. A green metal ring was discovered halfway up Gifford Hill, as if it had been left on the Carrying Place itself. The metal ring was an ornament from a Hudson Bay trading rifle in use during the 1820s to the 1840s.

The Wilson site is registered with the Ontario Ministry of Tourism, Culture, and Sport and designated as AlGq-46 in the provincial archaeological registry, part of Ontario's database of protected archaeological sites. However, to date there is still no absolute physical evidence defining the exact location of the Wilson homestead.

During the fall and winter of 2009–2010 there was further dredging of the harbour. The extracted material was trucked to Gifford Hill and dumped in a massive mound on Harbour Commission land, lying next to the Second Marsh. Heavy-duty vehicles carrying the waste material drove across a portion of the adjacent Wilson property and cut deeply into the top layers of earth on the historical site while en route to depositing their loads. The Ontario ministry responsible for the site alerted the Commission to the damage being done to the Wilson site, and in January 2010, after two months of heavy construction traffic over the Wilson site, the Commission completed the berm and spread construction debris of brick, stone, and concrete over the site. To date, there has been no official reprimand or compensation for damage caused.

On February 23, 2011, the City of Oshawa passed a motion recommending that an archaeological study of the Second Marsh and Gifford Hill be considered as part of the city's Waterfront Master Plan. However, since Gifford Hill belonged to the Oshawa Harbour Commission, as a

federal agency it is not subject to the municipal decision. A contro-
versy has been brewing since 2006, since the Harbour Commission
began its efforts to accommodate a private company called FarmTech
Energy Corporation, which is proposing to construct an ethanol plant
at Gifford Hill.

Since FarmTech submitted their proposal for the construction
of an ethanol plant on Gifford Hill, it first carried out a preliminary
archaeological assessment on the site, which, in its report, overlooked
the significance of the Wilson site, claiming that it was unimportant
archaeologically and did not examine the likelihood of potential resid-
ual burials from the Gifford Hill cemetery. The ministry, however, did
not accept this conclusion and ordered FarmTech to conduct a comprehensive archaeological investigation of the site. As of publication, a full
archaeological report has yet to be released on the Wilson site. It remains
unknown whether much of the site was left on Gifford Hill, or if during
the creation of the huge berms of harbour-dredged soil deposited on the
Wilson site, it was destroyed.

Over the last fifty years, the city and the Harbour Commission have
been embroiled in a power struggle over who controls the fate of Gifford
Hill. In 1998, Oshawa City Council requested that the 1,960 acres that

Archives of Ontario, C30-1, E59-659.

This aerial view of Gifford Hill shows it in relation to the harbour in the 1950s.
The Gifford farm is on the left and the cemetery is on the right.

were transferred to the Oshawa Harbour Commission be returned to the city. On July 16, 2010, Transport Canada announced that it would transfer the port's industrial activities from the west wharf to the east wharf in an agreement that transfers forty-eight acres of federal land to the city of Oshawa, including the return of some of the land the city had ceded to the Commission in 1966. On February 18, 2012, the federal government announced with a letter patent in the *Canada Gazettee* that the Oshawa Harbour Commission was henceforth to be known as the Oshawa Port Authority.

This pronouncement was followed by an announcement of the suspension of the environmental and archaeological assessments then underway, of the immediate construction of a railway spur line to the base of Gifford Hill, and that the start of construction of the ethanol plant on Gifford Hill would soon begin, in direct opposition to the designations of Oshawa City Council.

Back in 2008 the federal government had attempted to resolve the conflict over Gifford Hill between the Harbour Commission and the city by commissioning former, Toronto Mayor David Crombie to devise recommendations for a new system of management at the Oshawa Harbour. Crombie's report, *Recommendations for the Future of Oshawa Harbour*,[13] proposed that ownership of harbour lands be transferred to the City of Oshawa and that the federal government undertake an environmental evaluation and return all harbour lands to their pre-existing state. Crombie's report was ignored.

Leslie Frost had wanted Gifford Hill to become a historic site. When speaking at a luncheon at the Oshawa Kiwanis Club in 1972, just before his book describing the Scugog Carrying Place was published, he suggested that the Gifford Farm, then zoned for an industrial park, "should be set aside for historical purposes." At that luncheon Frost expressed regret that the Scugog portage "is a part of the forgotten history of Ontario," and said he was afraid that "we're rustling ahead and history is falling by the side."[14]

Some of the opposition to the harbour dredging in 2009–2010 and the proposed ethanol plant at Gifford Hill stems from potential negative effects on the neighbouring Second Marsh waterfowl, the potential of pollution, and the loss of a community-planned waterfront. These concerns are countered by business interests that espouse industrial development over environmental concerns, the emphasis being on maximizing economic growth. The struggle between these opposing forces of environmentalism and industrial development is not unlike the struggle of more than a century earlier between the advocates for temperance and those entrepreneurs that wished to profit from the building of mills and distilleries.

The old tavern entrepreneurs, such as Moody Farewell, discovered there was a price to pay for their economic initiatives that negatively affected both the Native and settler populations. Moody profited from his fur-trading business and his tavern, which he operated for a quarter century before closing it down due to his support for temperance. Perhaps the current entrepreneurs will also, in due time, realize that their quest for profit has a negative impact on the local population and will then advocate for more community-oriented enterprises along the Scugog Carrying Place.

FORGOTTEN BURIAL GROUNDS

Though the Rousseau cabin and the Wilson house were known to exist on the Scugog Carrying Place from the earliest days of European settlement, other aspects of the Carrying Place have eluded a fuller understanding of the trail. However, due to recent developments, some hidden aspects of the Scugog Carrying Place have come to light, suggesting that more remains to be discovered about the trail.

Incidentally, in 2007 two forgotten burial sites were found along the Scugog Carrying Place, one in the former community of Prince Albert, now a part of Port Perry, and another in Oshawa. In February 2007, at a spot on Old Simcoe Road along the Scugog Carrying Place, an examination by non-intrusive ground-penetration radar revealed the location of a possible twenty-nine burials. Though a recent cemetery was not known to exist on this site, archaeologists concluded that the interned likely were mostly First Nations people and possibly some Europeans. The early settler, Rueben Crandall, is reported to have been made aware that it was a First

Nations site. In his 1809–1810 survey notes for Reach Township, Samuel Wilmot mentions an "Indian Burial Ground" on the Fifth Concession in the general area where the 2007 examination took place.

The archaeological work on Old Simcoe Road was co-ordinated by Gordon Dibb of York North Archaeological Services and financed by the Mississauga of Scugog First Nations, with the support of the Lake Scugog Historical Society. The earliest settlers were buried at the Pine Grove cemetery in Prince Albert, suggesting that the distinct Prince Albert burials discovered in 2007 are that of a First Nations group. Three ten-by-ten-metre radar grids were taken on snow-covered and frozen ground, revealing the presence of burials. However, more archaeological work would need to be done in order to determine who is interned there.

In the summer of 2007, when a garage was levelled on King Street East, Oshawa, to make way for a new rectory for St. Gertrude's Roman Catholic Church, human bones were unearthed. These remains were found along the former course of the eastern branch of the Scugog Carrying Place, two miles north of the Oshawa Harbour and on the former Terwillegar farm north of Kingston Road. Construction on the project stopped and Ronald Williamson's Archaeological Services Inc. was called in to investigate. The company had conducted a number of archaeological recovery jobs in the area, including the excavation of the Grandview site and the relocation of several graves in the Farewell Cemetery, within a quarter mile of the St. Gertrude's site.

Williamson's crews sifted through the debris of the garage and adjacent property and found remains of several individuals. The archaeologists examined fifteen individual burials and determined that the minimum number of individuals buried there would have been thirty-four. The examined human remains consisted of two adult females, four adult males, one of whom is over sixty years in age, and nine sub-adults, including two newborns, one teenager, and four individuals between the ages of one and five.

The St. Gertrude's burials contained a few artifacts (pinched-toed coffins, screwed hinges, and flat nails), but no visible grave markers. In 1967 Blanche Meeker noted the discovery of burials, "in the late 20's [1920s] while excavating property on the Kingston Road, which property is now owned by the Catholic Church [St. Gertrude's], a number of graves were disturbed. These bones were reinterred in one grave, no doubt in some cemetery."[15] The archaeologists did find a number of burials that were co-mingled at St. Gertrude's Church burials, though the church had only acquired the property in 1951. Before that it was the property of Rolland Moffat, who had purchased the property in the early 1920s and built a house and garage there. Since the garage was constructed on top of the burials, a safe assumption would be that knowledge of these internments had been lost by then.

The St. Gertrude's burials are puzzling since another early pioneer cemetery lies less than a quarter mile away, almost within view on Harmony Road. The Farewell Pioneer Cemetery contains the remains of many of the local inhabitants, including those that lived on the property where the St. Gertrude's burials are found. The three earliest cemeteries in Oshawa are the Port Oshawa Pioneer Cemetery, the Farewell Pioneer Cemetery, and the Pioneer Memorial Garden Cemetery, which was used by the Wesleyan Methodist congregation. Except for a few earlier burials in these three cemeteries, the vast majority took place from 1840 onwards (Port Oshawa to 1926, Farewell to 1941, and Memorial to 1906), and primarily cover the latter half of the nineteenth century and into the early part of the twentieth. The St. Gertrude's burials, though identified as being also from the nineteenth century, do not show signs of later burials. The total number of burials for Port Oshawa, Farewell, and Memorial cemeteries is respectively 195, 148, and 292, while the St. Gertrude's burials only total thirty-four. This small number indicates the unusual nature of this burial ground and suggests that it was not used for more than a few decades.

St. Gertrude's may be the earliest European burial site in the Scugog Carrying Place area, since the artifacts contained within it appear to date from the earlier half of the nineteenth century. The presence of pinch-toed coffins (hexagonal coffins) and flat nails, all items known to be used in North American cemeteries well before 1850, suggest that this could be the case. For instance, at the Bethany Cemetery in Effingham County, Georgia, in use from 1757–1890, "stone grave markers ... were either marked with wooden slabs, or they had no markers at all" and hexagonal coffins predominated.[16] At a cemetery in Charleston County, South Carolina, dating from 1796 to 1832, only hexagonal coffins are found, and at a cemetery in Talbot County, Georgia, hexagonal coffin date to no later than the 1850s. In fact, in Georgia and South Carolina hexagonal coffins are uncommon after 1850.

It is believed that the burials at St. Gertrude's Church represent local inhabitants buried prior to 1850, possibly those who lived on that property and adjacent ones. The Terwillegar and Farewell families had owned much of this land during a large part of that period. Other nearby families, such as that of John Day, lived and worked here. However, the Terwillegars, Days, and other neighbouring families are accounted for in other early pioneer cemeteries. In fact, the Farewell family preferred to bury at the nearby cemetery in Harmony, within eyesight of the St. Gertrude Church burials where many of these local families are buried. To this day the burials at St. Gertrude's Church remain unidentified.

Gillian Gilchrist,[17] a retired Oshawa physician, attempted to solve the riddle of who was buried at St. Gertrude's. Some of her suggested burials (that of Charles Annis and Elizabeth Wilson, the wife of Benjamin Wilson), may match some of the fifteen individuals examined by Archeological Services Incorporated. Charles Annis is known to have died in Whitby Township in 1804, but his burial place is unknown, and Elizabeth Wilson died in 1840 on her son-in-law's farm, a mile north of this burial location, and was interned in a long-forgotten plot near the farm. We may never know precisely who was buried at St. Gertrude's in the early part of the nineteenth century, but we do know that they would have been some of the earliest settlers in the area.

HISTORICAL PLAQUES

There are modern reminders of the Scugog Carrying Place. A couple of existing plaques, and some still in the planning stages, help us to remember the trail's significance to the development of the Oshawa-Scugog corridor. Besides publishing his book on the Scugog Carrying Place, Leslie Frost, the sixteenth premier of Ontario, brought awareness of the Scugog Trail to future generations by initiating the creation of commemorative plaques.

Scugog Carrying Place

On November 14, 1971, a plaque was unveiled at the Soldiers' Memorial Park in Lindsay, Ontario, by the Ontario Department of Public Records and Archives. The plaque reads:

> The Scugog Route. This river and lake formed part of an Indian route from the Kawartha and Algonquin Park areas to Lake Ontario. During the French Regime efforts were made to prevent English traders from the Oswego area bartering with Indians who used such routes. Trading posts were established among the Mississauga by the beginning of the nineteenth century. In 1804 the killing on Washburn Island, Lake Scugog of trader John Sharp led to the subsequent loss on Lake Ontario of the Schooner *Speedy* bearing the accused Mississauga and trial officials.[18]

A year after this Scugog Route plaque was launched, Leslie Frost commissioned a second plaque of his own to commemorate *Cabane de Plomb* on the same spot. It states: "This ancient Scugog route which was used by the Hurons, Iroquois and Mississauga from prehistoric times commenced on Lake Ontario between Harmony and Oshawa Creeks where in the 18th century the French established a trading post known as *Cabane de Plomb*."[19]

More recently, Ken Ridge, an Oshawa resident, proposed that his city erect plaques to commemorate that portion of Scugog Carrying Place that lies within its borders. Acting on this advice, Heritage Oshawa, a cultural advisory body to the City of Oshawa, recommended that a plaque be created to recognize *Cabane de Plomb* and that it be placed at Lakeview Park, west of the Oshawa Harbour. On July 10, 2006, the Oshawa Development Services Committee, acting on the advice of Heritage Oshawa, put forward a recommendation that two plaques be created, one at the Purple Woods Conservation Area at the northern edge of Oshawa designating the Scugog Carrying Place, and a second one for the *Cabane de Plomb* at Lakeview Park. In October 2012, Heritage Oshawa dropped plans to commemorate *Cabane* with a plaque

*Leslie Frost at the dedication of the "Scugog Route" plaque in Lindsay on
November 14, 1971, (l–r) are George Oke of the Victoria County Historical
Society, the Honourable Leslie Frost, Robert Thompson, warden of Victoria
County, John Aikens, mayor of Lindsay, and William Ormsby.*

because of information gleaned through research for this book, though
they are still proceeding to determine the placement site for a plaque to
commemorate the Scugog Carrying Place.

Today, it is still possible to somewhat glimpse what the Scugog Carrying
Place must have been like. In its day the trail provided a transportation
corridor to funnel the Mississauga and Europeans between Lake Ontario
and Lake Simcoe and they crossed it on foot and by canoe. It is still possible to canoe along the Carrying Place in certain areas today. Since 1969
the Canoe the Nonquon race has been operated annually by the Scugog
Historical Society, partly funded by the Scugog Shores Museum, and has

raised $450,000 since its inception. The canoe race runs eleven miles of the Nonquon River and over five miles of water on Lake Scugog, ending at the docks in Port Perry. Because today's water levels are considerably lower than that of 100 years ago, the Oshawa and Farewell Creeks are now too shallow for canoeing. However, along the Beaver River canoeing is still viable with multiple access points off of the abutting roads.

It is also possible to get a sense of what the Carrying Place was like in its heyday by frequenting local trails along the Beaver River. The Beaver River Wetland Trail, a hiking, cycling, and cross-country ski trail, spans ten-and-a-half miles from the community of Backwater to the south of Woodville, and passes through the southern edge of Cannington. The trail runs on the bed of an abandoned railway line, which was purchased by the Lake Simcoe Region Conservation Authority in 1993. It traverses the west bank of the Beaver River and crosses to the east bank in Cannington. At its south end, the Beaver River trail merges with the Trans Canada Trail, the country's longest network of trails, which

Photograph by Grant Karcich.

Annual canoe race on the Nonquon River.

eventually will stretch from the Atlantic to Pacific coasts. Further south along the Oshawa Creek, a paved pathway provides for scenic walks along that stream, though the original Scugog Carrying Place often ran along higher ground to the east of the Creek.

Structures along the Scugog Carrying Place, such as the trading cabins at Lake Ontario and Lake Scugog, and the cabin near Raglan, have all disappeared. Even though Rousseau's cabin and Wilson's homestead have also disappeared, a number of heritage buildings still exist from the era before 1851. Today, they provide a physical link to the first fifty years of European settlement. These homes dating prior to 1851 can still be viewed in Oshawa and in the municipalities of Scugog and Brock. (See Appendix E for a list of heritage structures.) The best legacy of the Scugog Trail, however, exists in the modern roads, such as Simcoe Street, extending from Oshawa to Port Perry to Beaverton, which we travel on today.

This story of the trail, followed by the Scugog Carrying Place, was inspired by the recent dredging at Oshawa Harbour and its deleterious impact on the historic sites on Gifford Hill. At the time of writing it is uncertain whether the sites are still intact or have been destroyed. Though Bluff Point or *Min-ce-nan-quash* has disappeared and the precise locations of Rousseau's cabin and Benjamin Wilson's homestead have not been determined, they, and other aspects of the Scugog Carrying Place, continue to be remembered. It is hoped that this story will bring knowledge of this trail to a wider audience and thereby help preserve an understanding of its historical importance.

EPILOGUE

This book is dedicated to the memory of Samuel Pedlar (1831–1910), the trail's unacknowledged historian, without whom these pages could not have been written. After interviewing early settlers about the Scugog Carrying Place, Pedlar wrote, "it is therefore pretty certain that this Indian trail is no longer a myth — on the contrary, an interesting fact which at some time may form the basis of interesting information."[1]

Samuel Pedlar was born in England in 1831 and moved to Oshawa with his parents in 1841. His father, a successful entrepreneur, eventually

The only known image of Samuel Pedlar (1831–1910). From microfilm of Samuel Pedlar: Ancestral History of Charles Pedlar of Vauxhall, Cornwall, England, born about 1710 and his descendants, *1894.*

opened a hardware and tinplate business in Oshawa at the corner of Bond and Simcoe Streets. When Samuel Pedlar arrived at Skae's Corners, the community was no more than a small collection of buildings in the wilderness. A landscape of seemingly impenetrable forest surrounded the village. As a young man, Samuel witnessed the growth of Skae's Corners into the town of Oshawa and experienced the arrival of the first train in 1856.

During the early 1860s Samuel worked for publisher George Brown,[2] travelling as an agent in a one-horse rig, taking subscriptions for the *Daily Globe* and *Weekly Globe* newspapers that were published in Toronto. In 1865, when he became a manager for the Etna Life Insurance Company, which had its headquarters in Hartford, Connecticut, his territory was Toronto and Montreal and he became a pioneer in the insurance industry. But Samuel never forgot Oshawa. He returned to his hometown repeatedly. Upon retirement, he settled back in Oshawa and until his death in 1910 much of his time was given to the recording of his Cornish family history and researching local history.

Appendix A:

Archaeological Sites along the Scugog Carrying Place, Including the Farewell and Oshawa Creeks, and Nonquon and Beaver Rivers

Site/Bordon No.	Time Period	Location	Type	References
Wilson AlGq46	1793–1821	Whitby BF, lot 4	Homestead	Conant 1949
St. Gertrude's	1790–1850	Whitby Con.2 lot 5	Burials	Williamson 2009
Grandview AlGr-59	Middle to Late Iroquoian (A.D.1380–1450)	Oshawa Con.3 lot 3	Village	Williamson 2003
MacLeod	Late Iroquoian (A.D.1450)	Oshawa Con.2 lot 16	Village	Reed 1990
Pascoe	Iroquoian	Whitby Con. 9	Village	Min. Tourism
Prospect	Iroquoian	Reach Con. 2, lot 9/10	Village	Min. Tourism
Prince Albert	Unknown	Reach, Old Simcoe Rd.	Burials	Personal correspondence
Nonquon	Unknown	Scugog Island	Burials	Chamberlain 1889
Ball Point	Unknown	Lake Scugog	Burials	Coleman 1875
Washburn Island	Historic and A.D.1000–1300	Lake Scugog	Various	Kidd 1951
Seagrave Ossuary	Unknown	Reach Con.14, lot 17	Burials	Hvidsten 2004
Baird Ossuary BbGs-2	Unknown	Reach Con.14, lot 18	Burials	Min. Tourism

Site/Bordon No.	Time Period	Location	Type	References
Thomas	Late Iroquoian	Reach Con. 14, lot 18	Village	Donaldson 1962
Uxbridge Ossuary BbGt-1	Late Iroquoian A.D.1490	Uxbridge	Burials	Pfeiffer 1983
Markson BbGs-11	Middle or Late Iroquoian	Brock Con. 3, lot 7/8	Village	Min. Tourism
Corin & Bristow	Historic Huron	Thorah Island	Village	Sweetman 1990

* Min. Tourism data is from the Ontario Ministry of Tourism, Culture, and Sport.

APPENDIX B:

CARTOGRAPHY OF THE SCUGOG CARRYING PLACE

Date	Map	*Cabane de Plomb* (Bluff Point)	Lake Scugog	Remarks
1657	Bressani-Novae Franciae		Present; not named	
1699	Franquelin	*Cabane au Plomb*		First occurrence of *Cabane au Plomb*
1726	Léry Carte du Lac, Ontario	*Cabane au Plomb*		
1755	d'Anville	*Cabane de Plomb*	Present; not named	
1755	High Admiral Map			"Fr. Ft" (French fort) north near Lake Scugog
1757	Labroquerie	Presqu'ile petit ecort		
1775	d'Anville	*Cabane au Plomb*	Present; not named	
1785	La frontiere Map			Unnamed locality between Tegaogen and Ganaraské
1791	Jones Baseline survey	Min-ce-nan-quash		
1791–96	Jones Whitby Twp. C29			Long beach at L. Ontario

Date	Map	*Cabane de Plomb* (Bluff Point)	Lake Scugog	Remarks
1792	Lieut. Gov. Simcoe's Map	Les petites Escors		
1795	Jones Whitby Twp. C31	Bluff Point visible		Carrying Place marked
1799	D.W. Smith Plan			Two "Indian paths" shown
1807	Jones Whitby Twp. C30			Settlers listed to 1803
1810	Wilmot's Reach Twp.		Scugog shown	"Indian Foot Path"
1841	Baird Map	Bluff Point visible		
1841	Rankin Map		"Skugog"	Simcoe Street to Beaverton
1853	County Map		Scugog Shown	Scugog Road

Appendix C:

First Settlers along the Scugog Carrying Place, 1793–1844

Year of Arrival on Trail	Name	Location of Trail by Township, Concession, and Lot	Came From	Born
1793–1794	Benjamin Wilson	Whitby BF (4)	Vermont	Rehobeth, Mass.
	Eleazear Lockwood	Whitby BF (7)	New York	New York
1794–1795	Charles Annis	Whitby BF (6)	Susquehanna	New Hampshire
1794–1800	George Hall	Whitby BF (1)	Susquehanna	
1802–1803	A.M. Farewell	L. Scugog-Ball Island & Whitby Con. 1(4) in 1804		Vermont
1803	Mathew Terwilligar	Whitby Con. 1–6	Susquehanna	New York
1809	Jabez Lynde	Whitby 2 Con. (11)		Brookville, Mass.
1816	John Kerr	Whitby 2 Con. (11)	Duffin's Creek	New York
	John Henry	Whitby BF (8)		Drumlees, Cavan, Ireland
	Abraham Coryell	Whitby		
1817	John McGregor	Whitby Con. 1(11)		
	Benjamin Stone	Whitby Con. 2 (7/8)	Eastern Townships	Massachusetts
1821–1825	Joseph Wiley	Whitby 8th Con.		
1821	Reuben Crandell	Reach Con. 2	Prince Edward Co.	Saratoga Co., N.Y.

Year of Arrival on Trail	Name	Location of Trail by Township, Concession, and Lot	Came From	Born
1821	Samuel Dearborn	Whitby BF (10)	Highland Creek	New York
	George McGill	Whitby Con. 3 (7)	Paisley, Scotland	
	John Dickie	Whitby Con. 3 (8)	Paisley, Scotland	
	J. Widdifield	Whitby Con. 4 (10)		
	John Edward White	Thorah Con. (13–14)	Ireland	Bandon Co., Cork
	William Turner	Thorah Con. 1 (21)	Ireland	
	John M. Fralick	Whitby Twp.		
1823	John Rae	Reach Con. 2 (11)		
	John Sproul(e)	Reach Con. 12 (17)		
1824	Abner Hurd	Reach Con. 2 (17)		United States
	Daniel Dayton	Reach Con. 2 (17)	United States	Massachu-setts
1825	Chester Webster	Whitby Con. 5 (10)		
	Jacob Smith	Whitby Con. 5 (10)	Fredericksburg, Ont.	
	John Brandon	Brock Con. 13 (18)	Hallowell, U.P.	Fermanagh, Ireland
1826	Isaac Fralick	Southwest of Raglan	United States	Germany
1827	George Fisher	Whitby Con. 7 (12)	Fredericksburg, Ont.	New York State
	Richard Morden	Brock		
1827–1828	Henry Hicks	Whitby at Columbus		Luxillian, Cornwall
1828	Joseph Gorham	Whitby Con. 1 (11)		
	John Bruce	Beaverton	Islay, Scotland	
	Alex Calder	Thorah Con. 4 (10)	Scotland	

Year of Arrival on Trail	Name	Location of Trail by Township, Concession, and Lot	Came From	Born
1828–1831	Donald Christie	Reach Con. 4 (11)	Scotland	
	Archie McDermid	Reach Con. 5 (11)		
	Peter Christie	Reach Con. 5 (11)		
	John McKerchen	Reach Con. 4 (12)		
	Charles Stevens	Reach Con. 5 (10)		
1829	Thomas Wilcockson	Whitby Con. 6 (12)	Lincolnshire, Eng.	England
	Irvine Johnston	Brock Con. 12 (19)		
	Samuel Dearborn	Whitby Con. 3 (11)	Gibbs Mills	
	Henry Walker	Reach Con. 4 south of Manchester		
1830	Edward Skae	Whitby Con. 1 (11)	Scotland	
	Thomas Graham	Reach Con. 3 (14)		
	John Aston	Reach S. Manchester	Ireland	
	Joel Horner	Brock		
	Elias Williams	Reach Con. 6 (19/20)	Colborne, U.P.	
	Solomon Orser	Reach	Kingston	
1831	Andrew Mason	Whitby Con. 5 (10)	Kerr's Creek	
	Artemas Thompson	Thorah Con. 6 (13)	Prince Edward Co.	Utica, New York
	Harvey Kerr	Whitby Con. 5 (11)	Kerr's Creek	
1832	Martin Shaw	Whitby Con. 2 (11)		
	Joseph Adams	Whitby Con. 5 (10)	Devonshire, Eng.	

Year of Arrival on Trail	Name	Location of Trail by Township, Concession, and Lot	Came From	Born
	Robert Aston	Whitby Con. 5(10)	Clovelly, Eng.	
	Thomas Hodgson	Whitby Con.8 (11/12)	Westmoreland, Eng.	
1833	Charles Johnston	Brock Con. 12 (16)	Prince Edward Co.	Fermanagh, Ireland
1834	Elisha Doolittle	Whitby Con.6 (5–13)		
	Richard Luke	Whitby Con. 5 (9)	Plymouth, Eng.	St. Austell, Eng.
	James Burns	Whitby Con.9 (9)	Scotland	
	Peter McCuaig	Thorah Con 5 (11)	Scotland	
1836	Joseph Moore	Whitby B.F.(4–5)	United States	
1837	M. Weir	Brock Con.4 (16)	Scotland	
1838	James Shand	Whitby Con.5 (10)	Scotland	
	George Lee	Brock Con.5 (5)		Canada
1840	James Fox	Brock Con.5 (5)		Canada
1841	David Leask	Brock Con.13 (21)	Scotland	
1844	George Ormiston	Brock Con. 9 (10)	Scotland	

Appendix D:

Mills, Distilleries, Factories, and Tanneries on Tributaries near the Scugog Carrying Place to 1860

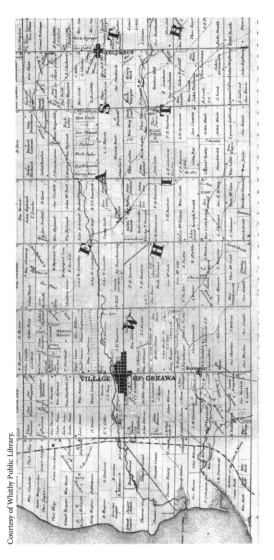

The Tremaine map of 1860 depicts the various commercial structures along the route that replaced the Scugog Carrying Place. From Tremaine's Map of the County of Ontario, Upper Canada.

WHITBY TOWNSHIP

Year	Type	Builder/Operator	Location
1825	Sawmill*	David Annis	BF Con., lot 10
	Fanning mill*		BF Con., lot 10
	Flour mill*	James Cooper/A. Small	BF Con., lot 10, Raglan Mills
	Mill	Thomas Haywood	1 Con., lot 2-SE Harmony
	Sawmill	Ralph Robinson	1 Con., lot 2-SE Harmony
1813	Gristmill*	A.M. Farewell	1 Con., lot 4 Harmony
1817	Distillery* & Brewery*	John McGregor	1 Con., lot 11
1821	Gristmill*	Samuel Dearborn	1 Con., lot 11 South Oshawa
1821	Sawmill*	Samuel Dearborn	1 Con., lot 11 South Oshawa
1822	Woollen mill*	Joseph Gorham	1 Con., lot 11 South Oshawa
1825	Distillery*	E. Smith	1 Con., lot 11 South Oshawa
1836	Tannery*	Bartlett Brothers	1 Con., lot 11 South Oshawa
1841	Foundry*	Robert Moscrip	1 Con., lot 11
	Leather factory	Johnathan & Wm. Bartlet	1 Con., lot 15
1841	Brewery*	Spalding	1 Con., lot 11
1843	Foundry*	Munroe Brothers	1 Con., lot 11
1817	Distillery*	John Kerr	2 Con., lot 11
1837	Flour mill and Distillery*	J.B. Warren	2 Con., lot 11
1842	Woollen mill*	Ethan Card	2 Con., lot 11
1829	Sawmill*	Winterfield (Widdifield)	4 Con., lot 11
1841	Four mill*	Ambrose Morris	4 Con., lot 10-E Osh Ck
	Sawmill*		4 Con., lot 10-E Osh Ck

Year	Type	Builder/Operator	Location
	Flour mill	James Ewart	4 Con., lot 10, 1/2 mi. S
	Sawmill		4 Con., lot 10, 1/2 mi. S
	Gristmill & Distillery	Peter Taylor	4 Con., lot 11
	Sawmill	Richard Luke	5 Con., lot 9-E Osh Ck.
	Sawmill	Daniel Cridiman	6 Con., lot 9 SE Columbus
	Gristmill	Thomas Coutts	6 Con., lot 9
	Flour mill	Wm. Starr/Rob. Parker	6 Con., lot 13 SW Columbus
	Sawmill		6 Con., lot 16 W Columbus
1835	Woollen factory	Mathewson/Ratcliff	6 Con., lot 16
	Woollen mill	Jos.Bowerman/Thomas Cunningham	6 Con., lot 18
	Grist/Flour mill	Bickle/Coulter/Peter Taylor	6 Con., lot 18
1831	Gristmill	W.H. Gibb	Columbus
	Leather factory	George Hepburn	7 Con., lot 13-N Columbus
	Flour mill	Walter Hill	7 Con., lot 15 Genoa Mills
	Sawmill	John Green	8 Con., lot 7 E Osh Ck.
	Sawmill		8 Con., lot 14 SW Raglan
	Gristmill	Samuel Hayward/ Henry Neville/Ralph Harnden	8 Con., lot 14 Norfolk Mills
	Leather factory		8 Con., lot 14 SW Raglan
	Sawmill	Ira Brown	8 Con., lot 14(centre)
	Sawmill	Luther Harnden	8 Con., lot 14 (front)

Year	Type	Builder/Operator	Location
	Sawmill		8 Con., lot 18 W Osh Ck.
1824	Sawmill	John/Timonthy Fralick	8 Con., lot 18
	Sawmill	William Clark	9 Con (front)
	Sawmill	David Bedford	9 Con., lot 13 N Raglan

REACH TOWNSHIP

Year	Type	Builder/Operator	Location
1846	Sawmill	Daniel Way	4 Con., lot 5
	Sawmill	Daniel Way	4 Con., lot 6
	Sawmill		4 Con., lot 7
	Gristmill	John Hicks	4 Con., lot 9
	Sawmill	Jacob Bongard	5 Con., lot 7
1831	Sawmill*	Squire Hurd	5 Con., lot 17
	Tannery	Joshua Wright	5 Con., lot 17 Prince Albert
1841	Distillery	Lockart & Wilson	6 Con., lot 19
1846	Sawmill*	Thomas & George Paxton	6 Con., lot 19 Port Perry
1847	Sawmill*	Paxton/Bigelow/Trounce	6 Con., lot 19 Port Perry
1850	Sawmill*	Samuel Hill/W.Sexton	6 Con., lot 19 Port Perry
1852	Saw & gristmill*	John Cameron	6 Con., lot 19 Port Perry
1853	Woollen mill*	Jacob & W.D. Bowerman	6 Con., lot 19 Port Perry
1853	Sawmill	Stephen Doty	6 Con., lot 19 Lake Scugog
	Sawmill		8 Con., lot 1
	Sawmill		9 Con., lot 7
	Sawmill	John Ianson	10 Con., lot 10

Year	Type	Builder/Operator	Location
	Sawmill	Isaac Cragg	10 Con., lot 12
	Flour & gristmill	John Beare/John Asling	10 Con., lot 13
	Sawmill		12 Con., lot 10
	Sawmill		12 Con., lot 14
	Sawmill		14 Con., lot 18
1846	Gristmill*	Edward Asling	Nonquon River
1854	Sawmill*	Abram Farewell	Seagrave, Nonquon River

BROCK TOWNSHIP

Year	Type	Builder/Operator	Location
	Sawmill		1 Con., lot 20
	Sawmill		2 Con., lot 20
	Steam Sawmill		2 Con., lot 20
	Gristmill*	J.B. Bolster	3 Con., lot 12
	Sawmill*	George Leask	3 Con., lot 12
	Sawmill		6 Con., lot 5
	Gristmill		10 Con., lot 9
	Sawmill*	William Thompson	10 Con., lot 18
	Gristmill		11 Con., lot 20
1830	Saw & Grist*	Joel Horner	11 Con., lot 20, McCaskill Mills
1849	Distillery*	Alex Munro	11 Con., lot 20, Cannington
	Woollen mill*	A. Card	12 Con., lot 22
	Sawmill*		13 Con., lot 18

THORAH TOWNSHIP

Year	Type	Builder/Operator	Location
1828–1830	Gristmill & Distillery*	Duncan Calder	Beaverton
	Saw & Oat mill*	Alexander Calder	Beaverton
1845	Carding & Fulling mills*	G. Proctor	Beaverton, Beaver River
	Wool factory	Rodrick Sillars	
	Lumber factory	William Bryanton	
	Sawmill	John Cameron	

LINDSAY

Year	Type	Builder/Operator	Location
1829–1830	Saw & Grist	William Purdy	Lindsay, Scugog River

*Mills, Distilleries, Factories, and Tanneries that are immediately adjacent to the Scugog Carrying Place trail

Note: Arranged geographically from south to north.

Sources: Canada West Census 1851; County of Ontario Map, Termaine, 1860; Pedlar 1895; Kaiser 1921; Farmer 1934

APPENDIX E:

PRE-1860 HERITAGE BUILDINGS STILL STANDING IN THE FORMER EAST WHITBY (OSHAWA), REACH, BROCK, AND THORAH TOWNSHIPS

Address	Year Built	Name
80 Peace St., Cannington	1825–35	Brandon Cabin
Lot 4, Con. 4, Brock Township	1825	Log Cabin
Darlington Provincial Park	1820s	Suggitt Cabin
707 Harmony Rd. N., Oshawa	1835	
824 Simcoe St. S., Oshawa	1835	Cedardale United Church
744 Thornton Rd. N., Oshawa	1837	Beckett House
62 King St. W., Oshawa	1838	Oshawa House Hotel
4150 Harmony Rd. N., Oshawa	1839	
Durham Rd. 15, Beaverton	1840	Stone Church (St. Andrew's Presbyterian Church)
306 Conlin Rd. E., Oshawa	1840	
809 Simcoe St. S, Oshawa	1840	
344 Thornton Rd. N., Oshawa	1840	
284 Simcoe St., Beaverton	1840s	Log Cabin
1446 Simcoe St. S., Oshawa	circa 1840	Henry House
1320 King St., Port Perry	1842	Christie Homestead
475 Cragg Rd., Scugog	1843	John Beare Residence
1618 King St., Port Perry	1845	Rowan Tree Hall
1450 Simcoe St. S., Oshawa	circa 1845	Guy House
3622 Simcoe St. N., Oshawa	1846	
4161 Grandview St. N., Oshawa	1847	
67 King St. E., Oshawa	1848	

Address	Year Built	Name
284 Simcoe St., Beaverton	1848	Old Stone Jail
61 Brock St. E., Oshawa	1850	
42 Brock St. W., Oshawa	1850	
103 Brock St. W., Oshawa	1850	
20 Colborne St. E., Oshawa	1850	
1600 Conlin Rd., Oshawa	1850	
1629 King St., Port Perry	1850	Aaron Ross
80 Peace St., Cannington	1850s	Log Cabin
143100 Old Simcoe Rd., Port Perry	1850	James McBrien-Heartland
15238 Old Simcoe Rd, Port Perry	1851	Palmer Homestead
32 Albert Street, Sunderland		Doble House
1454 Simcoe St. S., Oshawa	*circa* 1857	Robinson House

Note: Arranged chronologically by date.

Sources: Heritage Oshawa Municipal Heritage Committee Inventory, March 2006; Township of Scugog Municipal Heritage Register; Data from the Beaverton Thorah Eldon Historical Society, the Cannington Historical Society, and the Sunderland Historical Society.

NOTES

CHAPTER 1: EARLY DESCRIPTION

1. Samuel Pedlar, *Samuel Pedlar Manuscript*, Oshawa Public Library, transcribed from a microfilm of the original in 1970 and published in 2004, not paginated. *(*Frame numbers in citations for this manuscript refer to the frame they appear on in the microfilm.)*
2. Leslie Miscampbell Frost (1895–1973) was first elected to the Ontario legislature in 1937. He served as the sixteenth premier of Ontario from 1949 to 1961 and was the chancellor of Trent University from 1967 to 1973.
3. Percy Robinson, *Toronto during the French Régime: A History of the Toronto Region from Brûlé to Simcoe, 1615–1793* (Toronto: Ryerson Press, 1965), 150.
4. The tombstone inscription of John Fralick reads, "In memory of John M. Fralick who settled in Whitby 1821, then an almost unbroken wilderness, and endured all. Died May 18, 1858, AE 63 years, respected by all who knew him." It is in Hubbell's Cemetery, at Myrtle, now part of Whitby, Ontario.
5. *Samuel Pedlar Manuscript*, frame 38. From a letter from Wm. Bateman to S. Pedlar, November 2, 1894, stating that the name Oshawa was applied to the locality of Oshawa and that the original pronunciation was "Oshwe, Oshwa-e."
6. Donald B. Jones, "Jones, Augustus," *Dictionary of Canadian Biography, Volume VII 1836 to 1850* (Toronto: University of Toronto Press, 1988), 450–52.

7. Alexander Fraser, *Third Report of the Bureau of Archives for the Province of Ontario 1905* (Toronto: L.K. Cameron, 1906), 323–24.

8. Augustus Jones, Field Book No. 1, Survey Notes & Diary, 1791–2, Survey Records (L & F) Original Notebook No. 828, January 1791–September 17, 1791/September 7, 1792–October 25, 1792 (Ontario Ministry of Natural Resources). Copyright: 2011 Queens Printer, Ontario.

9. Archives Ontario, David William Smith, Surveyor General, Instructions to A. Jones, April 24, 1795, Letters, MS 563/1 Vol. 3, 778.

10. Archives Ontario, Letter from Augustus Jones, Surveyor, to survey officials, dated Newark October 4, 1794, RG1 A-I-1 Vol. 32: 49–51.

11. Trent University Archives, D.F. McOuat, "Letter July 2, 1971 to Leslie Frost," Leslie Frost Fond, 77-024/27/3.

12. *Samuel Pedlar Manuscript*, frame 324.

13. *Ibid.*

14. *Ibid.*

15. *Samuel Pedlar Manuscript*, frame 325.

16. *Samuel Pedlar Manuscript*, frame 242.

17. *Samuel Pedlar Manuscript*, frame 325.

18. *Samuel Pedlar Manuscript*, frame 326.

19. Philip Sproule, "Cannington Centennial '78,'" *Cannington Gleaner*, 1978, 13.

CHAPTER 2: IROQUOIS AND MISSISSAUGA ON THE TRAIL

1. *Samuel Pedlar Manuscript*, frame 326.

2. Peter Jones, *History of the Ojebway Indian* (London: A.W. Bennett, 1861), 112–13.

3. P.S. Schmalz, "The Role of the Ojibwa in the Conquest of Southern Ontario, 1650–1701," *Ontario History*, Vol. 76, No. 4 (1988): 332.

4. Jon Parmenter, *The Edge of the Woods: Iroquoia, 1534–1701* (East Lansing, MI: Michigan State University Press, 2010), 185–207, 365–72.

5. Percy Robinson, *Toronto during the French Régime: A History of the Toronto Region from Brûlé to Simcoe, 1615–1793* (Toronto: Ryerson Press, 1965), 65, 91, 100, 118, 230.

6. D.B. Smith, "The Dispossession of the Mississauga Indians: A Missing Chapter in the Early History of Upper Canada," *Ontario History*, Vol. 73, No. 2 (1981): 74.

7.   Leo A. Johnson, "The Mississauga-Lake Ontario Surrender of 1805," *Ontario History* Vol. 83, No. 3 (September 1990): 244.

8.   Leo A. Johnson, *History of the County of Ontario, 1615–1875* (Whitby, ON: Corporation of the County of Ontario, 1973), 26.

9.   Conrad Heidenreich, *Huronia: A History and Geography of the Huron Indians, 1600–1650* (Toronto: McClelland & Stewart, 1971), 84.

10. Bruce G. Trigger, *The Children of Aataentsic: A History of the Huron People to 1660* (Kingston and Montreal: McGill-Queen's University Press, 1987), 156.

11. Frost, Leslie Miscampbell, *The Forgotten Pathways of the Trent*, 23, 25, 107–11.

12. Trigger, *The Children of the Aataentsic*, 588–89.

13. Ontario Iroquoians is an archaeological term to describe the prehistoric Iroquoian people who lived between A.D. 1300 and 1500. They were the ancestors of the Huron prior to their migration to Simcoe County. Using "Ontario Iroquoians" distinguishes them from the historic Iroquois of New York State.

14. A map of the sites can be found in Frost, *Forgotten Pathways*, 25–26.

15. *The Beaverton Story: Harvest of Dreams* (Beaverton: ON: Published for the BTEH Society [Beaverton Thorah Eldon Historical Society] by the Publishing Company Limited, 1984), 1.

16. Paul Sweetman, "The Corin Site, Thorah Island/Lake Simcoe, 1970–1989," *Arch Notes*, Vol. 90, Issue 2 (March/April 1990): 63.

17. R. Williamson, S. Austin, and S.C. Thomas, "The Archaeology of the Grandview site: A Fifteenth Century Iroquoian Community on the North Shore of Lake Ontario," *Arch Notes*, Vol. 8, Issue 5 (September/October 2003): 5–49.

18. *Ibid.*

19. J.V. Wright, *The Ontario Iroquois Tradition* (Ottawa: National Museums of Canada, 1966), 79.

CHAPTER 3: THE SEARCH FOR *CABANE DE PLOMB*

1.   *Samuel Pedlar Manuscript*, frame 348.

2.   Frost, *Forgotten Pathways of the Trent*, 22.

3.   Percy Robinson, *Toronto during the French Régime*, 76–77. J.T. Coleman, *History of the Early Settlement of Bowmanville and Vicinity* (Bowmanville, ON: West Durham Steam Printing and Publishing House, 1875).

4. J.T. Coleman, *History of the Early Settlement of Bowmanville and Vicinity* (Bowmanville, ON: West Durham Steam Printing and Publishing House, 1875), 4.

5. Frost, *Forgotten Pathways of the Trent*, 61.

6. E.A. Cruikshank, *The Correspondence of Lieut. Governor John Graves Simcoe with Allied Documents Relating to his Administration of the Government of Upper Canada*, Vol. 3 (Toronto: Ontario Historical Society, 1923), 203.

7. Percy Robinson, *Toronto During the French Régime*, 161–63.

8. Thomas Kaiser, *Historic Sketches of Oshawa*, 1921, 5.

9. Oshawa Community Museum and Archives, Bob Stephenson, "Information on the 'Cabane de Plomb,'" letter written by Bob Stephenson, dated February 29, 1996.

10. Charles M. Johnston, "Rousseaux St John, John Baptist," *Dictionary of Canadian Biography*, Vol. V, 1801 to 1820 (Toronto: University of Toronto Press, 1983), 724.

11. *Canada Indian Treaties and Surrenders, from 1680 to 1890*, Volume I (Ottawa: Brown Chamberlin Queen's Printer, 1891). Facsimile copy by Coles Publishing, 1971, 23, 34–37.

12. Charles M. Johnston, "Rousseaux St John, John Baptist," *Dictionary of Canadian Biography*, Vol. V, 1801 to 1820 (Toronto: University of Toronto Press, 1983) 725.

CHAPTER 4: YANKEES ON THE TRAIL

1. *Samuel Pedlar Manuscript*, frame 183.

2. D.B. Smith, "The Dispossession of the Mississauga Indians: A Missing Chapter in the Early History of Upper Canada," *Ontario History*, Vol. 73, No. 2 (1981): 80–81.

3. *Ibid.*, 76.

4. J.E. Farewell, *County of Ontario* (Whitby, ON: Gazette-Chronicle Press, 1907), 18.

5. *Ibid.*, 19.

6. Michael J. Thoms, "Oijbwa Fishing Grounds: A History of Ontario Fisheries Law, Science, and the Sportsmen's Challenge toAboriginal Treaty Rights, 1650–1900," MA thesis, University of British Columbia (2004), 63.

7. Broken Front refers to the front of the lot facing Lake Ontario, which, because of the shoreline, could be smaller or larger than a standard lot.

8. E.A. Cruikshank, *The Correspondence of Lieut. Governor John Graves Simcoe with allied documents relating to his administration of the government of Upper Canada* (Toronto: Ontario Historical Society, 1923), Vol. 3: 203.

9. A. Graham, "For restoration of a farm seized under New York title (May 23, 1785)," *State Papers of Vermont, General Petitions, 1778–1787*, edited by E. A. Hoyt, Vol. VIII (1952), 119–20.

10. Thomas Conant, *Life in Canada* (Toronto: William Briggs, 1903), 80.

11. *Ibid.*, 94–95.

12. Durham boats are flat-bottomed boats with keels first produced by the Durham Boat Company of Durham, Pennsylvania.

13. *Samuel Pedlar Manuscript*, frame 108.

14. J. Carruthers, *Retrospect of Thirty-Six Years Residence in Canada West, Being a Christian Journal and Narrative* (Hamilton: T.L. McIntosh, 1861), 204.

15. *Ibid.*, 204.

16. *Samuel Pedlar Manuscript*, frame 311.

17. "Memoir of the late A.M. Farewell," *Oshawa Vindicator*, December 8, 1869.

18. B. O'Brien, *Speedy Justice: The Tragic Last Voyage of His Majesty's Vessel Speedy* (Toronto: The Osgoode Society, 1992), 59, 61.

19. Archives Ontario, John Stegmann MS 1814, August 28, 1804.

20. I.M. Wellington and C.C. James. "Presqu'isle," *Ontario History: Papers and Records*, Vol. V. (1904): 65.

21. Ontario Land Registry Office (1835) Will of Robert Isaac Day Gray, Instrument number 12184, Microfilm H-429.

22. Kenneth A. Cassavoy, "HMS Speedy Project: The 1990 Fieldwork," *Second Annual Archaeological Report, Ontario 1991*, Vol. 2 (1991): 125–30. See also E.V. Burtt, "H.M.S. Speedy Project — Ontario," *Fifth Annual Archaeological Report, Ontario 1994*, Vol. 5 (1994): 167–71.

CHAPTER 5: PREACHERS ON THE TRAIL

1. *Samuel Pedlar Manuscript*, frame 107.

2. Peter Jones, *Life and Journals of KAH-KE-WA-QUO-NÃ-BY* (Toronto: Anson Green, 1860), 45.

3. *Ibid.*, 197.

4. *Ibid.*
5. Mae Whetung-Derrick, *History of the Ojibwa of the Curve Lake Reserve and Surrounding Area*, Vol. 1 (Curve Lake Band #35, 1976), 68.
6. "Christian, Washington," *Dictionary of Canadian Biography*, Vol. VII (1836 to 1850) (Toronto, University of Toronto Press, 1988), 181–82.
7. The Bible Christian Church was a Methodist denomination founded in 1815 by William O'Bryan, a Wesleyan Methodist preacher in England. The Bible Christians came in Canada to administer to immigrants from Devon and Cornwall in Whitby Township.
8. Elizabeth Muir, "Dart, Elizabeth (Eynon)," *Dictionary of Canadian Biography*, Vol. VIII (1851 to 1860) (Toronto, University of Toronto Press, 1985), 200–01.
9. William R. Wood, *Past Years in Pickering: Sketches of the History of the Community* (Toronto: William Briggs, 1911), 36.
10. J. Carruthers, *Retrospect of Thirty-Six Years Residence in Canada West, being a Christian Journal and Narrative* (Hamilton, ON: T.L. McIntosh, 1861), 127.
11. Reverend Adolphus Egerton Ryerson (1803–1882), clergyman, journalist, and educator, was born near Vittoria, Ontario. He established Ontario's present system of public education.
12. J.T. Coleman, *History of the Early Settlement of Bowmanville and Vicinity* (Bowmanville, ON: West Durham Steam Printing and Publishing House, 1875), 19–20.
13. B.H. Roberts, *The Life of John Taylor, Third President of the Church of Jesus Christ of Latter-Day Saints* (Salt Lake City, UT: George Q. Cannon & Sons, 1892).
14. *Samuel Pedlar Manuscript*, frame 107.
15. *Ibid.*, frame 167.

CHAPTER 6: EXPANDING EUROPEAN SETTLEMENT

1. *Samuel Pedlar Manuscript*, frame 322.
2. *Ibid.*, frame 188.
3. Alexander Fraser, *Eleventh Report of the Bureau of Archives for the Province of Ontario, 1914* (Toronto: L.K.Cameron, 1915), 307, 312, 395.
4. W.H. Smith, *Smith's Canadian Gazetteer; Comprising Statistical and General*

Information Respecting All Parts of the Upper Province, or Canada West (Toronto: H. and W. Rowsell, 1846), 63.

5.   W.H. Smith, *Canada: Past, Present and Future*, Vol. 2 (Belleville: Mika Publishing, 1974), 29–30. Originally published in 1852 by Thomas Maclear, Toronto.

6.   *Ibid.*, 26.

7.   "Great flood and great destruction," *Globe*, Toronto, April 13, 1850. Reprinted in the *Oshawa Reformer*.

8.   Sybil C. Lynde Stirling, *To a House in Whitby: The Lynde Family Story 1600 to 1900* (self-published, 1998), 135.

9.   A pathmaster supervised the building of roads. Property owners were required to provide labour annually for the improvement of the roads in their area.

10.   Conant, *Life in Canada* (Toronto: William Briggs, 1903), 77.

11.   J.S. Williamson, "Darlington History," *Canadian Statesman*, Bowmanville, April 19, 1917.

12.   *Ibid.*

13.   *Samuel Pedlar Manuscript*, frame 222.

14.   Frank Chapell, "Oshawa through Maturity to Civic Dignity," *Oshawa Daily Times*, January 24, 1948, 9.

15.   *Samuel Pedlar Manuscript*, frames 35–40.

16.   W.H. Higgins, *The Life and Times of Joseph Gould* (Toronto: C. Blackett Robinson, 1887), 162.

17.   P.A. Henry, *Memoir of Rev. Thomas Henry: Christian Minister, York Pioneer, and Soldier of 1812* (Toronto: Hill & Weir Steam Printers, 1880), 93.

18.   Thomas Kaiser, *Historic Sketches of Oshawa* (Oshawa, ON: Hill & Weir Steam Printers, 1921), 25–28.

19.   Pearcy G. Fletcher, *Oshawa's Earliest Church: A Christian Heritage* (Oshawa, ON: Centennial United Church, 1975), 20.

Chapter 7: Settlers Migrate Northward

1.   *Samuel Pedlar Manuscript*, frame 232.

2.   W.H. Higgins, *The Life and Times of Joseph Gould* (Toronto: C. Blackett Robinson, 1887), 32.

3.   J.E. Farewell, *County of Ontario*, 38.

4. S. Farmer, *On the Shores of Scugog* (Port Perry, ON: *Port Perry Star*, 1934), 203.
5. Johnson, *History of the County of Ontario, 1615–1875*, 130.
6. Archives Ontario, Samuel Wilmot, "Diary taken on the survey of Township No. 1 immediately in rear of Reach between the 21st of March and 7th May 1817," MS924, reel 4.
7. Farewell, *County of Ontario*, 7.
8. Alexander Fraser, *Sixteenth Report of the Bureau of Archives for the Province of Ontario, 1920* (Toronto: Clarkson W. James, 1921), 154.
9. Between 1828 and 1856, Scottish-born David Gibson surveyed much of Simcoe, Grey, Huron, and Bruce Counties. He was also involved with William Lyon Mackenzie in the 1837 Rebellion and following the defeat uprising of the rebels he hid for a month in Oshawa before escaping to the United States. His Toronto home, Gibson House, is now a museum.
10. Lucille Campey, *The Scottish Pioneers of Upper Canada, 1784–1855: Glengarry and Beyond* (Toronto: Natural Heritage Books, 2004), 102, 309.
11. W. H. Higgins, *Life and Times of Joseph Gould* (Toronto: C. Blackett Robinson, 1887), 36–38.
12. Mary Houston Ritchie, *A Township on the Lake: Beaverton and Thorah 1820–1952* (Beaverton, ON: self-published, 1952), 3–4.
13. J. Carruthers, *Retrospect of Thirty-Six years Residence in Canada West Being a Christian Journal and Narrative* (Hamilton: T.L. McIntosh, 1861), 36.

CHAPTER 8: MARGINALIZATION OF FIRST NATIONS COMMUNITIES

1. *Samuel Pedlar Manuscript*, frame 327.
2. *Ibid.*, frame 205.
3. *Ibid.*, frame, 233.
4. Michael J. Thoms, *Oijbwa Fishing Grounds: A History of Ontario Fisheries Law, Science, and the Sportsmen's Challenge to Aboriginal Treaty Rights, 1650–1900* (Vancouver: University of British Columbia, 2004), 140.
5. Smith, *Canada: Past, Present and Future*, 34–35.
6. *Ibid.*, 215.
7. Mae Whetung-Derrick, *History of the Ojibwa of the Curve Lake Reserve and Surrounding Area* (Curve Lake Band #35, 1976), Vol. 1, 68.
8. J. Carruthers, *Retrospect of Thirty-Six Years Residence in Canada West*, 104–05.

9. Gordon Dibb, *A Stage I-II archaeological/heritage assessment of lands proposed for development as an aggregate pit by Robert Carpenter in part lots 17 and 18, Concession XII, Brock Township, Regional Municipality of Durham* (Peterborough: York North Archaeological Services, 1998), 9–11.

10. The statistics for aboriginal populations 1818–1850 are from W.H. Smith 1846 (pages 3, 158, 243) and W.H. Smith 1852 (Volume II, pages 34, 35, 38, 109, 214, 215). The 1818 figure for Rice Lake includes Mud Lake and the 1818 figure for Narrows and Rama incudes an additional group on Lake Huron.

11. Gordon Dibb, *A stage I-II archaeological/heritage assessment of lands proposed for development as an aggregate pit*, 9.

12. Statistics Canada (*statcan.gc.ca*) and Aboriginal Affairs and Northern Development Canada (*www.aandc-aadnc.gc.ca*).

CHAPTER 9: GROWTH OF COMMUNITIES IN WHITBY TOWNSHIP

1. *Samuel Pedlar Manuscript*, frame 316.
2. *Ibid.*, frame 157.
3. The Honourable Gordon D. Conant (1885–1953) was elected to the provincial legislature in 1937, and in 1943 became the twelfth premier of Ontario after the resignation of Mitch Hepburn. A provincial plaque in his honour is in Lakeview Park, Oshawa.
4. *Samuel Pedlar Manuscript*, frame 307.
5. *Ibid.*
6. *Samuel Pedlar Manuscript*, frame 308.
7. Smith, *Smith's Canadian Gazetteer* (1846), 63.
8. Farewell, *County of Ontario*, 36.
9. J. Douglas Ross, *Education in Oshawa: From Settlement to City* (Oshawa, ON: self-published, 1970), 4.
10. Farewell, *County of Ontario*, 19.
11. *Samuel Pedlar Manuscript*, frame 195.
12. Farewell, *County of Ontario*, 19–20.
13. "Great flood and great destruction," *Globe*, Toronto, April 13, 1850. From the *Oshawa Reformer*.
14. Johnson, *History of the County of Ontario, 1615–1875*, 92–93.
15. "Death of William Glenney," *The Gazette and Chronicle* (Whitby), 1912.
16. *Samuel Pedlar Manuscript*, frame 285.

17. *Literary News Letter* (Oshawa), August 23, 1849.

18. Smith, *Smith's Canadian Gazetteer* (1846), 136.

19. Smith, *Smith's Canadian Gazetteer* (1846), Fourth Edition, 136–37.

20. J. Lovell, *The Canada Directory for 1857–58* (Montreal: J. Lovell, 1857), 482.

21. Johnson, *History of the County of Ontario, 1615–1875*, 137.

22. Farewell, *County of Ontario*, 77.

23. *Samuel Pedlar Manuscript*, frame 225.

24. Smith, *Smith's Canadian Gazetteer* (1846), 38.

25. Smith, *Canada: Past, Present and Future*, Vol. 2, 30.

26. "To be sold or let on a term of years," *Globe*, Toronto, November 27, 1849.

27. Trent University Archives, Thomas Bouckley, "Letter May 17, 1971, to Leslie Frost," Leslie Frost Fond, 77-024/26/1. Thomas Llewellyn Bouckley (1904–1988) was born in Blackpool, England, and came to Canada as an infant. As an avid photographic historian, he amassed a large quantity of photographs depicting Oshawa from its early years to the 1980s. The Robert McLaughlin Gallery in Oshawa houses his collection of over 4,000 prints and negatives.

CHAPTER 10: VILLAGES FURTHER NORTH ON THE TRAIL

1. *Samuel Pedlar Manuscript*, frame 319 and frame 351.

2. Smith, *Smith's Canadian Gazetteer* (1846), 153.

3. Smith, *Canada: Past, Present and Future* (1852), 32–33.

4. Peter Perry (1792–1851) was born in Erneston (Bath), Upper Canada, and died in Saratoga Springs, New York. He is buried in Union Cemetery, Oshawa. His Loyalist father immigrated to Canada following the American Revolution. Perry's interest in the rights and interests of the people of Upper Canada led to his involvement in politics and ultimate election to the colonial assembly in 1825. His most significant political contribution involved a bill permitting clergymen of every legally recognized denomination to perform the marriage ceremony. After losing the election of 1836, he moved to Whitby Township and became a general merchant with his eye on the potential of the harbour at Windsor (Port Whitby). Perry was instrumental in having a road built between the harbour and Lake Scugog, ultimately purchasing both. Although he came from a Loyalist family, he did have some sympathies to the United States. In 1849, as a member of the provincial legislature, he flirted with the concept of the annexation of Ontario to the United States.

5. J. Lovell, *The Canada Directory for 1857–58* (Montreal: J. Lovell, 1857), 527.

6. Farewell, *County of Ontario*, 40.

7. Michael Helms, *Sunderland: A Small Town Case Study* (Sunderland, ON: self-published, 1991), 1–2.

8. Isaly Lambert, *Call Them Blessed: A History of Cannington, 1817–1971* (Lindsay, ON: Corp. of the Village of Cannington, 1971), 18.

9. Smith, *Canada: Past, Present and Future* (1852), 32–33.

10. Isaly Lambert, *Call Them Blessed: A History of Cannington, 1817–1971* (Lindsay, ON: Corp. of the Village of Cannington, 1971), 57.

11. BTEH Society. *The Beaverton Story: Harvest of Dreams* (Beaverton, ON: Ontario Publishing Company Limited, 1984), 5.

12. Smith, *Smith's Canadian Gazetteer* (1846), 13.

13. BTEH Society. *The Beaverton Story*, 61.

14. *Ibid.*

15. Smith, *Smith's Canadian Gazetteer* (1846), 13.

16. *Ibid.*

17. Smith, *Canada: Past, Present and Future*, 33.

18. J.C. Conner and J.W. Coltson, *The County of Ontario Directory for 1869–70* (Toronto: Hunter: Rose and Company, 1869), 11.

19. Sources for population chart: Johnson 1973: 72, (Whitby, Reach, Thorah from 1820 to 1840); Beaverton based on 1848 census. Smith 1846: 20: (Brock in 1842), 38: (Columbus for 1846), 97 (Lindsay), 153 (Prince Albert for 1846), 159 (Reach in 1842), 190 (Thorah in 1842), 219 (Whitby Twp. in 1842); Smith 1852: 32 (Reach for 1842 and 1850); 33 (Brock for 1842 and 1850); 33 (Thorah for 1842 and 1850).

CHAPTER 11: DEATH AND TEMPERANCE ON THE TRAIL

1. *Samuel Pedlar Manuscript*, frame 195.

2. The life expectancies for the Uxbridge Ossuary population is similar to other Ontario Iroquoian populations such as the Fairty Ossuary in Markham, but differs from the Moatfield Ossuary in Toronto. However, it's likely that the Moatfield study used a different method in calculating life expectancy that increased it beyond the common range.

3. C.M. Godfrey, *The Cholera Epidemics in Upper Canada 1832–1866* (Toronto: Seccombe House, 1968), 51–54.

4. *Samuel Pedlar Manuscript*, frame 262.

5. *Globe*, July 31, 1849, page 1, "A man by the name of William Townsend, a resident of Oshawa, was found dead on Sunday last in Mr. R. Woon's garden. A Coroner's inquest resulted in the decision that he had been seized with an apopletic fit."

6. *Samuel Pedlar Manuscript*, frame 352.

7. *Literary News Letter*, August 23, 1849. Reproduced in the *Ontario Reformer*, April 4, 1902.

8. Conant, *Life in Canada*, 66–67.

9. Gordon Conant, "Oshawa Lore Tales of Pioneer Days," *Oshawa Times-Gazette*, March 26, 1949, 13.

10. Conant, *Life in Canada*, 120–21.

11. Donald B. Smith, *Sacred Feathers: The Reverend Peter Jones (Kahkewaquonaby) and the Mississauga Indians* (Toronto: University of Toronto Press, 1987), 38, 67–68.

12. Peter Jones, *Life and Journals of KAH-KE-WA-QUO-NÃ-BY* (Toronto: Anson Green, 1860), 81.

13. E. Ryerson, and J.G. Hodgins, *The Story of My Life by the Late Rev. Egerton Ryerson, D.D., LLD: Being Reminiscences of Sixty Years' Public Service in Canada* (Toronto: William Briggs, 1884), 72.

14. "Whitby Temperance Society," *The Christian Guardian* (Toronto), June 2, 1834.

15. W. Jackson, *Early History of the Presbyterian Church in Ontario County* (Oshawa, ON: W. Jackson, 1971), 41.

16. Johnson, *History of the County of Ontario, 1615–1875*, 217.

17. S. Farmer, *On the Shores of Scugog* (Port Perry, ON: Port Perry Star, 1934), 105, 107.

18. George Washington Bungay, *Pen Portraits of Illustrious Abstainers, Vol. 1* (New York: The National Temperance Society and Publication House, 1881), 174–77.

19. *Samuel Pedlar Manuscript*, frame 381.

20. "Temperance reformer, John B. Gough (1817–1886), was an international celebrity during his own lifetime, who delivered some 9,000 lectures to more than nine million people throughout the United States, England, Scotland, Ireland, Wales, Canada, France, and Switzerland." See *www.teachushistory. org/second-great-awajeminh-age-reform/resources/sketch-john-goughs-life*.

21. *Samuel Pedlar Manuscript*, frame 382.

CHAPTER 12: THE LEGACY OF THE TRAIL

1. *Samuel Pedlar Manuscript*, frame 156.
2. Archives Ontario, Augustus Jones. Surveyor's Letters (103), July 4, 1796, RG1-2-1 Vol. 32, "Names of the Rivers, and Creeks, as they are called by the Mississaugas,"
3. Farewell, *County of Ontario*, 19.
4. *Samuel Pedlar Manuscript*, frames 155–56, 186.
5. "Oshawa pioneer cemetery to be moved next month," *Toronto Star*, July 17, 1975.
6. Jim Wilkes, "195 Graves Transferred from Oshawa's Pioneer Cemetery," *Oshawa Times*, November 1, 1975.
7. Alexander Fraser, *Nineteenth Report of the Department of Public Records and Archives of Ontario* (Toronto: Herbert H. Ball, 1931), 54.
8. Kaiser, *Historic Sketches of Oshawa*, 1921, 7.
9. Gordon Conant, "Oshawa lore tales of pioneer days," *Oshawa Times-Gazette*, March 26, 1949, 13.
10. Elise M. Cleverdon, "An East Whitby Mosaic," a booklet published by the East Whitby Centennial Committee in 1967, 7.
11. Blanche Meeker, *The Story of Benjamin Wilson, Our First Settler*, 12.
12. David Crombie, "*Recommendation for the Future of Oshawa Harbour: A Report by The Honourable David Crombie, P.C., O.C. February 21, 2008*," a federal report commissioned by the Ministry of Transport, Infrastructure and Communities, 2008.
13. "Gifford Farm belongs to history, says Frost," *Oshawa Times*, November 1, 1972.
14. Blanche Meeker, *The Story of Benjamin Wilson*, 12.
15. Daniel T. Elliot and Rita F. Elliot, *Bethany Cemetery, Effingham County, Georgia*, Ebenezer Archaeological Report Series, No. 2 (Athens, GA: The Ebenezer Group, 1989), 4, 15.
16. Gillian Gilchrist, "Harmony Village: Remembering the Settlers & a Lost Cemetery," a spiral-bound booklet published by the Oshawa Historical Society in 2010, 2–4.
17. Frost, *Forgotten Pathways of the Trent*, 93.
18. *Ibid.*, 93.
19. The original rail line was the Toronto Nipissing Railway built in 1871–72, which was later acquired by the Grand Trunk Railway. Cannington lost its

train station in 1968 and the railway stopped providing rail service to the community by 1989.

EPILOGUE

1. *Samuel Pedlar Manuscript*, frame 205.
2. George Brown (1818–1880) was a journalist and politician. He began the Toronto-based *Globe* newspaper in 1844 and is remembered as one of the fathers of Confederation.

BIBLIOGRAPHY

PRIMARY SOURCES (MANUSCRIPTS)

Archives Ontario:

C 277-1. Whitby Township Plan.

MS251 [Smalley, Arad]. "Inspection report of Thorah 1830," reel 1.

MS563/1. D.W. Smith, Instructions to A. Jones, April 24, 1795.

MS924, reel 4. Wilmot S., "Diary taken on the survey of Township No. 1 immediately in rear of Reach between the 21st of March and 7th May 1817."

MS924, reel 4. Wilmot S., "Diary of the survey of Township of Brock in the
Home District 12 Nov.–31 Dec. 1817," OA, MS924, reel 4.

MS1814. Stegmann John to William Chewett, August 28, 1804.

MS7294, Series F493. Woodhouse, T. Roy. "The Romance and tragedy of Jean
Baptiste Rousseau."

RG1 A-I-1 vol. 32. Augustus Jones. Letter dated Newark, October 4, 1794.

RG1-2-1 vol. 32. Augustus Jones. Surveyor's Letters (103), July 4, 1796, "Names
of the Rivers, and Creeks, as they are called by the Mississaguas."

Ontario Land Registry Office:

1835 Will of Robert Isaac Day Gray, Instrument number 12184, Microfilm H-429.

Oshawa Community Museum and Archives:

Dyl, J.S. *Oshawa Harbour Area History 1790–1870*. Oshawa: n.p., 1971.

Pedlar, Samuel. "Samuel Pedlar Manuscript." Oshawa, ON: Oshawa Public Library, 2004, not paginated. This collection comprises material collected and compiled by Samuel Pedlar for his history of Oshawa and covers the period from 1790 to 1904. This version was purchased from the Archives Ontario by the City of Oshawa and transcribed from a microfilm of the original by Sharon Stark and Margaret Egerer, July/August 1970. The original source is: Archives Ontario, Samuel Pedlar collection, accession number 3309.

Stephenson, Bob. "Information on the 'Cabane de Plomb'" (letter), February 29, 1996.

Oshawa Public Library

Pedlar, Samuel. *Samuel Pedlar Manuscript*. Oshawa, ON: Oshawa Public Library, 2004, not paginated. This collection comprises material collected and compiled by Samuel Pedlar for his history of Oshawa and covers the period from 1790 to 1904. This version was purchased from the Archives Ontario by the City of Oshawa and transcribed from a microfilm of the original by Sharon Stark and Margaret Egerer, July/August 1970. The original source is: Archives Ontario, Samuel Pedlar collection, accession number 3309.

Royal Ontario Museum:

Kidd, K.E. Washburn Island Lake Scugog, 1951.

Smith, D.W. The Council Book: Petitioners Names: B 11, page 11, [1793].

Trent University Archives:

Leslie Frost fond. Baird, Hugh. "Letter December 10, 1971."

Leslie Frost fond. Bouckley, Thomas. "Letter May 17, 1971."

Leslie Frost fond. McOuat, D.F. "Letter July 2, 1971."

PRINTED PRIMARY SOURCES

Canada Indian Treaties and Surrenders, from 1680 to 1890, Vol. I. Ottawa: Brown Chamberlin Queen's Printer, (1891). Facsimile copy by Coles Publishing, 1971.

Carruthers, J. *Retrospect of Thirty-Six Years Residence in Canada West being a Christian Journal and Narrative*. Hamilton: T.L. McIntosh, 1861.

Chamberlin, A.F. *Archaeology of Scugog Island*, 1889, n.p.

———. *The Language of the Mississaga Indians of Skugog: A Contribution to the Linguistics of the Algonkian Tribes of Canada*. Philadelphia: MacCalla & Company, 1892.

Chapell, Frank. "Oshawa through maturity to civic dignity." *Oshawa Daily Times*, January 24, 1948.

"Cholera has made its appearance in the vicinity of Oshawa…," *Literary News Letter*, August 23, 1849, reproduced in the Ontario Reformer, April 4, 1902.

Coleman, J.T. *History of the Early Settlement of Bowmanville and Vicinity*. Bowmanville, ON: West Durham Steam Printing and Publishing House, 1875.

Conant, T. *Life in Canada*. Toronto: William Briggs, 1898.

———. *Upper Canada Sketches*. Toronto: William Briggs, 1903.

Conner, J.C. and J.W. Coltson. *The County of Ontario Directory for 1869–70*. Toronto: Hunter: Rose and Company, 1869.

"Death of William Glenney." *Gazette and Chronicle*. Whitby (1912).

"Eleizur Lockwood." *Firelands Pioneer* (June 1865). See *http://wc.rootsweb. ancestry.com/cgi-bin/igm.cgi?op=GET&db=eland&id=I656*, April 12, 2010.

Farewell, J.E. *County of Ontario: short notes as to the early settlement and progress of the County and brief references to the pioneers and some Ontario County men who have taken a prominent part in provincial and dominion affairs*. Whitby, ON: Gazette-Chronicle Press, 1907.

"Gifford Farm belongs to history, says Frost," *Oshawa Times*, November 1, 1972.

Graham, A. "For restoration of a farm seized under New York title (May 23, 1785)." In *State Papers of Vermont, General Petitions 1778–1787*, edited by E. A. Hoyt. Montpelier, VT: Secretary of State, on publication, 1952, Vol. VIII: 119–20.

"Great flood and great destruction (From the Oshawa Reformer). *The Globe*, Toronto, April 13, 1850: 178.

"Insurance Pioneer Dead." *The Globe*, Toronto (1910).

Lovell, J. *The Canada Directory for 1857–58: containing names of professional and businessmen, and of the principal inhabitants, in the cities, towns and villages throughout the Province, alphabetical directories of banks ... Post Office Department, Post Offices ... and railway and steamboat routes throughout Canada, corrected to November 1857.* Montreal: J. Lovell, 1857.

Mayne, W. "Diary of Journey from Niagara to Kingston in November and December 1794." In *The Correspondence of Lieut. Governor John Graves Simcoe with allied documents relating to his administration of the government of Upper Canada,* edited by E. A. Cruikshank. *Ontario Historical Society.* Vol. 3 (1923): 203.

"Memoir of the late A.M. Farewell." *Oshawa Vindicator,* December 8, 1869.

Moore, Wm. F. "Whitby Temperance Society." *The Christian Guardian* (Toronto), June 2, 1834.

"Oshawa pioneer cemetery to be moved next month." *Toronto Star,* July 17, 1975.

Pedlar, S. *Ancestral history of Charles Pedlar of Vauxhall, Cornwall, England, born about 1710, and his descendants [microform] : also Edward Morrish of St. Stephens, Cornwall, England, born about 1765, and his descendants.* Toronto: by Hunter, Rose Co., 1894.

Roberts, B.H. *The Life of John Taylor, Third President of the Church of Jesus Christ of Latter-Day Saints.* Salt Lake City, UT: George Q. Cannon & Sons, 1892.

Ryerson, E. and J.G. Hodgins. *The story of my life by the late Rev. Egerton Ryerson, D.D., LLD.: being reminiscences of sixty years' public service in Canada.* Toronto: William Briggs, 1884.

Smith, W. H. *Smith's Canadian Gazetteer; comprising statistical and general information respecting all parts of the upper province, or Canada West.* Toronto: H&W Rowsell, 1846.

"To be sold or let on a term of years." *The Globe,* Toronto (November 27, 1849): 3.

Traill, C.P. *The Canadian Settler's Guide.* Toronto: Old Countryman Office, 1855.

Walton, G. *The City of Toronto and the Home District Commercial Directory and register with almanack and calendar for 1837.* Toronto: T. Dalton and W.J. Coates, 1837.

SECONDARY SOURCES

A Century of Service Kingsway College. Oshawa, 2003.

Archaeological mitigation of the Farewell (Harmony Road) Pioneer Cemetery, City of Oshawa, Regional Municipality of Durham. Toronto: Archaeological Services Inc., 1994.

Arculus, P. *The Merchants of Old Port Perry*. Port Perry: *Port Perry Star*, 1999.

Beaverton Thorah Eldon Historical Society. *The Beaverton Story: Harvest of Dreams*. Beaverton, ON: Ontario Publishing Company Limited, 1984.

Building Harmony: The Archaeology of the Grandview Site. Toronto: Archaeological Services Inc., 1999.

Becker, John. "Early Land Surveys in Southern Ontario." *Families*, February 2007.

Beers, J.H. *Illustrated Historical Atlas of the County of Ontario*. Toronto: J.H. Beers & Co., 1877.

Bouckley, T. *Pictorial Oshawa*, Vol. 1. Oshawa, ON: Alger Press, 1975.

Bridges, P. "*The Short Site and Area: A preliminary Report, 14.*" 1972.

Brown, G. *Brown's Toronto City and Home District Directory, 1846–1847*. Halton-Peel Branch, Ontario Genealogical Society, 1989. Originally published by George Brown, Toronto, 1846.

Bungay, George Washington. *Pen Portraits of Illustrious Abstainers*, Vol. 1. New York: The National Temperance Society and Publication House, 1881.

Burtt, E.V. "H.M.S. *Speedy* Project — Ontario." *Fifth Annual Archaeological Report, Ontario 1994*, Volume 5 (1994): 167–71.

Cassavoy, Kenneth A. "HMS Speedy Project: The 1990 Fieldwork." *Second Annual Archaeological Report, Ontario 1991*, Vol. 2 (1991):125–30.

"Christian, Washington," *Dictionary of Canadian Biography*, Vol. VII, 1836–1850. Toronto: University of Toronto Press, 1988, 181–82.

Cleverdon, Elise M. *An East Whitby Mosaic*. East Whitby Centennial Committee, 1967.

Conant, G. D. "Oshawa lore: tales of pioneer days." *Oshawa Daily Times-Gazette*, March 12, 1949.

Crombie, David. "Recommendation for the Future of Oshawa Harbour: A Report by The Honourable David Crombie, P.C., O.C. February 21, 2008." Ottawa: Ministry of Transport, Infrastructure and Communities, 2008. See also *www.tc.gc.ca/programs/ports/crombie.htm*.

Cruikshank, Ernest Alexander. *Documents Relating to the First Settlement 1778–1783*. Niagara Historical Society, 1927: n.p.

Development Services Committee. "Proposal for Scugog Place and the Cabane de Plomb (French Trading Post) in the City of Oshawa, 2006." Development Services Committee, City of Oshawa.

Dibb, Gordon. "A stage I-II archaeological/heritage assessment of lands proposed for development as an aggregate pit by Robert Carpenter in part lots 17 and 18, Concession XII, Brock Township, Regional Municipality of Durham." Peterborough, ON: York North Archaeological Services, 1998. A report on file with the Ontario Ministry of Tourism, Culture and Sport.

Donaldson, W. "The Thomas Site: A Late Prehistoric Village in Ontario County." *Ontario Archaeology*, Vol. 7 (1962): 21–38.

Dudar, J.C. "Reconstructing population history from past peoples using ancient DNA and historic records analysis: the Upper Canadian pioneer and land resources." Unpublished MA Thesis, McMaster University, Hamilton Ontario, 1998.

Elliot, Daniel T. and Rita F. Elliot. *Bethany Cemetery, Effingham County, Georgia: Ebenezer Archaeological Report Series, Number 2*. Athens, GA: 1989.

Farmer, S. *On the Shores of Scugog*. Port Perry, ON: *Port Perry Star*, 1934.

Fletcher, Percy G. *Oshawa's Earliest Church: A Christian Heritage*. Centennial United Church, 1975.

Fraser, Alexander. *Third Report of the Bureau of Archives for the Province of Ontario 1905*. Toronto: L.K. Cameron, 1906.

———. *Eleventh Report of the Bureau of Archives for the Province of Ontario, 1914*. Toronto: L.K. Cameron, 1915.

———. *Sixteenth Report of the Bureau of Archives for the Province of Ontario, 1920*. Toronto: Clarkson W. James, 1921.

———. *Nineteenth Report of the Department of Public Records and Archives of Ontario*. Toronto: Herbert H. Ball, 1931.

Fraser, Marguerite J. *A Place Called Solina*. Oshawa, ON: Maracle Press, 1975.

Frost, L.M. *Forgotten Pathways of the Trent*, Don Mills, ON: Burns & MacEachern, 1973.

Garland, M.A. and J.J. Talman. "Pioneer Drinking Habits and the Rise of the Temperance Agitation in Upper Canada prior to 1840." In H.A. Stevenson and J.D. Wilson. F.H. Armstrong, ed. *Aspects of Nineteenth Century Ontario*. Toronto: University of Toronto Press, 1974.

Gilchrist, Gillian. "Harmony Village: Remembering the Settlers & A Lost Cemetery." Oshawa Historical Society, 2010.

Godfrey, C.M. *The Cholera Epidemics in Upper Canada 1832–1866*. Toronto: Seccombe House, 1968.

Gordon, Jack A. *Green Pastures of Old Brock*. Lindsay, ON: Hall Printing, 2001.

Grover, F. *"Some Indian Landmarks of the North Shore."* Chicago Historical Society, 1905, 267–69.

Guillet, E.C. *Early Life in Upper Canada*. Toronto: University of Toronto Press, 1933.

H. Belden & Co. *Illustrated Historical Atlas of Counties Northumberland and Durham Ont*. Bellville, ON: Mika Silk Screening, 1972.

Harsell, F. "Oshawa Pioneer Memorial Gardens Cemetery: 185–201 Bond Street, Oshawa, Ontario, Canada." Whitby-Oshawa Branch, Ontario Genealogical Society, 1982.

Heidenreich, Conrad. *Huronia: A History and Geography of the Huron Indians, 1600–1650*. Toronto: McClelland & Stewart, 1971.

Helms, Michael. *Sunderland: A Small Town Case Study*. Sunderland, ON: self-published, 1991.

Henry, P.A. *Memoir of Rev. Thomas Henry: Christian Minister, York Pioneer, and Soldier of 1812*. Toronto: Hill & Weir Steam Printers, 1880.

Higgins, W.H. *The Life and Times of Joseph Gould*. Toronto: C. Blackett Robinson, 1887.

Hodder, E.M. *The Harbours and Ports of Lake Ontario in a Series of Charts*. Toronto: Maclear & Co., 1857.

Hoig, D.S. *Reminiscences and Recollections: An Interesting Pen Picture of Early Days, Characters and Events in Oshawa*. Oshawa, ON: Mundy-Goodfellow, 1933.

Hood, McIntyre. *Oshawa, "The Crossing Between the Waters: A History of Canada's Motor City."* Oshawa, ON: McLaughlin Public Library, 1967.

Hoyt, Edward A. ed. *General Petitions, 1778–1787*. Montpelier, VT: Secretary of State, 1952.

Hvidsten, J. Peter. *Scugog: The Early Years, 1821–1899*. Port Perry, ON: Observer Publishing, 2000.

Jackson, W. *"Early History of the Presbyterian Church in Ontario County."* Oshawa, ON: 1971.

Johnson, Leo A. *History of the County of Ontario, 1615–1875*. Whitby, ON: Corporation of the County of Ontario, 1973.

———. "The Mississauga-Lake Ontario Surrender of 1805." *Ontario History*, Vol. 83, No. 3 (1990): 233–53.

———. "Farwell, Abraham." *Dictionary of Canadian Biography*, Vol. XI

1881–1890. Toronto: University of Toronto Press, 1982.

———. "Gibbs, Thomas Nicholson." *Dictionary of Canadian Biography*, Vol. XI 1881–1890. Toronto: University of Toronto Press, 1982.

Johnston, Charles M. "Rousseaux St John, John Baptist." *Dictionary of Canadian Biography*, Vol. V 1801–1820. Toronto: University of Toronto Press, 1983.

Jones, Augustus. *Field Book No. 1, Survey Notes & Diary, 1791–2, Survey Records (L&F) Original Notebook No. 828, January 1791–September 17, 1791/ September 7, 1792–October 25, 1792*. Ontario Ministry of Natural Resources, Queens Printer Ontario, 2011.

Jones, Peter. *History of the Ojebway Indian*. Toronto: Anson Green, 1860. See also *http://en.wikisource.org/wiki/Life_and_Journals_of_ Kah-ke-wa-quo-n%C4%81-by/Chapter_VI*.

———. *Life and Journals of KAH-KE-WA-QUO-NÃ-BY*. London: A.W. Bennett, 1861. See also *http://www.archive.org/stream/historyofojebway00jonerich/ historyofojebway00jonerich_djvu.txt*.

Kaiser, T.E. *Historic Sketches of Oshawa*. Oshawa, ON: The Reformer Printing and Publishing Co. Ltd., 1921.

———. *Oshawa's History: Historical Sketches*. 1908.

Karcich, G. "American settlement of Durham Region." *Families*. Vol. 22, No. 4 (1983): 221–27.

Kirkconnell, Watson. *County of Victoria Centennial History*. Lindsay: Victoria County Council, 1967.

Konrad, Victor. "An Iroquois Frontier: The North Shore of Lake Ontario during the Late Seventeenth Century." *Journal of Historical Geography*, Vol. 7, No. 2 (1981): 129–44.

Lambert, Islay. *Call Them Blessed: A History of Cannington 1817–1971*. Lindsay, ON: Corp. of the Village of Cannington, 1971.

Leighton, Douglas. "Proulx, Jean-Baptiste." *Dictionary of Canadian Biography*, Vol. XI 1881–1890. Toronto: University of Toronto Press, 1982.

McLean, Elaine. *Artemas Thompson of Thorah Township, Ontario, His New England Ancestors and Canadian Descendants 1630–1974*. Don Mills, ON: self-published, 1995.

———. *Charles Johnston (1752–1845) of Brock Township, Ontario*. Don Mills, ON: self-published, 1999.

Meeker, Blanche. *The Story of Benjamin Wilson, Our First Settler*. Report prepared for the Oshawa and District Historical Society, 1967.

Moodie, Susanna. *Roughing It in the Bush*. London: Richard Bentley, 1852.

Muir, Elizabeth. "Dart, Elizabeth (Eynon)." *Dictionary of Canadian Biography*, Vol. VIII, 1851–1860. Toronto: University of Toronto Press, 1985.

O'Brien, B. *Speedy Justice: The Tragic Last Voyage of his Majesty's Vessel Speedy*. Toronto: The Osgoode Society, 1992.

Parmenter, Jon. *The Edge of the Woods: Iroquoia, 1534–1701*. East Lansing, MI: Michigan State University Press, 2010.

Pearce, Robert J. "Report on a background study of heritage resources for the GO A.L.R.T. extension (Whitby to Oshawa)." Museum of Indian Archaeology, 1983. *Report on the phase II archaeological investigation of selected areas on the GO ALRT extension: Whitby to Oshawa* (Government of Ontario Rapid Transit System). Report submitted to M.M. Dillon Ltd and the Ministry of Transportation and Communications, Toronto.

People of the Lakes. Alexandria, VA: Time-Life Books, 1994.

Pfeiffer, S. "Demographic Parameters of the Uxbridge Ossuary Population." *Ontario Archaeology*. Vol. 40 (1983): 9–14.

Reed, P. "*The MacLeod Site (AlGr-1) and a preliminary delination of the Lake Ontario Iroquois. Anthropology Department*. Unpublished report, McMaster University (1990): 179.

Reeve, Harold. *The History of the Township of Hope*. Cobourg, ON: Cobourg Sentinel-Star, 1967.

Ritchie, Mary Houston. *A Township on the Lake: Beaverton and Thorah 1820–1952*. Beaverton, ON: self-published, 1952.

Robinson, P.J. *Toronto during the French Régime: A History of the Toronto Region from Brûlé to Simcoe, 1615–1793*. Toronto: Ryerson Press, 1965. First edition printed in 1933.

Ross, J. Douglas. *Education in Oshawa: From Settlement to City*. Oshawa, ON: [publisher not identified], 1970.

"*St. Gertrude's May 1960 Dedication Book*." Oshawa, 1960.

Sabean, John. *Time Present and Time Past: A Pictorial History of Pickering*. Alton Editions, 2000.

———. *The Ojibwa of Southern Ontario*. Toronto: University of Toronto Press, 1991.

Schmalz, P.S. "The Role of the Ojibwa in the Conquest of Southern Ontario, 1650–1701." *Ontario History*. Vol. 76, No. 4 (1988): 326–52.

Smith, Donald B. "Jones, Augustus." *Dictionary of Canadian Biography*, Vol. VII 1836–1850. Toronto: University of Toronto Press, 1988.

———. "The Dispossession of the Mississauga Indians: a Missing Chapter in the Early History of Upper Canada." *Ontario History*, Vol. 73, No. 2 (1981): 67–87.

———. *Sacred Feathers: The Reverend Peter Jones (Kahkewaquonaby) and the Mississauga Indians*. Toronto: University of Toronto Press, 1987.

———. "Who Are the Mississauga." *Ontario History*. Vol. 67, No.4 (1975): 211–22.

Smith, W.H. *Canada: Past, Present and Future*. Belleville, ON: Mika Publishing, 1974. Originally published in 1852 by Thomas Maclear, Toronto.

Smith, W.L. *Up Bruce and Huron Way: The Pioneers of Old Ontario*. Toronto: George N. Morong, 1923.

Sproule, P. "Cannington Centennial '78," *Cannington Gleaner*, 1978, 13.

Stirling, S.C.L. *To a House in Whitby:The Lynde Family Story 1600 to 1900*. Privately published by Sybil Sterling, 1998.

Surtees, Robert J. *The Williams Treaties*. Treaties and Historical Research Centre, Indian and Northern Affairs Canada, 1986.

Sweetman, Paul W. "The Corin Site, Thorah Island Lake Simcoe, 1970–1989." *Arch Notes*, No. 90–2 (March/April 1990): 18–22.

Thoms, J. Michael. "Oijbwa Fishing Grounds: A History of Ontario Fisheries Law, Science, and the Sportsmen's Challenge to Aboriginal Treaty Rights, 1650–1900." Unpublished PhD Thesis, University of British Columbia, Vancouver, 2004.

Traill, Catharine Parr. *The Backwoods of Canada*. London: C. Knight, 1836.

Trigger, Bruce G. *The Children of Aataentsic: A History of the Huron People to 1660*. Kingston and Montreal: McGill-Queen's University Press, 1987.

Weir, F.G. *Scugog and Its Environs*. Port Perry, ON: Star Print, 1927.

Wellington, I.M. and C.C. James. "Presqu'isle." *Ontario History: Papers and Records*, Vol. V (1904): 65.

Whetung-Derrick, Mae. *History of the Ojibwa of the Curve Lake Reserve and Surrounding Area*. Curve Lake Band #35, 1976. Three volumes.

Whitford, Jacques. "Stages 1 and 2 Archaeological Assessment, proposed FarmTech Ethanol Facility, Oshawa, Ontario Part of Lots 4 and 5, Broken Front, Former Township of Whitby." Ontario Ministry of Tourism and Culture, 2008.

Wilkes, Jim. "195 graves transferred from Oshawa's Pioneer Cemetery." *Oshawa Times*, November 1, 1975.

Williamson, J.S. "Darlington History." Bowmanville: *Canadian Statesman*, April 19, 1917.

Williamson, R.F., Austin, S.J., and Thomas, S.C. "The Archaeology of the Grandview Site: A Fifteenth Century Iroquoian Community on the North Shore of Lake Ontario." *Arch Notes,* Vol. 8, Issue 5 (September/October 2003).

———. *Bones of the Ancestors: The Archaeology and Osteobiography of the Moatfield Ossuary.* Gatineau, QC: Canadian Museum of Civilization, 2003.

———. "Report on 690 King Street, 19th Century Cemetery." Archaeological Services Inc., 2009.

Wintemberg, W.J. "Artifacts from Ancient Graves and Mounds in Ontario." *Transactions of the Royal Society of Canada.* Vol. XXII, Section II (1928): 175–99.

Wood, William R. *Past Years in Pickering: Sketches of the History of the Community.* Toronto: William Briggs, 1911.

Wright, J.V. *The Ontario Iroquois Tradition.* Ottawa: National Museums of Canada, 1966.

INDEX

ABOUT THE AUTHOR

Grant Karcich has written articles on Canadian history and books on genealogy, and has given presentations on history and anthropology over the past ten years. Grant holds a master's degree in both library and information science, and anthropology and has worked as a librarian and information specialist. Having grown up along the Scugog Carrying Place route, he has long wanted to bring the story of this forgotten trail back to life. He resides in Oshawa, Ontario.